CONSUMING MODERNITY

CONSUMING MODERNITY

Public Culture in a South Asian World

CAROL A. BRECKENRIDGE, EDITOR

UNIVERSITY OF MINNESOTA PRESS

Minneapolis / London

Published by the University of Minnesota Press
111 Third Avenue South, Suite 290, Minneapolis, MN 55401 2520
Printed in the United States of America on acid-free paper
http://www.upress.umn.edu
Second Printing, 1998

Library of Congress Cataloging-in-Publication Data
Consuming modernity : public culture in a South As n world /
Carol A. Breckenridge, editor.
p. cm.
Includes index.
ISBN 0-8166-2305-8
ISBN 0-8166-2306-6 (pbk.)
1. Popular culture—India. 2. India—Social life and customs.
I. Breckenridge, Carol Appadurai, 1942- .
DS423.C577 1995
306'.0954—dc20   94-46772

Contents

v

~

Preface

In the mid-1980s, when the project reflected in this book was first conceived, it was clear that significant changes were under way in India. The consumer economy catering to an apparently growing middle class was a sure sign of a surplus in the domestic economy, and an avalanche of advertisements heralded major lifestyle changes. Rajiv Gandhi's government was speeding up privatization and the denationalization of industry, thus admitting a steady stream of multinational and transnational corporations into India with their products and projects. Signs that Nehruvian secularism was at risk were everywhere. It was becoming clear that the Indian diaspora in England and the United States could play a binational role in a changing world. Thus the term *nonresident Indian*—shortened to NRI—came to be used by the Indian state to lay claim to the skills, technologies, and finances of its "nationals" abroad by offering them favorable schemes for investment in India. And new fault lines in civil society were created by controversial events like the debate around the legal issues regarding Ayodhya's Babri Masjid, Muslim civil law in regard to the divorced woman Shahbano (1985), the immolation of Roop Kanwar on her husband's funeral pyre (1987), the publication of Salman Rushdie's *The Satanic Verses* (1989), the increase in bride burnings, and the Mandal Commission Report that proposed state-initiated changes in regard to caste in India.

The dilemma for the student of India working in the area studies tradition in the United States was to frame a project about India's new forms of public modernity that would not repeat the earlier, triumphalist errors of modernization theory. In 1986 and 1987, under the research rubric "public culture in late-twentieth-century India," Arjun Appadurai and I sought to open a space of debate in regard to the many issues associated with the enormous shifts under way in India. Along the way it became clear that the connection between public culture and global cultural flows was at the heart of the matter. In search of a framework for clarifying this connection comparatively and transnationally, we began the journal *Public Culture* in 1988.

Though the nation, the state, and the market represented other possible points of entry into these "postcolonial" issues, the idea of the public seemed more open, more inclusive, more flexible. Then and now (despite the subsequent publication of the English translation of Jürgen Habermas's book *The Structural Transformation of the Public Sphere* in 1989) the category of the public seemed an undertheorized aspect of collective life. Many of the changes we could see were informed by changes in global capital and in the cultural flows that it appeared to encourage. Thus the public sphere also looked like a promising entry into the local reception and transformation of global cultural flows.

At the same time it was clear that this project was larger than the two of us, and we sought colleagues who would join us to explore the cultural dynamics of contemporary India through the lens of public culture. To that end I organized a double panel at the South Asia Meetings of the University of Wisconsin at Madison in 1988, and we began discussions with the Joint Committee on South Asia of the Social Science Research Council (SSRC) and the American Council of Learned Societies. The Joint Committee supported a trip to India in late 1986 to discuss the public culture project with colleagues in Delhi and two workshops that we organized, one more generally on public culture in 1988 and the other on global advertising in 1991. Many of the essays in this volume began at the 1988 South Asia Meetings or at these SSRC workshops. I owe the authors an apology for the inordinate time that it has taken to see their work into print.

Many individuals have helped to shape the ideas contained in this volume over the past few years. But for their initial enthusiasm and encouragement, when the very idea of public culture seemed fragile and ambiguous, I wish to thank Bernard S. Cohn and Toby Volkman, whose support of this project continues unabated; for her patience and willingness to assume more than her share of the responsibility for the production process, I thank

Janaki Bakhle; and for their varying attention to other matters large and small, I am grateful to Sarah Diamond, Victoria Farmer, Ritty Lukose, Rob Mosimann, and Namita Gupta Wiggers.

Carol A. Breckenridge
Chicago, April 1994

CHAPTER ONE

Public Modernity in India

ARJUN APPADURAI AND CAROL A. BRECKENRIDGE

This is not a book for those who believe that Americanization or commodification or McDonald's (or some variation of all these) is seducing the world into sameness and creating a world of little Americas, unless they are prepared to change their minds. Neither is this a book for those die-hard adherents of modernization theory who believe that modernity is a single destination to which all lines of developmental traffic lead, and that all that matters is who gets there first and how high the price of their journey. Our assumption is that modernity is today a global experience (even if the term *modernity* is, in some sense, a category of Western history and reflexivity). It is further our assumption that this experience is as varied as magic, marriage, or madness, and thus worthy of scholarly attention and, more generally, of comparative study.

But there is a more compelling reason to study all the sites of modernity (including those of the West) on the same terms. Most societies today possess the means for the local production of modernity, and, as their members move around the world, these experiences inform and inflect one another, thus making even the paradigmatic modernity of the United States and Western Europe (itself not an unproblematic assumption) no more pristine. Koreans, Samoans, Turks, Indians, Chinese, Mexicans, Haitians, and Mongols now move to the countries of the West (and stay), not as folk ciphers

1

waiting to be imprinted with Euro-American modernity, but equipped with their own understandings of modernity to negotiate with the ones they encounter. There is thus no justification for regarding the modernities of the world as pale reflections of a Euro-American original, or of looking at them for enactments of a recipe we have lived through (or past) already. Modernity is now everywhere, it is simultaneously everywhere, and it is interactively everywhere. But it is not only everywhere, it is also in a series of somewheres, and it is through one such somewhere, India, that this volume enters the global reality of modernity, and for such a localized entry we propose another general category: public culture.

While there have been several now-classic discussions of public life that draw on European discourses surrounding privacy, citizenship, civility, and the state (Arendt 1951; Goffman 1963; Sennett 1976), the most influential recent discussion of the public sphere as a historical formation is contained in Jürgen Habermas's study *The Structural Transformation of the Public Sphere* (1989, German original 1962). Habermas views the structural transformation of the public sphere in the course of the nineteenth and twentieth centuries as one that involves a move "from a public critically reflecting on its culture to one that merely consumes it" (175). In this process, the strict separation of the public from the private realm gives way to a public sphere dominated by the mass media, in which public life is effectively depoliticized:

> Yet the more the original relationship between the intimate sphere and the public sphere in the world of letters is reversed and permits an undermining of the private sphere through publicity, the more decisions within this latitude can be influenced. In this fashion the consumption of culture also enters the service of economic and political propaganda. Whereas the relationship of the public sphere in the world of letters to that in the political realm was once absolutely constitutive for that central identification of "property owner" with "human being" as such, without therefore viewing them as coextensive, there prevails today a tendency toward the absorption of the plebiscitary "political" public sphere by one depoliticized through a preoccupation with consumption of culture. (177)

Habermas's sense of the degeneration of politics—as civil society and the bourgeois public sphere cease to be the pivots of public discussion—remains a tacit presupposition in his subsequent work and has been subjected to a variety of criticisms and refinements (Fraser 1990; Calhoun 1992; Hansen 1993; Negt and Kluge 1993; Robbins 1993). It is embedded in an account of the relationship between literacy, public communication, and politics, which greatly narrows the scope of a complex process. Norbert Elias (1978) and Michel Foucault (1972) have shown that the interplay of bodily practices,

disciplinary institutions, and discourses of knowledge is far more complicated than the rational communication assumptions of Habermas's earlier
and more recent work. Also, as John Keane (1988) has pointed out, Habermas's universalist pragmatics is deeply compromised by the highly artificial,
hypothetical, and abstract nature of the subject as Habermas derives it from
Kant. This idea of the subject prevents Habermas from linking language to
embodied practice, from recognizing the importance of what he calls sym-
bolic action as opposed to rational speech, and from investigating the links
between mass media and the emancipatory dimensions of art, display, and
performance. In general, though there were important distinctions between
Horkheimer, Adorno, Marcuse, and Benjamin, the Frankfurt school was
never able to free itself of the sense that mass media (and mass-mediated culture) were anything but the instruments of class domination under late capitalism (see Arato and Gebhardt 1990: 185-224).

Thus, though the category of public culture appears to share this concern
with the media and with modernity, it cannot be considered simply a new
way of talking about mass culture. The critique of mass culture carries many
of the presuppositions of the more general worldview of the Frankfurt
school, presuppositions that we do not in every case accept. Specifically, we
believe (following Foucault) that knowledge and power are mutually impli-
cated in ways that involve the structure and distribution of discursive formations, not just the power of images produced by the dominant classes
under late capitalism. These discursive formations can range from the explicitly theoretical and literary to the visual, the spectacular, and the experiential. More important, the consumers of mass-mediated cultural forms are
agents and actors, not merely objects and recipients. In this latter shift, we
build on a variety of approaches to cultural consumption as a political practice: the work of the (now dispersed) Birmingham school, which established
the capability of subaltern groups to resist through strategies of style (Hebdige 1979), the complexity of socialization into the culture of labor (Willis
1977), and the elaborate social conditions of reading in which certain images and icons became popular (Bennett, Mercer, and Woollacott 1986). The
contribution of the Birmingham school to a more emancipatory sense of
the possibilities of mass media is supported by a variety of recent moves in
the study of readers, viewers, and spectators. We see now that gender, race,
and class can imply radically different practices of reading and pleasurable
viewing (e.g., A. Mattelart 1983; Radway 1984; Mulvey 1989); that the cultural improvisations of subaltern groups can involve resistance, co-optation,
and critique of commodified master forms (Feld 1988); that readers are not

isolates but form communities of response and judgment (Fish 1980; Smith 1988); and that texts themselves contain the seeds of alternative readings, contested cultural assumptions, and subversive political possibilities (Hunt 1989). A great many of these views are contained in the extensive, and ongoing, work of the "subaltern studies" group, who have transformed the study of colonial India. In a sense our interest is to extend this perspective to India considered as a "postcolony" (compare Mbembe 1992a, 1992b).

In general, we are committed to the sense of the viewer, the reader, and the spectator in relation to the experience of modernity as involving complex forms of subjectivity, agency, pleasure, and embodied experience. The adjective *mass* in relation to contemporary culture appears destined to elide these complexities of reception. Building on some countercurrents in twentieth-century culture theory (e.g., Benjamin 1976; Kracauer 1987; Liebman 1988; Iser 1989), we are interested in moving toward a theory of reception that is global and oriented to the interaction of media in the experience of viewers regarded as varieties of subject.

But if the adjective *mass* fails to capture the complex negotiations between cultural producers and consumers, and rests on too anemic a sense of the viewing subject, the adjective *popular* poses a different set of problems. In the past fifteen years, the term *popular culture* has undergone a complicated set of shifts, expansions, and critiques that start with the straightforward use of the term among European social historians to refer to the history of the inarticulate. There is now much greater self-consciousness about the politics of the term *popular culture* (Hall 1982; Chartier 1984; Shiach 1989; Mukerji and Schudson 1991). The study of the popular by historians is now linked to the problematics of the public sphere (Freitag 1989b, 1991), of community politics (Yeo and Yeo 1981), of class, and of conflict (Crow 1985; Hunt 1989). Particularly among historians of India, there is a growing awareness of the political trajectory that unites subaltern consciousness, the transformation of leisure and work, communitarian politics, and the dynamics of decolonization (Breckenridge and van der Veer 1993; Niranjana, Dhareshwar, and Sudhir 1993; Freitag 1989c; Kumar 1988; Guha and Spivak 1988).

This volume seeks in part to loosen the link between the word *public* and the history of civil society in Europe, and to agree that it be used to refer to a set of arenas (compare Freitag 1989a) that have emerged in a variety of historical conditions and that articulate the space between domestic life and the projects of the nation-state—where different social groups (classes, ethnic groups, genders) constitute their identities by their experience of mass-mediated forms in relation to the practices of everyday life (compare Lee 1993). *Public* in this usage ceases to have any necessary or predetermined relationship to formal politics, rational communicative action, print capitalism, or the dynamics of the emergence of a literate bourgeoisie. Thus the term becomes emancipated from any specific Euro-American master narrative and indicates an arena of cultural contestation in which modernity can become a diversely appropriated experience.

The term *public culture* thus allows us to describe not a type of cultural phenomenon but a *zone* of cultural debate (Appadurai and Breckenridge 1988; for other uses of the term *public culture,* see Bender 1989 and Horne 1986). This zone cannot be understood apart from the general processes of globalization that we cited at the beginning. From this point of view, the contestatory character of public culture has much to do with the tensions and contradictions between national sites and transnational cultural processes. These tensions generate arenas where other registers of culture encounter, interrogate, and contest one another in new and unexpected ways. Thus national culture seeks to co-opt and redefine more local, regional, or folk cultural forms. Commercial culture (especially in the cinema, television, and the audio industry) seeks to popularize classical forms. Mass cultural forms seek to co-opt folk idioms. This zone of contestation and mutual cannibalization—in which national, mass, and folk culture provide both mill and grist for one another—is at the very heart of public modernity in India. In identifying the public modernity of any given national space, we are obliged to identify the broad dynamics that characterize the local dynamics of the site.

The Society of Consumption in India

There are several ways to approach the contested space within which public modernity is visible in contemporary India (see Kapur 1991). In the observations that follow, we privilege consumption as an activity and a modality of social life. In part, this is because we assume that in trying to understand the political imaginary of modernity, it is important to engage with the subjective experience of modern life, which is closely tied up with particular sorts of pleasure, desire, and agency. Consumption, conceived as "the work of the imagination" (Appadurai 1990, forthcoming), is an activity that simultaneously captures the distinctive disciplines of modernity and draws attention to new forms of expenditure and social identity. The relation of consumption practices to new forms of class politics and national narrative requires separate treatment, but it is a sense of consumption as a profound basis for group identity that informs the discussion that follows.

In recent years, many observers of the South Asian scene have noticed that Indians are engaged in forms of consumption, recreation, and entertainment that resemble cosmopolitan cultural forms in other parts of the contemporary world (Kemper 1993). The growing national frenzy over sports such as cricket, the palpable growth in domestic tourism, the dynamism of the food and restaurant industries (Appadurai 1988), the rapid inroads made by television and videocassettes into the domain of the cinema, the penetration of the countryside by voracious media and advertising forces, and the general commodification of cultural objects are all part of this process, which has many other expressions as well.

Yet this emergent public culture is not the same as Indian national culture, for national culture itself is a contested mode, embattled, on the one hand, by transnational cultural messages and forces (which sometimes threaten the nation-state) and, on the other hand, by indigenous critiques, from various sectors, that continuously threaten the cultural hegemony of the nation-state. National culture in countries like India is the site of an uneasy collaboration between the cultural agencies of the nation-state and the private, largely commercial agencies that dominate certain kinds of cultural production. Today, in India, the control of cultural production is shared in a fragile and variable way between the state and private enterprise, depending on the kind of cultural product that is involved.

Public culture in late-twentieth-century India is thus a contested terrain. The actors and interests in the contest are a variety of producers of culture and their audiences; the materials in the contest are the many cultural modalities—sport, television, cinema, travel, radio, and museums—discussed in this volume; and the methods, increasingly shared by *all* parties, involve the mass media and related mechanical modes of reproduction. What is at stake in the contest is, of course, no less than the consciousness of the emergent Indian public. The messages of public culture are therefore directed to audiences without regard to the limits of family, locality, or social category. This does not mean that the new images are directed to a homogeneous and universal Indian but that they are designed to appeal to a consciously diverse audience.

The embattled arena of culture we define as public has behind it particular social, political, and economic forces and interests. The hardest of these interests to pin down is the burgeoning middle class, which is vigorously pursued by market research firms employed by entrepreneurial (and electoral) interests in India. In fact, the ruthless and intense competition between market research firms such as Marg and IMRB is itself a tribute to the urgency of the hunt for the middle-class market. Even at the most conservative estimates, there are at least a million Indians who already have disposable incomes that make them the economic support of new forms of cultural consumption. But such estimates are not necessarily meaningful from a cultural point of view, for many more Indians who live in cities or in small towns and villages that have access to print and visual media are also targets of the media and are affected to some degree by their messages, values, and priorities. This middle class—both actual and potential—is the social basis of public culture formations.

In addition to the middle classes, another key interest group in the shaping of public culture is the variety of entrepreneurs and commercial institutions that constitute what have been referred to elsewhere as the "culture industries." Included here would be all those who have floated new magazines, both in English and in the vernaculars; the entire film and closely related music industry, with all its technical adjuncts; the tourist industry; and, cutting across all of these, the burgeoning advertising industry.

The media boom in contemporary India is part of a worldwide explosion whose cultural contours are barely understood. Critical to this boom are the older cinematic and print forms, and the newer television and videocassette recorder technologies (Manuel 1993). In India, each of these media technologies has distinctive capabilities and functions, and each interacts in a different way with older modes of organizing and disseminating information in Indian society. In the case of print media, the most notable recent development is the enormous increase in the number of periodical newsmagazines, both in English and in the vernacular languages. This boom creates and feeds an extraordinary hunger for a variety of sorts of information, opinion, and news directed toward the interests of different audiences. Competition in the newsmagazine business is intense. The central thrust of these newsmagazines appears to be the bringing together of gossip, politics, cinema, sport, and investigative journalism within the same purview. At the same time, there is a multiplication of specialized magazines directed at particular tastes, interests, and fashions.

Equally important, magazines both support and extend the empire of advertising. As in other parts of the world, advertising links media to changes in the marketplace and constitutes a critical vehicle for the shaping of public taste more generally and in regard to such traditional cultural forms as the martial arts more specifically (see Zarrilli in this volume).

Magazines also provide a lively forum for the expression of reader views and thus constitute an agency for interaction between the small town and rural audiences of many of these magazines and their more cosmopolitan publishers, writers, and reporters (see Talwar 1989; Chanda 1991; Wolf 1991). It is in and through the pages of these magazines that Indians of a variety of classes and regions are learning where and how they can gain access to knowledge of the emergent lifestyles.

Finally, the state plays a key role in the making and sustaining of public culture. The state is an active competitor in the marketplace of cultural images and productions—in important aspects of the travel industry, in the radio entertainment industry, and, most of all, in its growing organization of national as well as regional cultural centers, spectacles, and publications. The state is also a crucial gatekeeper and referee in the contest of private cultural entrepreneurs, through its powers of licensing and censorship and through its control of a variety of regulations involving public morality and order. Nowhere is this better seen than in the phenomenal current powers of the "mandarins of Mandi House," the bureaucrats who decide what soap operas, documentaries, and other features the Indian television viewer will see (Rajagopal 1993).

The commercial cinema provides a powerful emotional and aesthetic framework within which an Indian form of "capitalist realism" (compare Schudson 1984) is learned. That is, in the narratives and images of cinema, Indians experience a new polyglot image of glamour, fashion, and mobility centered on the lifestyles of heroes and heroines. Heightened by the musical, visual, and auditory intimacies of the theater, Indian films contain models of celebrity and of consumption that are pivotal to the new public culture.

With major production centers in Bombay and Madras, film is perhaps the single strongest agency for the creation of a national mythology of heroism, consumerism, leisure, and sociality (see Thomas and Dickey in this volume; see also Binford 1989; Das Gupta 1980; Dickey 1993; Dissanayake 1987, 1988, 1992; Mazumdar 1991; Niranjana 1991; Rajadhyaksha 1986; Shah 1950; Vachani 1989). The Hindi film industry in particular (though also to some extent the Tamil and Bengali cinemas) is not only very popular in India but is also a very successful export to Africa, the Middle East, Southeast Asia, and the Far East, where the films are subtitled in Indian as well as in non-Indian languages. Like Hollywood in its heyday, the Indian commercial film industry is built around stars, an aesthetically distinctive world of stage settings and billboards (Haggard 1989; Srivatsan 1991), a lively magazine industry, and a closely linked commercial music industry. The culture of cinema in contemporary India affects almost every arena of public life. Yet the power of cinema in India today can only be understood in relation to the arrival of television. The visual landscape of Indian films is a dream landscape. Television and its sister technology, video recordings, have entered India in a big way and constitute a new threat to the cultural hegemony of cinema, while at the same time they extend the reach of cinematic forms to the smaller towns and poorer citizens of India (Ganley and Ganley 1987; Boyd, Straubhaar, and Lent 1988). Though substantially regulated by the Indian state (just as David Lelyveld has shown radio broadcasting to be; see chapter 3 in this volume), Indian television programming already has a large component of privately produced soap operas, docudramas, and other forms of televised entertainment. This is, of course, in addition to a fairly large amount of state-sponsored and state-controlled programming, which ranges from news programs (still largely state-controlled) to live sports programs, cultural performances, and informational programs (informed by development communications on everything from birth control to new cropping techniques for farmers). In general, though a number of the most popular serials on Indian television have operated on variations of the Hindi film formula, many television programs have a historical, cultural, or documentary dimension.

In television, above all, it is the Indian heritage that is turned into spectacle. The most striking examples of this process are the three most popular television series of the past few years: *Buniyaad,* which concerned the trials and tribulations of the partition of India and Pakistan as experienced by a large Punjabi extended family; and the television serializations of the two great Indian epics, the *Ramayana* (Lutgendorf 1990) and the *Mahabharata* (see Mankekar 1993), for whose weekly time slot the whole television-watching audience of India apparently dropped everything. Domestic travel and museums are now important parts of a generalized, mass-media-provoked preoccupation with heritage and with a richly visual approach to spectacles. The relationship between state-controlled television and the growing force of private producers from India as well as major interests from outside (such as Star TV) are far too volatile and complex to discuss in this context. The visual culture of this new, and public, modernity is dominated by what we call "nationalist realism," that is, an array of images, symbols, scripts, and plots in which the nation is figured as central to the project of modernity. The nation, sometimes as figure, sometimes as ground, is never absent from this transnationally constituted visual field (Abu-Lughod 1993).

This centrality of the national narrative is not, however, a sign of the uncontested cultural hegemony of the state. The political economy of public life in India thus involves a complex interaction between the triangulated forces of the middle classes of Indian cities, towns, and villages, the entrepreneurs involved in the culture industries, and various organs of the state; all of these forces seek to maneuver around, through, and with the agencies and forms of transnational cultural flows. India's burgeoning public sphere is neither entirely benign nor entirely democratic. Like other forms of politics, it involves the marginalization of those who cannot afford the price of entry into this world and those who prefer to remain outside it.

As is evident from the essays in this volume, public culture in contemporary India involves the overlap and interpenetration of diverse modes and sites of cosmopolitan experience, interrelated by the modern media, by consumption, and by technology. To enter into the discursive world of the new public modernity, Indians have to buy its vehicles of dissemination. They must purchase subscriptions to magazines (or rent them from small neighborhood shops in the bazaar, which sometimes double as recyclers of newsprint), buy tickets to cricket matches and cinema shows, gain access to television sets, and pay for meals at restaurants. In consuming the array of media-dominated images and symbols associated with these settings, they are drawn into the commodity world more generally. Film, television, and video technologies are at the heart of the new cosmopolitanism, for they provide the visual tentacles that draw the largest number of Indians into this world, at least as viewers and spectators, if not as critics or as producers.

Television is at the cutting edge of the privatization of leisure in contemporary India (as elsewhere). As public spaces grow more violent, disorderly, and uncomfortable, those who can afford it consume their spectacles in the company of their friends and family, on television. This is true of the two great passions of the mass audience: sport and cinema. In the one case through live coverage and in the other through reruns and videocassettes, the stadium and the cinema hall are being replaced by the living room as the setting for spectacle. In this process, the public space of stadia and cinema halls is being abandoned by the middle classes and left to the working-class audience. Test matches are still well attended, but the crowds that attend them are more volatile (see chapter 2 in this volume). No longer a complex shared experience between the rich and the poor, the stadium spectacle is a more polarized and jagged experience, which many do not prefer to the cool, private, and omniscient television screen. As it is elsewhere in the world, the (working-class) audience of live matches and other large-scale spectacles is itself a prop in a larger performance staged for the benefit of television audiences. It is there not to enjoy the "liveness" of the spectacle but to provide evidence of it for the television audience. It is an audience of the spectacle from its own point of view; on television it becomes part of the spectacle for those at home.

But though certain aspects of public culture are experienced within domestic settings, this should not be interpreted to mean that the new middle classes are moving massively indoors. Travel is a central part of the new cosmopolitanism, and it has a glitzy, upmarket dimension (as Barbara Ramusack's essay in this volume suggests) as well as a more proletarian dimension (Breckenridge 1987).

Museums, travel, and heritage are anything but cool aspects of leisure and self-cultivation in contemporary India. Throughout India, the images that Indians see on television, the efforts of politicians to stimulate group consciousness outside the ambit of the state, and the efforts of the state to control the construction of heritage form an explosive mix. In the state of Uttar Pradesh, for example, the state government is engaged, like that of many other Indian states, in expanding tourism on a massive basis, partly by advertising the historical and cultural treasures of Uttar Pradesh. But Uttar Pradesh is also the setting of perhaps the major battle between Hindus and Muslims in India over the past few years, the case of what is known as the Babri Masjid, which Hindu revivalist organizations see as the heart of Hindu Ayodhya, a territory crucial to the traditional sacred geography of Hinduism. As groups like the Vishwa Hindu Parishad (a major communal organization working sometimes in cahoots with the state and sometimes against it) moved to "restore" a Hindu shrine to Rama adjacent to the Muslim shrine of the Babri Masjid, the entire nation viewed this local battle in the context of its feverish recent consumption of the televised Hindu epic, the *Ramayana*. While the televised epic was not openly incendiary in regard to religious sentiments, and while it is alleged that many Muslims also watched this quintessentially Hindu mythological drama, there can be no question that the electronic rediscovery of the Hindu epics gave tremendous leverage to Hindu religious nationalists as they escalated the communal stakes in places like Ayodhya. While the result is a series of extremely difficult political and law-and-order problems both for the state and the central government in Delhi, there is no easy answer, since the state (at both levels) is also massively involved in the heritage industry in an effort to shore up state structures by bolstering the imagined community of "Indians." It was in part this landscape of contestation that shaped the debated reception of Salman Rushdie's *The Satanic Verses* in 1989.

The gaze of Indian viewers and spectators is certainly caught up in what

we have elsewhere called an "interocular" field (Appadurai and Breckenridge 1992). This interocular field is structured so that each site or setting for
the socializing and regulating of the public gaze is to some degree affected by
the experiences of the other sites. The interweaving of ocular experiences,
which also subsumes the substantive transfer of meanings, scripts, and symbols from one site to another (in surprising ways), is a critical feature of
public culture in contemporary India. This can be seen, for example, in the
world of sport in contemporary India, where leisure, spectacle, stardom, and
nationalism come together in a volatile way.

In a world shaped by media representation and images, sport provides a
cultural form employed by India to package the spectacular for both national and international audiences (as is shown in this volume by Phillip
Zarrilli with regard to the martial arts). The changing sport culture of India
is stimulated in part by popular energy, private enterprise, and media interest, and in part by the state through its commitment (meager though it is) to
sport education and to international sports. Though the conventional patrons of modern sport have come from the princely states and private urban
clubs, those who achieve public recognition in sport as stars, champions,
and medal winners are as likely to come out of the Indian railways or the Indian army, where organized sport is promoted and encouraged, or from the
playing fields of the North Indian state of Punjab.

Two public aspects of sport in India can be seen in cricket and the Commonwealth Games, on the one hand, and in the competitive sport of the
Olympics and the Asian Games, on the other. Both are related to and shaped
by international sport; both have their roots in the colonial ecumene; and
both are now dominated by media hegemony, which is facilitated by the
electronic age of the late twentieth century. While problems of patronage,
heritage, leisure, and commodification affect almost every aspect of organized sport in India, our discussion here (and the essay by Arjun Appadurai in
this volume) focuses on cricket, since it is such an overwhelming feature of
the Indian landscape today.

In general, the coevolution of these experiences (reinforced with the in-
terocularity we referred to earlier) is a crucial part of the emergence of the
new Indian consumer-citizen. The experiences that Indians have of cosmopolitan life and the debates that surround them create a constantly shifting
relationship between backdrops and foregrounds, between *experiences of
reading* (books, pamphlets, newspapers, brochures, billboards) and the *readings of experience* that are to be found in films, museums, archaeological sites,
and televised epics. Converging here with the recent suggestions of Bennett

and Woollacott (1987: 260-69) regarding what they call "reading formations" (a concept that breaks down the sharp boundary between intratextual
and intertextual properties), we propose that public culture is a shifting array
of texts and experiences, which constitute evolving contexts for each other. In
such a situation, everyday life (compare de Certeau 1984) is no longer a sep-
arable domain defined by structures "outside" public culture and brought to
bear upon it, but a complex experiential field in which the lives of particular
agents, readers, and subjects are interwoven with the shared texts and moments of public culture. This volume is intended as a prolegomenon to the
study of everyday lives and biographical and ethnographic specificities
under the emergent modern regime that public culture constitutes.

We have not discussed here—for it would take us far beyond the scope of
this essay—the major question of how the new visual fields we have discussed, the "nationalist realisms" they often mediate and the new capabilities
to consume, interact with the emergence of the Hindu right in India in the
past decade. In general, we have not addressed how the new forms of public
modernity with which we are concerned interact with the present crisis of
secularism in countries like India. Yet there is no doubting that one large
marker of the half-century since India became independent is a sense that
the Nehruvian project of big science, triumphal secularism, and mass democratic participation is in crisis. Instead, electoral politics has grown increasingly violent, big science is under attack by many kinds of activists and social
critics, and the space of secularism has suffered massive inroads from the
discourse of Hinduization. Perhaps not unconnected to all these developments, the vigorous and optimistic socialistic discourse of the fifties and sixties has given way to all sorts of discourses of privatization, liberalization,
and Hinduization. In some sense, India here seems to join the general script
of the world after 1989—a world of high-speed capitalism, violent ethno-
nationalisms, and corrupt mass politics. The story of how postcolonies like
India fit into the new post-1989 global order has yet to be told, but one in-
gredient of this story will surely be the sort of public modernity that many
Indians have come to experience and engage. That this modernity is closely
tied up with increased religious violence and political cynicism on the part
of the major parties is a problem that we can pose here but hardly resolve.

Modern Worlds

Since part of our concern is with looking at modernity as a historical emergent in societies such as India, we point the reader especially to the essays by

Appadurai, Conlon, Lelyveld, and Ramusack. It is quite clear that none of the forms and expressions that are involved in the zone of the public sphere arrive full blown or uninflected in contemporary India. Each of them has a direct history that goes back to the early part of this century, or to the nineteenth century and sometimes to a protohistory of cognate indigenous expressions that goes back much further. Thus cricket has a history in India that goes back into the eighteenth century, while cinema goes back to the early part of this century. Similarly, while tourism may be a relatively recent form, it is not obvious when and how the transition from pilgrimage to tourism may have occurred. We have therefore paid special attention to the trajectories that different expressions of public culture have taken in order to better account for the configuration of this cultural zone today.

The experience of modernity is local, but locality itself has undergone a fundamental set of changes over the past five hundred years. We are in the process of witnessing a fundamental transformation in the very nature of world systems and global processes. Various forms of global interaction have always been with us, and so have various forms of world system. Even before maritime expansion of the West in the sixteenth century, complex global formations did exist (Abu-Lughod 1989), but we are only now beginning to theorize the shifts from these early modern global processes to those that constitute global processes today (Appadurai 1990, 1991; Featherstone 1990).

The global processes of the present, like those of the past five centuries, have economic forces at their heart, but the nature of these economic processes and their relationship to social, cultural, and organizational forms are now very uncertain. Capitalism appears to be increasingly flexible (Harvey 1989) and even "disorganized" (Urry and Lash 1987); social movements seem alienated and "rhizomic" (Deleuze and Guattari 1987); the relations between states seem in a radical sense to be "turbulent" (Rosenau 1990); national narratives seem to exceed the capacities of states to contain them (Bhabha 1990). If there is one major example of the complexities of the relationship between economics, politics, and media, it is the anticommunist tide that has swept Eastern Europe and seems likely to reconfigure the global political stage.

This volume does not pretend to offer a sweeping account of these changes in the nature of global processes and formations, but it does show that locality and parochiality are no longer necessarily mutual correlates. To put it another way, the imagination has emerged as a new force in social life, largely as a result of the spread of electronic media, in the context of rapid flows of resources, images, and persons across national boundaries. There is much interesting work on the implications of modern media flows, and the debate between those who see the media as large scale instruments of global capitalist hegemony (A. Mattelart 1979, 1983; Schiller 1976) and those who see the heterogeneity of the cultural forms generated by the spread of media (Appadurai 1990; Feld 1988; Hannerz 1989, 1992) has only just begun.

Few students of global modernities would deny that the media (in particular the electronic media) have transformed the meaning of locality by creating complex images of distance, self, other, and social transformation that extend to the remotest societies of the world the capability to construct imagined worlds. Not all these imagined worlds are created equal, nor is the creation of them everywhere a product of democratic processes. Indeed, the battle between states and subjects, between ethnic separatisms and new "majorities," between image makers and image receivers in any given nation-state is at least as heated as the battle between these imagined worlds.

Thus India is a locality, but it is better described as a "site" (Soja 1989), or a spatial vortex, in which complex historical processes come into conjunction with global processes that link such sites together. Appadurai has described these sites as the confluences of history and genealogy (1991), where what is being generated are prismatic structures of modernity, which are peculiar in the shape of the cultural and historical trajectories they bring to the present and thus to the way they refract (or inflect) the worlds they imagine. Prismatic modernities are local, but they are also fundamentally interactive with other such structures, which taken together constitute not a network of localities, as in traditional central-place models or dependency theory, but a global structure for the continuous (and potentially infinite) flow of images and ideologies through particular sites.

This volume describes the structure and dynamics of one such prismatic site, namely, India. These essays show how Indian history and its own civilizing logics (in the sense of Elias 1978) provide the stage on which imagined worlds are constructed. These essays also show that the process of building these prisms and negotiating their structure is neither simply emancipatory nor simply repressive. Constructing and experiencing these processes draws together social groups in unexpected ways, creating new solidarities but also new distinctions and oppositions.

The spread of modernity is no longer (if it ever was) merely an aspect of technology transfer, whether in India or elsewhere. Every national society now creates its own ways of playing with modernity (Holston 1989; Ivy 1988; Mattelart and Mattelart 1990; Miyoshi and Harootunian 1989; Niranjana, Dhareshwar, and Sudhir 1993; Siegel 1986) in the way that Western observers once thought was true largely for Japan. As far as this sort of play with the "means of modernity" (see Appadurai in this volume) is concerned, the advanced capitalist countries may have a head start, but they are no longer gatekeepers. The genie is out of the bottle, and as localities turn into "sites" throughout the world, particular societies become locations not of pristine cultures, but rather of complex and specific negotiations between history and globality. These negotiations have a very specific cultural sociology (as we show for India in this volume), but this specificity has little to do with the idea of cultural distinctiveness as rooted in boundable groups, fixable norms, and persistent customs.

The new forms of specificity that characterize sites in today's world are prismatic and interdependent, and they involve unique configurations of knowledge, history, and discourse, in the realm we have called "public culture." In this view, what is distinctive about any particular society is not the fact or extent of its modernity, but rather its distinctive debates *about* modernity, the historical and cultural trajectories that shape its appropriation of the means of modernity, and the cultural sociology (principally of class and state) that determines who gets to play with modernity and what defines the rules of the game.

References

Abu-Lughod, Janet L. 1989. *Before European Hegemony: The World System A.D. 1250-1350.* New York: Oxford University Press.

Abu-Lughod, Lila, ed. 1993. Screening Politics in a World of Nations. *Public Culture* 5 (3) (guest edited by Lila Abu-Lughod).

Appadurai, Arjun. 1988. How to Make a National Cuisine: Cookbooks in Contemporary India. *Comparative Studies in Society and History* 30 (1): 3-24.

———. 1990. Disjuncture and Difference in the Global Cultural Economy. *Public Culture* 2 (2): 1-24.

———. 1991.Global Ethnoscapes: Notes & Queries for a Transnational Anthropology. In *Recapturing Anthropology,* edited by R. G. Fox. Santa Fe, N.M.: School of American Research Press.

———. Forthcoming. *Modernity at Large: Cultural Dimensions of Globalization.* Minneapolis: University of Minnesota Press.

Appadurai, Arjun, and Carol A. Breckenridge. 1988. Why Public Culture? *Public Culture* 1 (1): 5-9.

———. 1992. "Museums Are Good to Think: Heritage on View in India." In *Museums and Communities,* edited by I. Karp, S. Levine, and C. Mullen Kreamer, pp. 34-55. Washington, D.C., and London: Smithsonian Institution Press.

Arato, Andrew, and Eike Gebhardt, eds. 1990. *The Essential Frankfurt School Reader.* New York: Continuum.

Arendt, Hannah. 1951. *The Origins of Totalitarianism.* New York: Harcourt, Brace.

Bender, Thomas. 1989. Metropolitan Life and Public Culture. In *Power, Culture and Place: Essays in New York City History,* edited by John Mullenkopk. New York: Russell Sage.

Benjamin, Walter. 1976. The Work of Art in the Age of Mechanical Reproduction [German original 1936]. In *Illuminations*, translated by Harry Zohn, edited by Hannah Arendt, pp. 217-51. New York: Schocken.

Bennett, Tony, and Janet Woollacott. 1987. *Bond and Beyond: The Political Career of a Popular Hero*. New York: Methuen.

Bennett, Tony, Colin Mercer, and Janet Woollacott, eds. 1986. *Popular Culture and Social Relations*. Milton Keynes and Philadelphia: Open University Press.

Bhabha, Homi K., ed. 1990. *Nation and Narration*. New York: Routledge.

Binford, Mira Reym, ed. 1989. Indian Cinema. *Quarterly Review of Film and Video* 11 (3): 1-108.

Boyd, Douglas A., Joseph D. Straubhaar, and John A. Lent. 1988. *Videocassette Recorders in the Third World*. New York: Longman.

Breckenridge, Carol A. 1987. The Work of Leisure, the Culture of Place: Video and the Humble Geographies of Tourism in India. Unpublished manuscript.

Breckenridge, Carol A., and Peter van der Veer, eds. 1993. *Orientalism and the Postcolonial Predicament*. Philadelphia: University of Pennsylvania Press.

Calhoun, Craig, ed. 1992. *Habermas and the Public Sphere*. Cambridge, Mass., and London: MIT Press.

Chanda, P. Sita. 1991. Birthing Terrible Beauties: Feminisms and "Women's Magazines." *Economic and Political Weekly* 26 (43): WS67-WS70.

Chartier, Roger. 1984. "Culture as Appropriation: Popular Cultural Uses in Early Modern France." In *Understanding Popular Culture: Europe from the Middle Ages to the Nineteenth Century*, edited by Steven L. Kaplan, pp. 229-54. Berlin: Mouton.

Crow, Thomas E. 1985. *Painters and Public Life in Eighteenth Century Paris*. New Haven, Conn.: Yale University Press.

Das Gupta, Chidananda. 1980. *Talking about Films*. New Delhi: Orient Longman.

de Certeau, Michel. 1984. *The Practice of Everyday Life*. Translated by Steven Rendell. Berkeley: University of California Press.

Deleuze, G., and F. Guattari. 1987. *A Thousand Plateaus: Capitalism and Schizophrenia*. Translated by B. Massumi. Minneapolis: University of Minnesota Press.

Dickey, Sara. 1993. *Cinema and the Urban Poor in South India*. Cambridge and New York: Cambridge University Press.

Dissanayake, Wimal, ed. 1987. Self and Modernization in Malayalam Cinema. *East-West Film Journal* 1 (2): 60-77.

———. 1988. *Cinema and Cultural Identity: Reflections on Films from Japan, India, and China*. Lanham, Md.: University Press of America.

———. 1992. *Sholay: A Cultural Reading*. New Delhi: Wiley Eastern.

Elias, Norbert. 1978. *The Civilizing Process*. Translated by Edmund Jephcott. Oxford: Basil Blackwell.

Featherstone, Mike, ed. 1990. *Global Culture: Nationalism, Globalization and Modernity*. London: Sage.

Feld, Steven. 1988. Notes on World Beat. *Public Culture* 1 (1): 31-37.

Fish, Stanley. 1980. *Is There a Text in This Class? The Authority of Interpretive Communities*. Cambridge, Mass.: Harvard University Press.

Foucault, Michel. 1972. *Power/Knowledge: Selected Interviews and Other Writings, 1972-1977*. Edited by Colin Gordon. New York: Pantheon.

Fraser, Nancy. 1990. Rethinking the Public Sphere: A Contribution to the Critique of Actually Existing Democracy. *Social Text*, no. 25/26: 56-80.

Freitag, Sandria B. 1989a. *Collective Action and Community: Public Arenas and the Emergence of Communalism in North India*. Berkeley and Los Angeles: University of California Press.

———. 1989b. Popular Culture in the Rewriting of History: An Essay in Comparative History and Historiography. *Peasant Studies* 16 (3): 169-98.

———. 1991. Aspects of the Public in Colonial South Asia. *South Asia: Journal of South Asian Studies*, n.s. 14 (1) (special issue edited by Sandria Freitag).

Freitag, Sandria B., ed. 1989c. *Culture and Power in Banaras: Communication, Performance, and Environment, 1800-1980*. Berkeley and Los Angeles: University of California Press.

Ganley, Gladys D., and Oswald H. Ganley. 1987. *Global Political Fallout: The First Decade of the VCR 1976-1985*. Cambridge, Mass.: Harvard University Press.

Goffman, Erving. 1963. *Behavior in Public Places: Notes on the Social Organization of Gatherings*. New York: Free Press of Glencoe.

Guha, Ranajit, and Gayatri Chakravorty Spivak, eds. 1988. *Selected Subaltern Studies*. New York: Oxford University Press.

Habermas, Jürgen. 1989. *The Structural Transformation of the Public Sphere: An Inquiry into a Category of Bourgeois Society* [German original 1962]. Cambridge, Mass.: MIT Press.

Haggard, Sunil. 1989. Mass Media and the Visual Arts in Twentieth-Century South Asia: Indian Film Posters 1947-Present. *South Asia Research* 8 (1): 71-88.

Hall, Stuart. 1982. "The Recovery of Ideology: The Return of the Repressed in Media Studies." In *Culture, Society and the Media*, edited by Michel Gurevitch et al., pp. 56-90. London: Methuen.

Hannerz, Ulf. 1989. Notes on the Global Ecumene. *Public Culture* 1 (2): 66-75.

———. 1992. *Cultural Complexity*. New York: Columbia University Press.

Hansen, Miriam. 1993. Unstable Mixtures, Dilated Spheres: Negt and Kluge's *The Public Sphere and Experience*, Twenty Years Later. *Public Culture* 5 (2): 179-212.

Harvey, David. 1989. *The Condition of Postmodernity: An Enquiry into the Origins of Cultural Change*. Oxford: Basil Blackwell.

Hebdige, Dick. 1979. *Subculture: The Meaning of Style*. London: Methuen.

Holston, James. 1989. *The Modernist City: An Anthropological Critique of Brasilia*. Chicago: University of Chicago Press.

Horne, Donald. 1986. *The Public Culture: The Triumph of Industrialism*. London: Pluto.

Hunt, Lynn, ed. 1989. *The New Cultural History*. Berkeley and Los Angeles: University of California Press.

Iser, Wolfgang. 1989. *Prospecting from Reader Response to Literary Anthropology*. Baltimore, Md.: Johns Hopkins University Press.

Ivy, Marilyn. 1988. Tradition and Difference in the Japanese Mass Media. *Public Culture* 1 (1): 21-29.

Kapur, Geeta. 1991. Place of the Modern in Indian Cultural Practice. *Economic and Political Weekly* 26: 2803-6.

Keane, John. 1988. *Democracy and Civil Society: On the Predicaments of European Socialism, the Prospects for Democracy, and the Problem of Controlling Social and Political Power*. London: Verso.

Kemper, Steven. 1993. The Nation Consumed: Buying and Believing in Sri Lanka. *Public Culture* 5 (3): 377-93.

Kracauer, Siegfried. 1987. Cult of Distraction: On Berlin's Picture Palaces. *New German Critique* 40: 91-96.

Kumar, Nita. 1988. *The Artisans of Banaras: Popular Culture and Identity, 1880-1986*. Princeton, N.J.: Princeton University Press.

Lee, Benjamin. 1993. Going Public. *Public Culture* 5 (2): 165-78.

Liebman, Stuart, ed. 1988. Alexander Kluge: Theoretical Writings, Stories, and an Interview. *October* 46 (special issue edited by Stuart Liebman).

Lutgendorf, Philip. 1990. Ramayan: The Video. *Drama Review* 34 (2): 127-76.

Mankekar, Purnima. 1993. Television Tales and a Woman's Rage: A Nationalist Recasting of Draupadi's "Disrobing." *Public Culture* 5 (3): 469-91.

Manuel, Peter. 1993. *Popular Music and Cassette Culture in North India.* Chicago: University of Chicago Press.

Mattelart, Armand. 1979. *Multinational Corporations and the Control of Culture: The Ideological Apparatuses of Imperialism.* Translated by Michael Chanan. Sussex: Harvester.

———. 1983. *Transnationals and the Third World: The Struggle for Culture.* South Hadley, Mass.: Bergin and Garvey.

Mattelart, Armand, and Michèle Mattelart. 1990. *The Carnival of Images: Brazilian Television Fiction.* Translated by David Buxton. New York, Westport, Conn., and London: Bergin and Garvey.

Mattelart, Michèle. 1983. "Notes on 'Modernity': A Way of Reading Women's Magazines." In *Communication and Class Struggle. Vol. 1, Capitalism, Imperialism,* edited by Armand Mattelart and Seth Siegelaub, pp. 158-70. Great Britain: International General Editions.

Mazumdar, Ranjani. 1991. Dialectic of Public and Private: Representation of Women in *Bhoomika* and *Mirch Masala. Economic and Political Weekly* 26 (43): WS81-WS84.

Mbembe, Achille. 1992a. The Banality of Power and the Aesthetics of Vulgarity in the Postcolony. Translated by Janet Roitman. *Public Culture* 4 (2): 1-30.

———. 1992b. Prosaics of Servitude and Authoritarian Civilities. Translated by Janet Roitman. *Public Culture* 5 (1): 123-45.

Miyoshi, Masao, and H. D. Harootunian, eds. 1989. *Postmodernism and Japan.* Durham, N.C.: Duke University Press.

Mukerji, Chandra, and Michael Schudson, eds. 1991. *Rethinking Popular Culture: Contemporary Perspectives in Cultural Studies.* Berkeley: University of California Press.

Mulvey, Laura. 1989. *Visual and Other Pleasures.* Bloomington: Indiana University Press.

Negt, Oskar, and Alexander Kluge. 1993. *The Public Sphere and Experience: Toward an Analysis of the Bourgeois and Proletarian Public Sphere.* Foreword by Miriam Hansen. Translated by Peter Labanyi. Minneapolis: University of Minnesota Press.

Niranjana, Tejaswini. 1991. Cinema, Femininity and Economy of Consumption. *Economic and Political Weekly* 26 (43): WS85-WS86.

Niranjana, Tejaswini, Vivek Dhareshwar, and P. Sudhir, eds. 1993. *Interrogating Modernity: Culture and Colonialism in India.* Calcutta: Seagull.

Radway, Janice A. 1984. *Reading the Romance: Women, Patriarchy, and Popular Literature.* Chapel Hill: University of North Carolina Press.

Rajadhyaksha, Ashish. 1986. Neo-Traditionalism: Film as Popular Art in India. *Framework,* no. 32/33: 20-67

Rajagopal, Arvind. 1993. The Rise of National Programming: The Case of Indian Television. *Media, Culture and Society* 15 (1): 91-112.

Robbins, Bruce, ed. 1993. *The Phantom Public Sphere.* Minneapolis and London: University of Minnesota Press.

Rosenau, James N. 1990. *Turbulence in World Politics.* Princeton, N.J.: Princeton University Press.

Schiller, H. 1976. *Communication and Cultural Domination.* White Plains, N.Y.: International Arts and Sciences.

Schudson, Michael. 1984. *Advertising, the Uneasy Profession: Its Dubious Impact on American Society.* New York: Basic Books.

Sennett, Richard. 1976. *The Fall of Public Man.* New York: Knopf.

Shah, Panna. 1950. *The Indian Film.* Bombay: Motion Picture Society of India.

Shiach, Morag. 1989. *Discourse on Popular Culture: Class, Gender and History in Cultural Analysis, 1730 to the Present.* Cambridge: Polity Press.

Siegel, James T. 1986. *Solo in the New Order: Language and Hierarchy in an Indonesian City.* Princeton, N.J.: Princeton University Press.

Smith, Barbara Herrnstein. 1988. *Contingencies of Value: Alternative Perspectives for Critical Theory.* Cambridge, Mass.: Harvard University Press.

Soja, Edward W. 1989. *Postmodern Geographies: The Reassertion of Space in Critical Social Theory.* London and New York: Verso.

Srivatsan, R. 1991. Looking at Film Hoardings: Labour, Gender, Subjectivity and Everyday Life in India. *Public Culture* 4 (1): 1-24.

Talwar, Vir Bharat. 1989. "Feminist Consciousness in Women's Journals in Hindi." In *Recasting Women: Essays in Colonial History,* edited by Kumkum Sangari and Suresh Vaid. New Delhi: Kali for Women.

Urry, John, and Scott Lash. 1987. *The End of Organized Capitalism.* Madison: University of Wisconsin Press.

Vachani, L. 1989. *Narrative, Pleasure and Ideology in the Hindi Film: An Analysis of the Outsider Formula.* M.A. thesis, Annenberg School of Communication, University of Pennsylvania.

Willis, Paul E. 1977. *Learning to Labour: How Working Class Kids Get Working Class Jobs.* Aldershot, England: Gower.

Wolf, Gita. 1991. Construction of Gender Identity: Women in Popular Tamil Magazines. *Economic and Political Weekly* 26 (43): WS71-WS73.

Yeo, Eileen, and Stephen Yeo, eds. 1981. *Popular Culture and Class Conflict 1590-1914.* Atlantic Highlands, N.J.: Humanities Press.

PART I

The Historical Past

CHAPTER TWO

Playing with Modernity

The Decolonization of Indian Cricket

ARJUN APPADURAI

For the ex-colony, decolonization is a dialogue with the colonial past, and not a simple dismantling of colonial habits and modes of life. Nowhere are the complexities and ambiguities of this dialogue more evident than in the vicissitudes of cricket in countries that were once part of the British Empire. In the Indian case, the cultural aspects of decolonization deeply affect every domain of public life, from language and the arts to ideas about political representation and economic justice. In every major public debate in contemporary India, one underlying strand is always the question of what to do with the shreds and patches of the colonial heritage. Some of these patches are institutional; others are ideological and aesthetic.

Malcolm Muggeridge once joked that Indians were "the last living Englishmen," thus capturing the fact—true at least of the urbanized and Westernized elites of India—that while England itself became gradually denatured as it lost its empire, aspects of its heritage took deep root in the colonies. In the areas of politics and economics, the special relationship between India and England has very little meaning anymore, as England strives to overcome economic disaster and Indians reach out increasingly to the United States, the Middle East, and the rest of the Asian world. But there is a part of Indian culture today that seems forever to be England, and that is cricket. It is therefore worth examining the dynamics of decolonization in this sphere, where the urge to cut the ties with the colonial past seems weakest.

The process by which cricket gradually became indigenized in colonial India can best be envisioned by making a distinction between "hard" and "soft" cultural forms. "Hard" cultural forms are those that come with a set of links between value, meaning, and embodied practice, links that are difficult to break and hard to transform. "Soft" cultural forms, by contrast, are those that permit relatively easy separation of embodied performance from meaning and value, and relatively successful transformation at each level. In terms of this distinction, I would suggest that cricket is a "hard" cultural form that changes those who are socialized into it more readily than it is itself changed.

One reason cricket is not easily susceptible to reinterpretation as it crosses social boundaries is that the values it represents are, at their heart, puritan ones, in which rigid adherence to external codes is a part of the discipline of internal moral development (James 1963: chapter 2). Form closely follows (moral) function here. To some extent, all rule-governed, competitive sport has some of this "hard" quality, but it is arguably more notably present in competitive forms that come to encapsulate the core moral values of the society in which they are born.

Thus, cricket, as a "hard" cultural form, ought to resist indigenization. In fact, counterintuitively, it has become profoundly indigenized and decolonized, and India is often seen as suffering from a veritable cricket "fever" (Puri 1982). There are two ways to account for this puzzle. The first, recently suggested by Ashis Nandy (1989), is that there are mythic structures beneath the surface of the sport that make it profoundly Indian, in spite of its Western historical origins. The alternative approach (though it is not entirely inconsistent with many of Nandy's insights) is that cricket became indigenized through a set of complex and contradictory processes that parallel the emergence of an Indian "nation" from the British Empire. The argument developed in this essay is that indigenization is often a product of collective and spectacular experiments with modernity, and not necessarily of the subsurface affinity of new cultural forms with existing patterns in the cultural repertoire.

The indigenization of a sport like cricket has many dimensions: it has something to do with the way the sport is managed, patronized, and publicized; it has something to do with the class background of Indian players and thus with their capability to mimic Victorian elite values; it has something to do with the dialectic between team spirit and national sentiment, which is inherent in the sport and is implicitly corrosive of the bonds of empire; it has something to do with the way in which a reservoir of talent is created and nurtured outside the urban elites, so that the sport can become internally self-sustaining; it has something to do with the ways in which media and language help to unyoke cricket from its "Englishness"; and it has something to do with the construction of a postcolonial male spectatorship that can charge cricket with the power of bodily competition and virile nationalism. These processes interacted with one another to indigenize cricket in India in a way that is distinct from the parallel process in other British colonies (for some sense of the diaspora of cricket through the empire as a whole, see Allen 1985).

Obviously, the story of cricket depends on the vantage point from which it is told. The remarkable implications of the history of cricket in the Caribbean have been immortalized in the work of C. L. R. James (especially 1963; see also Diawara 1990 and Birbalsingh 1986). Australians have had a long struggle—dramatized in cricket—to break free of the sanctimonious and patronizing way in which they are regarded by the English. South Africa finds in cricket yet another conflicted way to reconcile its Boer and English genealogies. But it is in the colonies occupied by black and brown peoples that the story of cricket is most anguished and subtle: in the Caribbean, in Pakistan, in India, and in Sri Lanka (on the last, see Roberts 1985). I do not pretend that what cricket implies about decolonization from the Indian perspective holds good for all former colonies, but it is surely one part of the larger story of the construction of a postcolonial and global cultural framework for team sport.

The Colonial Ecumene

It is no exaggeration to suggest that cricket came closer than any other public form to distilling, constituting, and communicating the values of the Victorian upper classes in England to English gentlemen, as part of their embodied practices, and to others as a means for apprehending the class codes of the period. Its history in England goes back into the precolonial period, and there is little doubt that the sport is English in origin. In the second half of the nineteenth century, when cricket acquired much of its modern morphology, it also took shape as the most powerful condensation of Victorian elite values. These values, about which much has been written, can be summarized as follows. Cricket was a quintessentially masculine activity and expressed the codes that were expected to govern all masculine behavior: sportsmanship, a sense of fair play, thorough control over the expression of strong sentiments by players on the field, subordination of personal sentiments and interests to those of the side, unquestioned loyalty to the team.

Though cricket became a central instrument of socialization for the Victorian elite, it contained from the start a social paradox. It was honed as an instrument of elite formation, but like all complex and powerful forms of play, it both confirmed and created sporting sodalities that transcended class. Thus it was always open to the most talented (and useful) among the lower and middle classes who stumbled into it. Those among the great unwashed in Victorian England who were capable of subjecting themselves to the social and moral disciplines of the playing field could enter into a limited intimacy with their superiors. The price of admission was complete dedication to the sport and, usually, great talent on the field. Cricket was, in Victorian England, a limited road to social mobility. Of course, no amount of shared cricket would make an Englishman confuse an Oxford Blue with a Yorkshire working-class professional cricketer. But on the playing field (where cooperation was necessary) there was some respite from the brutalities of class in England. It has also been noted that it was the presence of these lower-class players that allowed the Victorian elite to incorporate the harsh techniques required to win while retaining the idea that sportsmanship involved a patrician detachment from competitiveness. Lower-class professional players thus did the dirty subaltern "work" of winning so that their class superiors could preserve the illusion of a gentlemanly, noncompetitive sport (Nandy 1989: 19-20). This inherent paradox—an elite sport whose code of fair play dictated an openness to talent and vocation in those of humble origins—is a key to the early history of cricket in India.

For much of the nineteenth century in India, cricket was a segregated sport: Englishmen and Indians played on opposite teams when they played together at all. Cricket was associated with clubs, the central social institutions of the British in India. Indian cricket clubs (and their associated teams) were largely a product of the last quarter of the nineteenth century, though there were a number of Parsi clubs based in Bombay starting in the 1840s. In this, as in other matters, the Parsis were the bridge community between Indian and English cultural tastes. Parsi teams from India toured England in the 1880s, and in 1888-89 the first English team toured India (though the majority of its matches were against teams wholly composed of Englishmen, and only a few were against teams composed of Indians). Bombay was the birthplace of cricket for Indians (and still retains a preeminent place in Indian cricket culture).

Though there was never a conscious policy in regard to the support of cricket by the colonial regime in India, cricket evolved into an unofficial instrument of state cultural policy. This was largely a result of the cultural commitments of those members of the Victorian elite who occupied key positions in Indian administration, education, and journalism, and who regarded cricket as the ideal way to transmit Victorian ideals of character and fitness to the colony. Lord Harris, governor of Bombay from 1890 to 1895, was perhaps the most crucial figure in the quasi-official patronage of cricket in India, and he was followed by a succession of governors, both in Bombay and in the other presidencies, who saw cricket as fulfilling the following range of tasks: solidifying the bonds of empire; lubricating state dealings between various Indian "communities," which might otherwise degenerate into communal (Hindu/Muslim) riots; and implanting English ideals of manliness, stamina, and vigor into Indian groups seen as lazy, enervated, and effete. In this regard, cricket was one of many arenas in which a colonial sociology was constructed and reified. In this sociology, India was seen as a congeries of antagonistic communities, populated by men (and women) with a variety of psychological defects. Cricket was seen as an ideal way to socialize natives into new modes of intergroup conduct and new standards of public behavior. Ostensibly concerned with recreation and competition, its underlying quasi-official charter was moral and political. The underlying contradiction, between "communally" organized teams and the ideal of creating broader civic bonds, underlay the development of cricket from its inception to the present, and is dealt with more fully in the next section of this essay.

On the whole, from about 1870 to 1930, in the high period of the Raj, there is no doubt that for Indians to play cricket was to experiment with the mysteries of English upper-class life. Whether it was by playing teams from England, which included men who had known each other at Eton and Harrow, Oxford and Cambridge, or in tours to England, a small segment of the Indian sporting population was initiated into the moral and social mysteries and rituals of Victorian cricket (Cashman 1980; Docker 1976).

The biographies and autobiographies of the finest Indian cricketers of this era, including Vijay Hazare (1976, 1981), L. P. Jai (Raiji 1976), and Mushtaq Ali (1981), who had active cricket careers into the 1940s, clearly show that they were exposed (in spite of their very diverse social backgrounds) to the value commitments associated with Victorian cricket—sportsmanship, self-effacement, team spirit—as well as to the hagiography and lore of cricket throughout the empire, but especially in England.

But class and race conspired in very complex ways in the "Victorian colonial ecumene" (Breckenridge 1988) and in its Edwardian successor structures. I have already suggested that Victorian cricket involved important class distinctions in England, distinctions that to this day affect the relations there between gentlemen and professional players, coaches and players, county and league cricket. Together, white males of all classes helped to create and embody a sporting code whose patrician moral dimensions were central to the upper classes, and whose "workmanlike" skills were pointers to the role of the working classes in the sport (Clarke and Clarke [1982: 82-83] offer an interesting treatment of the peculiar inflections of the idea of "manliness" in English sporting ideology). The complexity of this specific brand of colonial discourse also illustrates one variant of what has been seen, in a rather different context, as the ambivalence of colonial discourse (Bhabha 1984).

As in many other areas, including art, etiquette, language, and conduct, it is now increasingly clear that during the heyday of the modern colonialisms, a complex system of hegemonizing and hierarchizing values and practices evolved conjointly in the metropolis and its colonies (Cooper and Stoler 1989). In the case of cricket in India, the key to the complex flows that linked cricket, class, and race in the colonial ecumene was the story of patronage and coaching in India. The biographies referred to here, and an excellent synthetic account (Cashman 1980, chapter 2) make it clear that in the period between 1870 and 1930, British involvement in Indian cricket was very complex: it involved officers of the army stationed in India, businessmen from England, and senior government officials, all of whom helped to implant the idea of cricket in various Indian settings. At the same time, Indian princes brought English and Australian professional cricketers to India to train their own teams.

The princely phase in the patronage of Indian cricket is in some ways the most important in the analysis of the indigenization of cricket. First, cricket, as an elite sport, required the sort of time and money not available to the bourgeois elites of colonial India. The princes, on the other hand, were quick to see cricket as another extension of their royal traditions and absorbed such sports as polo, rifle shooting, golf, and cricket into their traditional aristocratic repertoires. This permitted them to offer new kinds of spectacle to their subjects (Docker 1976: 27), to link themselves to the English aristocracy in potentially new and fruitful ways, and to ingratiate themselves with the colonial authorities in India (such as Lord Harris), who favored cricket as a means for the moral disciplining of Orientals. The princes who supported cricket were often the less grand members of the Indian aristocracy, for cricket was somewhat cheaper than some other forms of royal patronage and spectacle. Cricket had three appeals as an adjunct to the lifestyle and ethos of petty kingship in India: (a) its role, especially in the North, as a manly art in the aristocratic culture of leisure; (b) its Victorian credentials, which opened doors in England that might otherwise be less well oiled (as in the case of Ranji); and (c) its role as a useful extension of other royal public spectacles that had been an important part of the obligations and mystique of royalty in India. Accordingly, minor and big princes in many parts of India throughout this century imported coaches from England, organized tournaments and prizes, subsidized teams and coaches, developed grounds and pitches, imported equipment and expertise, and hosted English teams.

Most important, they provided both direct and indirect support to many cricketers (or their families) from humble backgrounds, who were eventually able to make their way to bigger cities, to more important teams, and, some-times, to national and international visibility. For many Indian cricketers out-side the big colonial cities in the period before World War II, one or another form of subsidy from princely houses was the key to their entry into the cos-mopolitan world of big-time cricket. Such players were able to achieve some measure of mobility through cricket, and thus to introduce a considerable de-gree of class complexity into Indian cricket, a complexity that persists today.

The groundwork for the Indianization of cricket was therefore laid through the complex, hierarchical cross-hatching of British gentlemen in India, Indian princes, mobile Indian men who were often part of the civil services and the army, and, most important, those white cricketing profes-sionals (mainly from England and Australia) who actually trained the great Indian cricketers of the first decades of this century. These professionals, the most prominent of whom were Frank Tarrant, Bill Hitch, and Clarrie Grimmett, as well as the somewhat more socially established British army men, college principals, and businessmen who "coached" budding Indian cricketers, seem to have been the crucial links between stardom, aristocracy, and technical skill in the colonial cricketing world at large. What these pro-fessional coaches accomplished was to provide the technical skills that were crucial for the patronage fantasies of the Indian princes (which were in turn tied to their own fantasies of a monarchical/aristocratic ideal of empire) to be translated into competitive Indian teams actually composed of Indians. Although there is no decisive evidence for the following interpretation, it is highly likely that small-town boys like Mushtaq Ali, Vijay Hazare, and Lala Amarnath would have had a hard time entering the rarefied world of cricket (still dominated by English, and Victorian, sporting codes) without the translation of cricket into an embodied technical practice by these lower-class white professionals. Thus it is not the case that an Anglophone class drama was simply reproduced in India; in the circulation of princes, coaches, army officials, viceroys, college principals, and players of humble class origin between India and England (and Australia) a complex imperial class regime was formed. In this regime Indian and English social hierarchies were interlinked and cross-hatched to produce, by the 1930s, a cadre of nonelite Indians who felt themselves to be genuine cricketers and genuinely "Indian" as well.

In this light, the great princely batsman Ranjitsinhji (1872-1933) is probably a sad exception; for him cricketing and "Englishness" became so deeply connected that he could never take the idea of cricket as an Indian game very seriously. He was the *jamsaheb* of Nawanagar, a small kingdom in Saurashtra, on the west coast of India. Ranji has a mythic place in the annals of cricket, and is even today (along with a handful of others like W. G. Grace, Don Bradman, and Gary Sobers) considered to be one of the great batsmen of all time. It is worth spending a little time on Ranji, for he exemplifies what colonial cricket was all about. Ironically, it was probably just this profound identification with the empire and the Crown that allowed Ranji to become the quintessential and living trope of an "Oriental" form of cricketing skill.

Ranji was not simply a great run getter but was also seen in cricket circles as carrying a peculiar Oriental glow. The great C. B. Fry said of him that "he moved as if he had no bones; one would not be surprised to see brown curves burning in the grass where one of his cuts had travelled or blue flame shimmering round his bat, as he made one of his strokes." Neville Cardus said that "when he batted, strange light was seen for the first time on English fields." Clem Hill, an Australian test cricketer, simply said: "He is more than a batsman, he's a juggler!" Bill Hitch, the Surrey and England fast bowler, referred to him as "the master, the magician" (de Mellow 1979: chapter 10).

Ranji was seen to bring a peculiarly Indian genius to batting, hence the reference to magic and juggling, strange light and blue flames. Ranji in fact represented the glamorous obverse of the effeminacy, laziness, and lack of stamina that many colonial theorists thought Indians represented (Hutchins 1967: chapter 3; Nandy 1983). In Ranji, wile became guile, trickery became magic, weakness became suppleness, effeminacy was transformed into grace. This Orientalist glow, of course, had a great deal to do with Ranji's impeccable social credentials, his total devotion to English institutions (all the way from college to the Crown), and his unswerving loyalty to the empire. He thus not only revolutionized cricket and offered the crowds an extraordinary treat when he was at bat, but English audiences could always read in his performances a loyal and glamorous offering of the mysterious Orient to the playing fields of Eton. Ranji was the ultimate brown Englishman. There is no doubt, however, that he belonged to that generation of Indian princes for whom loyalty to the Crown and pride in being Indian were coextensive, although one recent analyst has suggested that Ranji's commitments may have been expressions of deep personal doubts and conflicts (Nandy 1989).

Ranji's story is only an extreme case of a more general irony: that the Indian princes, who patronized cricket as a way to enter the patrician Victorian world and were largely opposed to the nationalist movement, in fact laid the grounds for the mastery of cricket among ordinary Indians that was to blossom into a full-blown pride in Indian cricketing competence by the 1930s.

Cricket, Empire, and Nation

Today, the extraordinary popularity of cricket in India is clearly tied up with nationalist sentiment. But in the early history of the game in India, as we have noted already, cricket fostered two other kinds of loyalty. The first was (and is) to religious (communal) identities. The second, rather more abstractly instantiated in the sport, was loyalty to empire. The interesting question here is how the idea of the *Indian nation* emerged as a salient *cricketing* entity.

As far back as the first clubs organized by Parsis in Bombay in the mid-nineteenth century, membership in religious communities became the salient principle around which Indians banded together to play cricket. This organizing principle remained in place until it was dislodged in the 1930s. Hindus, Parsis, Muslims, the Europeans, and, eventually, the Rest (a label for bringing together communally unmarked groups into cricket teams) were organized into cricket clubs. There was much debate, from the very start, about the pros and cons of this "communal" organization of cricket. Though elsewhere in princely India the major patrons of sport were the princes, who paid no regard to communal principles in their recruitment of players, in the presidencies of British India, players were divided into religious/ethnic groupings, some of which included antagonists in public life more generally. Thus, cricket was an important arena in which players as well as crowds learned to think of themselves as "Hindu," "Muslim," and "Parsi," in contrast with the "Europeans."

There has been much good historical work to show that these social categories were both the creation and the instrument of a colonial sociology of rule (Appadurai 1981; Cohn 1987; Dirks 1987; Freitag 1989; Pandey 1990; Prakash 1990), but the fact is that they entered deeply into Indian self-conceptions and into Indian politics and cultural life. Though it is true that census classifications, the control of religious endowments, and the issue of separate electorates were the major official arenas in which issues of communal identity were reified as part of a colonial sociology of India, the role of cricket in this process must not be underestimated. At least in Western India, British officials like Governor Harris were complacent in their view of cricket as a safety valve for communal hostility and as a means for teaching Indians how to live amicably with communal diversity. But, deeply embedded as they were in their own fictions about the fragmentation of Indian society, what they did not realize was that in the playing field (as elsewhere) they were perpetuating communal conceptions of identity that in Indian cities might have become more fluid. Thus we have the paradox that in Bombay, perhaps the most cosmopolitan colonial city, the major elite sport was organized around communal lines.

This communal principle was bound to become otiose as the seriousness and quality of cricket in India increased. Unlike cricket in India, English cricket was organized around a system in which the nation was the exemplary unit, and "counties," not communities, were its lower-level constituencies. In other words, territory and nationhood for England, community and cultural distinctiveness for "India" (Appadurai 1993). Thus when English teams began to tour India, the question was how to construct an "Indian" team that was a fitting opponent. In the early tours, in the 1890s, "Indian" teams were largely composed of Englishmen, but as more Indians began to play the game, and as more patrons and entrepreneurs began to organize teams and tournaments, it was inevitable that the full pool of Indian talent be drawn upon to construct a first-rate Indian team. This process, whereby Indians increasingly came to represent "India" in cricket, follows, not surprisingly, the history of the evolution of Indian nationalism as a mass movement. Cricket in the Indian colonial context thus casts an unexpected light on the relationship between nationhood and empire. Insofar as England was not simply identical with the empire, there had to be other parallel entities in the colonies against which the English nation-state could play; thus "India" had to be invented, at least for the purposes of colonial cricket.

Yet there was surprisingly little explicit communication between those who were responsible for organizing cricket in India on an all-India basis and those in the all-India Congress Party (and elsewhere) who (beginning in the 1880s) were professionally committed to the idea of a free Indian nation.

The idea of "Indian" talent, an "Indian" team, and "Indian" competition in international cricket emerged relatively independently, under nonofficial stimulation by its patrons and publicists. Thus "cricket nationalism" emerged as a paradoxical, though logical, outgrowth of the development of cricket in England. Rather than being a spin-off of the "imagined community" of nationalist politicians in India, nationally organized cricket was an internal demand of the colonial enterprise, and thus required cognate national or protonational enterprises in the colonies.

Nevertheless, as cricket became more popular in the first three decades of this century, and as the nationalist movement, particularly with Mahatma Gandhi and the Indian National Congress, gathered momentum in the same period, cricket nationalism and explicitly nationalist politics as such did come into contact in the ordinary lives of young Indians. Thus, N. K. P. Salve, a major Indian politician and cricket entrepreneur, recalls how, in the early thirties, he and his friends were intimidated and prevented from playing on a fine cricket pitch in Nagpur by a certain Mr. Thomas, an Anglo-Indian sergeant in charge of the pitch, who "looked like an African cape buffalo, massive and hefty in size, otherwise possessed of offensive, uncouth and vulgar characteristics" (Salve 1987: 5). After several scary and abusive episodes involving Thomas (a classic subaltern figure keeping native urchins away from the sacrosanct spaces of imperial performance), Salve's father and his friends, all influential local followers of Gandhi, intervened on behalf of the young boys with a senior British official in Nagpur and won them the right to use the pitch when it was not in "official" use. Throughout Salve's narration of this story we get a strong sense of his fear of the Anglo-Indian subaltern, the sensuous attraction of playing on an "official" pitch, the outrage of Indians being kept out of a public space, and the nationalist flavor of their resentment. It is probable that cricket nationalism and official nationalist politics were rarely wedded in conscious public debates or movements, but that they affected the lived experience of play, skill, space, and rights for many young Indians in the small towns and playing fields of India before independence. But the growth of cricket consciousness and cricket excitement cannot be understood without reference to the role of language and the media.

Vernacularization and the Media

The media have played a crucial role in the indigenization of cricket, first through the English-language cricket commentaries aired by All-India Radio starting in 1933. Largely in English during the thirties, forties, and fifties (Cashman 1980: 145-46), radio commentary starting in the sixties was increasingly in Hindi, Tamil, and Bengali, as well as in English. Multilingual radio commentary is probably the single most important instrument in the socialization of the Indian mass audience into the subtleties of the sport. While commentary on the test matches (involving India and other countries) has been confined to English, Hindi, Tamil, and Bengali, other first-class matches are accompanied by radio commentary in all the major languages of the subcontinent. No systematic study has been made of the role of vernacular cricket commentary in socializing nonurban Indians into the cosmopolitan culture of cricket, but it was evidently a major factor in the indigenization of the sport.

Through radios, which are very widely available and which attract large crowds in train stations, cafeterias, and other public places, Indians have absorbed the English terminology of cricket, especially its noun structure, into a variety of vernacular syntactic structures. This type of sports pidgin is crucial to the indigenization of the sport for it permits contact with an arcane form at the same time as the form is linguistically domesticated. Thus, the elementary vocabulary of cricket terms in English is widely known throughout India (increasingly even in villages).

The complex linguistic experiences that emerged in the context of vernacular broadcasts are exemplified in the following narrative taken from Cashman (1980: 147):

> During the 1972-73 series the following conversation between Lala Amarnath, the expert, and the Hindi commentator took place after Ajit Wadekar had straight driven Pocock for four off the front foot. This conversation illustrated this hybrid language and some of the hazards of its use:
>
> HINDI COMMENTATOR: Lalaji, aap wo back foot straight drive ke bare me kya kahena chahte hain?
>
> AMARNATH: Wo back foot nahin front foot drive thi . . . badi sunder thi . . . wristy thi.
>
> COMMENTATOR: Han Badi risky thi. Wadekar ko aisa nahin khelna chahiye.
>
> AMARNATH: Commentator sahib, risky nahin wristy. Wrist se mari hui.
>
> (Translation)
>
> COMMENTATOR: Lala, what would you like to say about that straight drive off the back foot?
>
> AMARNATH: That was a front and not a back foot drive . . . it was beautiful . . . was wristy.
>
> COMMENTATOR: So that was risky. Wadekar shouldn't have played like that.
>
> AMARNATH: Mr. Commentator, risky is not wristy. It was hit with the wrist.

Although Cashman's translation is not entirely sensitive, it makes it quite clear that the vernacularization of cricket has its linguistic pitfalls, but what he does not note is that it is through the discussion of such errors that Hindi speakers domesticate a relatively esoteric cricket term like *wristy.*

The media hegemony of cricket (often a source of complaint on the part of partisans of other sports) has been deepened since the arrival of television. After a very modest start with small audiences in the late 1960s, television has now completely transformed cricket culture in India. Cricket, as several commentators have pointed out, is perfectly suited for television, with its many pauses, its spatial concentration of action, and its extended format. For audience as well as advertisers it is the perfect television sport.

Television reduces foreign teams and stars to manageable size; it visually domesticates the exotic nature of the sport (particularly for those who might previously only have "heard" matches on the radio). And, for a country whose cinema stars are its major celebrities, television lends cinematic authority to the sports spectacle. In a civilization where "seeing" (*darsan*) is the sacred instrument of communion, television has intensified the star status of the great Indian cricket players. Indian test cricketers have never been the objects of greater adulation than in the past decade of intense television viewing of major games.

Television has deepened the national passion for cricket nurtured by radio, but both radio commentary and television watching have been reinforced, from the viewpoint of audience reception and participation by a vast growth in books, newspaper coverage, and sports magazine consumption, not just in English, but also in the vernaculars.

The proliferation of news, biographies of stars, commentaries, and instructional literature, especially in the major cricket-playing areas, provides the critical backdrop for the special force of television. While this vernacular material is "read" and "heard" by those who do not themselves read, radio is "heard" and "imagined" in live form, while television coverage makes the transition to spectacle. These mass-mediated forms have created a public that is extremely large, is literate in many different senses in the subtleties of the sport, and can bring to cricket the passions generated by reading, by hearing, and by seeing.

The role of the mass vernacular literature in this process is crucial, for what these books, magazines, and pamphlets do is to create a bridge between the vernaculars and the English language, put pictures and names of foreign players into Indic scripts and syntax, and reinforce the body of "contact" terms, English terms transliterated into Hindi, Marathi, or Tamil, heard on the radio. Some of these materials also are instructional and contain elaborate diagrams and verbal texts that explain the various strokes, styles, rules, and logics of cricket to readers who may know no English. This vernacularization process, which I have examined most closely with a body of materials in Marathi,[1] provide a verbal repertoire that allows large numbers of Indians to experience cricket as a linguistically familiar form, thus liberating cricket from the very "Englishness" that first gave it its moral authority and intrigue.

Vernacular commentary on radio (and later on television) provides the first step to the domestication of the vocabulary of cricket because it provides not just a contact vocabulary, but also a link between this vocabulary and the excitement of the heard or seen drama of the game, its strokes, its rhythm, its physical excitement. The "Englishness" of cricket terminology is drawn into the world of Hindi, Marathi, Tamil, and Bengali but is simultaneously brought into intimate contact with the actual playing of the game throughout the streets, playgrounds, and building lots of urban India and the free spaces of many villages as well. Thus, the acquisition of cricket terminology in the vernacular reinforces the sense of bodily competence in the sport, which in turn is given a hefty boost by watching the sport regularly on television. The great stars of cricket are imitated, children are nicknamed after them, and the terminology of cricket, its strokes and its stars, its rules and its rhythms, become part of vernacular pragmatics and a sense of lived bodily competence.

The vast corpus of printed materials in the vernaculars reinforces this link between terminological control and bodily excitement and competence by providing large amounts of information, statistics, and lore that further reinforce the linguistic and pictorial competence of Indians who are only partially comfortable in the Anglophone world. In the many books, magazines, and pamphlets in the vernaculars, the rules, strokes, and terminology of cricket (most often transliterated directly from the English, so that they remain part of the linguistic ecumene of international cricket) are often accompanied by schematic diagrams. Discussing at length the lives and styles of cricketers both Indian and foreign and embedding these discussions in detailed debates and dialogues about matters of judgment and regulation (such as "neutral umpiring"), these materials hitch cricket terminology to the body as a site of language use and experience. In addition, by embedding these instructional materials in news, gossip, stars, and sensational events surrounding cricket, cricket is drawn into a wider world of celebrities, controversies, and contexts outside of sport, which further embed it in linguistically familiar terrain.

The Hindi-language magazine *Kriket-Kriket* provides an excellent example of the "interocular" (Appadurai and Breckenridge 1991) world of the vernacular reader, for this magazine contains advertisements for Hindi pulp fiction, for Hindi comic books, for various body products like contact lenses and indigenous lotions, and for photo albums of cricket stars. There are also advertisements for various kinds of how-to and self-help pocket books, most dealing with skills like electrical wiring and shorthand as well as more esoteric subjects like methods of making lubricating grease for machinery. Finally, many lavish color photos of cricket stars and numerous news items on specific matches and tournaments embed cricket in a splendid world of semicosmopolitan glitz in which cricket provides the textual "suture" for a much more diverse collage of materials having to do with modern lifestyles and fantasies. Since magazines such as *Kriket-Kriket* are relatively cheaply produced and sold, their paper and graphics quality is low, and therefore it is not at all easy to distinguish various kinds of news and opinion pieces from the advertisements for other kinds of literature and services. The total effect is of a seamless web of verbal and visual impressions of cosmopolitanism in which cricket is the connective tissue. Other vernacular magazines are more chaste and less interocular than this one, but taken together with other printed materials, and especially with the additional experiences of radio, television, and film newsreels of cricket matches, they testify that the culture of cricket consumed by semi-Anglophone readers is decisively postcolonial and polyglot.

Perhaps even more important are the newspaper and magazine stories, as well as the books, that tell the cricketing life stories of various stars both old and new. These cricket life stories in the vernacular locate the skills and excitement of the sport in linguistically manageable narratives, thus making not just comprehensible stars but also proximate cricketing "lives." These readable lives then become the basis for a renewed intimacy in the reception of radio and television coverage of cricket events, and the bodily hexis of even the most rustic boy, playing with poor equipment on a fallow field, is tied at the level of language and the body to the world of high-powered cricket spectacles. The fact that many of these books and pamphlets are either ghostwritten or written in association with professional writers does not detract from their force as tools for understanding cricket for many readers outside the Anglophone world. Tying the life of a star to known places, events, schools, teachers, coaches, and fellow players creates a narrative structure in which cricket becomes enlivened just as its "stars" are made graspable (for an excellent example, see Shastri and Patil 1982).

The general force of the media experience is thus powerfully synesthetic. Cricket is read, heard, and seen, and the force of daily life experiences of cricket, occasional glimpses of live cricket matches and stars, and the more predictable experiences of the cricket spectacle on television all conspire not just to vernacularize cricket but also to inject the master terms and master tropes of cricket into the bodily practices and body-related fantasies of many young Indian males. Print, radio, and television reinforce each other powerfully and create an environment in which cricket is simultaneously larger than life (because of its stars, its spectacles, and its association with the glamour of world tests and international intrigue) and close to life (because it has been rendered into lives, manuals, and news that are no longer English-mediated). As Indians from various linguistic regions in India see and hear the cricket narratives of television and radio, they do so not as neophytes struggling to grasp an "English" form, but as culturally literate viewers for whom cricket has been deeply vernacularized. Thus, through a complex set of experiential and pedagogical loops, the "reception" of cricket becomes a critical instrument of subjectivity and agency in the process of decolonization.

The Empire Plays Back

Decolonization at the reception end involves the acquisition of cultural literacy in cricket by a mass audience, and this side of decolonization involves the sort of appropriation of competence that we are all inclined to applaud. But there is also a production dimension to decolonization, and here we enter the complex world of entrepreneurship and spectacle, of state sponsorship and vast private profits.

While it is true that poorer and less urbane Indian men were able to enter the cosmopolitan world of cricket through royal or official support in the period before World War II, the relatively wide class base of even the best Indian teams would not have lasted after the war had it not been for the fascinating and quite unusual pattern of patronage of cricket by major business corporations, especially in Bombay but also throughout India.

Corporate patronage of cricket is a fascinating factor in the sociology of Indian sport, and its essentials are these: many prestigious companies hired (and still do) outstanding cricket players early in their careers, gave them considerable freedom to maintain the rigorous practice schedules ("at the nets") to assure their staying in form, and, most important, assured them secure employment as regular members of their staffs after their cricket careers ended. Such employment of cricketers was seen, originally in Bombay in the 1950s, as a beneficial form of social advertising, accruing goodwill to the company by its support of an increasingly popular sport, of some "stars," and of the health of the national image in international competition. Corporate employment of cricketers has meant support of talent not just in the big cities; the State Bank of India (a huge public-sector operation) recruited and hired excellent cricketers in branches throughout India, so that this patron was single-handedly responsible for the nurturance of cricket far from its urban homes. Thus corporate patronage of cricket is not only responsible for providing a quasi-professional means of security for a sport whose deepest ideals are "amateur," it also provides a steady initiative for drawing in aspiring young men from the poorer classes and from semirural parts of India.

In turn, corporate support has meant that the state has been able to make a relatively low investment in cricket yet reap a large profit in terms of national sentiment. While the patronage of cricket since World War II has been largely a commercial investment on the part of major corporations (as part of their public relations and advertising budgets), the state in India has been generous with its extension of media support to the game. This alliance between state-controlled investments—through media and the provision of law and order, through private commercial interests in providing career security to players, and through a complex public (though not governmental) body called the Board of Control—provided the infrastructure for the transformation of cricket into a major national passion in the four decades since Indian independence in 1947.

The television phase in the history of Indian cricket, of course, is part of the intense recent commercialization of cricket and the associated commodification of its stars. Like other sports figures in the capitalist world, the best-known Indian cricket stars are now metacommodities, on sale themselves while they fuel the circulation of other commodities. The sport itself is increasingly in the hands of advertisers, promoters, and entrepreneurs, with television, radio, and print media feeding the national passion for the sport and its stars. Such commodification of public spectacles appears at first glance to be simply the Indian expression of a worldwide process, and thus to represent neither decolonization nor indigenization but recolonization by the forces of international capital. But what it mostly represents is the aggressive mood of Indian capitalists in seizing the potential of cricket for commercial purposes.

Transformed into a national passion by the processes of spectacle, cricket in the past two decades has become a matter of mass entertainment and mobility for some, and thereby has become wrapped up with winning (Nandy 1989). Indian crowds have become steadily more greedy for Indian victories in test matches and steadily more vituperative about losses, both at home and abroad. Thus players, coaches, and managers walk a tighter rope than ever before. While they reap the benefits of stardom and commercialization, they have to be increasingly solicitous of critics and the crowd, who do not tolerate even temporary setbacks. This has meant a steady growth in the pressure for technical excellence.

After a serious slump from the mid-fifties to the late sixties, Indian cricketers won some extraordinary victories in 1971 over the West Indies and over England, both on the home grounds of their opponents. Though the 1971 national team was hailed by crowds and critics alike, there were suggestions that the victories owed much to luck and the poor form of the opposing teams. Nevertheless, 1971 marked a turning point for Indian cricket, under the leadership of Ajit Wadekar. Though there were some real setbacks after that, Indian cricketers had shown that they could beat their former colonial masters on their home grounds, and beat the formidable Caribbean players on theirs. The 1971 victories marked the psychological inauguration of a new boldness in Indian cricket.

The seventies were a period in which every test team was humbled by the West Indies, who seemed too powerful to touch, with their brilliant batsmen, their extraordinary (and scary) fast bowlers, and their speed in the field. Cricket had become the Caribbean sport; everyone else was struggling to stay in the picture. In this context, the sweetest moment for Indian cricket was the victory over a strong West Indies team in 1983. With that victory, India established itself as a world force in international cricket whose real competition was the West Indies and Pakistan rather than England and Australia. South Africa, New Zealand, and Sri Lanka remained largely outside the top rank in test cricket. By 1983 England appeared to be a spent force in test cricket (in spite of occasional stars like Ian Botham) and India a major one.

But it is important not only that the black and brown ex-colonies now dominate world cricket. It is significant that their triumph coincides with a period in which the impact of media, commercialization, and national passion have almost completely eroded the old Victorian civilities associated with cricket. Cricket is now aggressive, spectacular, and frequently unsporting: audiences thirst for national victory, and players and promoters are out for the money. It is hard to escape the conclusion that the decolonization of cricket would not have occurred without detaching the sport from its Victorian moral integument. Nor is this process restricted to the colonies: it has been noticed that Thatcherism in England has done much to erode the ideology of "fair play" that once dominated cricket in its home country (Marshall 1987).

Cricket now belongs to a different moral and aesthetic world, far from the one imagined by Thomas Arnold of Rugby. Nothing marks this change in ethos as much as the arrival of the professionalized, strictly commercial phenomenon of World Series Cricket (WSC), a global, media-centered cricket package created by an Australian named Kerry Packer. Packer's WSC was the first major threat both to the colonial ecumene of amateur sportsmanship and to the post-World War II ethic of cricket nationalism, centered as it was on the major innovation in the sport since World War II—one-day cricket, in which a single day's play (as opposed to five or more days) settles the outcome. One-day cricket encourages risk taking, aggressiveness, and bravado while suiting perfectly the intense attention appropriate to high-powered television advertising and a higher turnover of events and settings. Packer's WSC bypassed national loyalty in the name of media entertainment and fast economic benefits for players. West Indian, English, Australian, and Pakistani cricketers were quick to see its appeals. But in India, players were slower to respond, since the structure of patronage gave them much more security than their counterparts enjoyed elsewhere. Still, Packer's bold enterprise was the signal that cricket had moved into yet another, postnationalist, phase in which entertainment value, media coverage, and the commercialization of players would transcend the national loyalty of the early postindependence period and the Victorian amateur ethic of the colonial period.

Today, Indian cricket represents a complex configuration of each of these historical transformations. The rule structure of the game and the codes of behavior on the field are still nominally regulated by the classic Victorian values of restraint, sportsmanship, and amateurism. At the same time, national loyalty is a powerful counterpoint to these ideals, and victory at any cost is the demand of crowds and television audiences. From the point of view of players and promoters, both the Victorian code and nationalist concerns are subordinated to the transnational flow of talent, celebrity, and money.

The new ethos is best captured in the recently created Australasia Cup, hosted by the tiny Persian Gulf emirate of Sharjah, which has a considerable population of Indian and Pakistani migrants. This cup brings out both the commercial and the nationalist logic of contemporary cricket. In an extremely exciting final sequence in the decisive match in 1986, watched by a television audience of 15 million, Pakistan needed four runs to win and achieved them in one stroke against the last ball of the match. The live audience for the game included film stars and other celebrities from India and Pakistan as well as South Asian migrants making their living on Gulf money.

The Sharjah cup is a long way from the playing field of Eton. The patronage of oil money, the semiproletarian audience of Indian and Pakistani migrant workers in the Persian Gulf, film stars from the subcontinent sitting on a sports field created by Islamic oil wealth, an enormous television audience in the subcontinent, prize money and ad revenue in abundance, bloodthirsty cricket: here, finally, is the last blow to Victorian upper-class cricket codes, and here is a different global ecumene. After Sharjah, all cricket is Trobriand cricket, not because of the dramatic rule changes associated with that famous form of cricket, but because of the successful hijacking of a ritual from its original English practical hegemony and its Victorian moral integument. From the perspective of Sharjah, it is the Etonians who seem like Trobrianders today.

Part of the decolonization of cricket is the corrosion of the myth of the Commonwealth, the loose fraternity of nations united by their previous status as parts of the British Empire. The Commonwealth has largely become a community of sport (like the Ivy League in the eastern United States). Politically, it represents a faint shadow of the civilities of empire. In trade, politics, and diplomacy it has become a farce: Fijians drive Indian immigrants out of the Fijian polity; Sinhalas and Tamils kill each other in Sri Lanka (while Sinhala cricket teams tour India); Pakistan and India teeter continuously on the edge of war; the new nations of Africa fight a variety of internecine battles; South Africa is a site of new interracial anxieties; and England is embarrassed by Bradford Muslims and Salman Rushdie.

Yet the Commonwealth Games are a serious and successful international enterprise, and global cricket is still on the face of it an affair of the Commonwealth. But the Commonwealth that is constituted by cricket today is not an orderly community of former colonies held together by common adherence to a Victorian and colonial code. It is an agonistic reality in which a variety of postcolonial pathologies (and dreams) are played out on the landscape of a common colonial heritage. No longer an instrument for socializing black and brown men into the public etiquette of empire, it is now an instrument for mobilizing national sentiment in the service of transnational spectacles and commoditization.

The peculiar tension between nationalism and decolonization is best seen in the cricket diplomacy between India and Pakistan, which involves multiple levels of competition and cooperation. Perhaps the best example of cooperation in the spirit of decolonization is the very complex process through which politicians and bureacrats at the highest levels of the two an tagonistic nations cooperated in the mid-1980s to shift the venue of the prestigious World Cup from England to the subcontinent in 1987, with the financial backing of the Reliance Group of Industries (one of the biggest, most aggressive business houses in contemporary India) and the encouragement of the leaders of the two countries (Salve 1987). Yet in Sharjah, as well as in every venue in India, in Pakistan, and elsewhere since Partition, cricket matches between India and Pakistan are thinly disguised national wars. Cricket is not so much a release valve for popular hostility between the two populations as a complex arena for reenacting the curious mixture of animosity and fraternity that characterizes the relations between these two previously united nation-states. England, in any case, is no longer part of the equation, whether in the tense politics of Kashmir or on the cricket grounds of Sharjah.

Recent journalistic coverage of the Australasia Cup matches in Sharjah (Tripathi 1990) suggests that the Gulf States have moved into increasing prominence as venues for international cricket, and that the national rivalry between India and Pakistan has been deliberately both highlighted and contained in order to create a simulacrum of their current tension over Kashmir. While the armies face each other across the borders of Kashmir, the cricket teams provide a star-studded simulacrum of warfare on the cricket field.

Conclusion: The Means of Modernity

It remains now to return to the general issues set out in the introduction to this essay. The example of cricket suggests something of what it takes to decolonize the production of culture in regard to what were earlier characterized as "hard" cultural forms. In this case, particularly from the Indian vantage point, the key forces that have eroded the Victorian moral and didactic framework of cricket are the indigenization of patronage, in the sense of finding both indigenous patrons whose styles can accommodate the form and audiences who can be drawn into the spectacle; state support through massive media subsidies; and commercial interest either in the standard contemporary possibilities for commodification forms or in the slightly more unusual form of company patronage for players. It is only this strong alliance of forces that, in the case of India, has permitted the gradual unyoking of cricket from its Victorian value framework and its animation by new forces associated with merchandising and with spectacle.

Yet all these factors do not get to the heart of our problem: Why is cricket a national passion? Why is it not just indigenized but the very symbol of a sporting practice that seems to embody India? Why is it watched with rapt attention in stadia from Sharjah to Madras and in every media context as well? Why are the stars of cricket worshipped perhaps even more than their counterparts in the cinema?

Part of the answer to these questions doubtless lies in the profound links between the idea of "play" in human life (Huizinga 1950), of organized sport in mobilizing simultaneously powerful sentiments both of nation and of humanity (MacAloon 1984, 1990), and of agonistic sport in recalibrating the relationship between leisure and pleasure in modern industrial societies (Elias and Dunning 1986; Hargreaves 1982). Cricket, from these perspectives, can be seen as a form of agonistic play that has captured the Indian imagination decisively.

But to account for the central place of cricket in the Indian imagination, one must understand how cricket links gender, the nation, fantasy, and bodily excitement. It is true that among the Indian upper classes, especially insofar as they are able to insulate themselves from the masses (either in their homes or in special viewing sections) while they watch cricket, women have become both players and aficionados. Yet for the nation at large, cricket is a male-dominated activity in terms of players, managers, commentators, aficionados and live audiences. Male spectators, even when they do not dominate audiences at either live or televised games, are the "preferred viewers" of the game, since the biggest spectacles—test matches and major one-day matches—involve only male players. The Indian female gaze, at least thus far, is twice removed: watching males play, but also watching males watching other males play. For the male viewer, watching cricket is a deeply engaged activity, at the level of bodily hexis (Bourdieu 1977), since most Indian males under the age of forty have either seen cricket games at first hand, have played themselves in some local version of the game, or have read about it and seen it played. Thus the pleasure of viewing cricket for the Indian male, as with virtually no other sport, is rooted in the bodily pleasure of playing, or imagining playing, cricket.

But since cricket has, through the convergence of state, media, and private-sector interests, come to be identified with "India," with "Indian" skill, "Indian" guts, "Indian" team spirit, and "Indian" victories, the bodily pleasure that is at the core of the male viewing experience is simultaneously part of the erotics of nationhood. This erotics, particularly for working-class and lumpen male youth throughout India, is connected deeply to violence, not just because all agonistic sport taps the inclination to aggressiveness but also because the divisive demands of class, of ethnicity, of language, and of region in fact make the nation a profoundly contested community. The erotic pleasure of watching cricket, for Indian male subjects, is the *pleasure of agency* in an imagined community that in many other arenas is violently contested (see Mitra 1986 for a slightly different angle on this process). This pleasure is neither wholly cathartic nor wholly vicarious, since playing cricket is close to, or part of, the experience of many Indian males. It is, however, magnified, politicized, and spectacularized without losing its links to the lived experience of bodily competence and agonistic bonding. This set of links between gender, fantasy, nation, and excitement could not occur without a complex set of historical contingencies involving empire, patronage, media, and commerce, contingencies that set the stage for the current embodied excitement about cricket in India.

We can now return to the puzzle with which we began. How did cricket, a "hard" cultural form tightly yoking value, meaning, and embodied practice, become so profoundly Indianized, or, from another point of view, de-Victorianized? Because, in the process of its vernacularization (through books, newspapers, radio, and television), it became an emblem of Indian nationhood at the same time that it became inscribed, as practice, into the Indian (male) body. Decolonization in this case involves not only the creation of "imagined communities" through the workings of print capitalism, as Anderson (1983) has suggested, but also the appropriation of agonistic bodily skills that can then further lend passion and purpose to the community so imagined. This may be the special contribution of spectator sport (as opposed to the many other forms of public culture) to the dynamics of decolonization.

One can still ask—since gender, body, and the erotics of nationhood can come into powerful conjuncture through other sports (soccer and hockey are very strong popular sports in India even today)—why cricket? Here I must make a speculative leap and suggest that cricket is the ideal focus for national attention and nationalist passion because it affords the experience of experimenting with what might be called the "means of modernity" for a wide variety of groups within Indian society. To those groups who constitute the state, particularly through their control of television, it offers the sense of being able to manipulate nationalist sentiment. To the technocrats, publicists, journalists, and publishers who directly control the media, it provides the sense of skill in handling the techniques of televising sports spectacles, of manipulating private-sector advertising, of controlling public attention, and, in general, of mastering the media themselves. To the private sector, cricket affords a means for linking leisure, stardom, and nationalism, thus providing a sense of mastery over the skills of merchandising and promotion. To the viewing public, cricket affords the sense of cultural literacy in a "world" sport (associated with the still not erased sense of the technological superiority of the West) and the more diffuse pleasure of association with glamour, cosmopolitanism, and national competitiveness. To the upper-middle-class viewer, it affords the privatized pleasures of bringing stardom and nationalist sentiment within the safe and sanitized environs of the living room. To working-class and lumpen youth, it offers the sort of sense of group belonging, potential violence, and bodily excitement that characterizes football passion in England. To rural viewers, readers, and listeners, finally, cricket (appropriately vernacularized) gives a sense of participation in the lives of stars, the fate of nations, and the electricity of cities. In all these cases, while the ends of modernity may be understood (and contested) variously as world peace, national skill, individual fame, and team virility or mobility, the *means of modernity* contained in cricket involve a confluence of lived interests where cricket producers and consumers can share the excitement of Indianness without its many divisive scars. Finally, though perhaps least consciously, cricket gives all these groups and actors the sense of having hijacked the game from its English habitus into the colonies at the level of language, body, and agency as well as competition, finance, and spectacle. If cricket did not exist in India, something like it would certainly have been invented for the conduct of public experiments with the means of modernity.

Notes

I am grateful to John MacAloon and to the participants at the First International Conference on the Olympics and East/West and North/South Cultural Exchanges in the World System, Seoul, Korea, August 17-19, 1987. An earlier version of this essay was written for that conference, and was presented at the South Asia Meetings in Madison, Wisconsin, in November 1987 and at the annual meetings of the American Anthropological Association in 1988. This earlier version was published in Shin-Pyo, MacAloon, and Da Matta 1988. I am grateful to participants on all these occasions for criticisms, anecdotes, and encouragement of all sorts. Finally, Carol Breckenridge raised several major questions that forced me to radically revise and strengthen the earlier version of this essay.

1. These materials include the Marathi-language magazines *Chaukar, Ashtapailu, Kriket Bharati,* and *Shatkar,* which have counterparts in Tamil, Hindi, and Bengali. These magazines provide gossip on cricket stars, reviews of cricket books in English, and news and analysis of cricket in England and elsewhere in the Commonwealth; they sometimes also cover other sports, as well as cinema and other forms of popular entertainment. In them, therefore (both in the texts and in the advertisements), cricket is textually simultaneously vernacularized and drawn into the glamour of cosmopolitan life. A detailed analysis of these materials would war-

rant a separate study. These magazines, along with books by cricketers—such as *Shatak aani Shatkar* (ghostwritten Marathi autobiographies of Ravi Shastri and Sandip Patil)—form the basis of the linguistic and readerly decolonization of cricket. I am deeply grateful to Lee Schlesinger, who hunted out some of these materials for me in the bookstores and byways of Pune.

References

Ali, S. Mushtaq. 1981. *Cricket Delightful.* Delhi: Rupa.

Allen, David R. 1985. *Cricket on the Air.* London: British Broadcasting Corporation.

Anderson, Benedict. 1983. *Imagined Communities: Reflections on the Origin and Spread of Nationalism.* London: Verso and NLB.

Appadurai, Arjun. 1981. *Worship and Conflict under Colonial Rule.* New York: Cambridge University Press.

———. 1993. Number in the Colonial Imagination in India. In *Orientalism and the Post-Colonial Predicament,* edited by C. A. Breckenridge and P. van der Veer, pp. 314-39. Philadelphia: University of Pennsylvania Press.

Appadurai, Arjun, and Carol A. Breckenridge. 1991. "Museums Are Good to Think: Heritage on View in India." In *Museums and Their Communities: The Politics of Public Culture,* edited by I. Karp, C. Mullen Kreamer, and S. Levine, pp. 34-55. Washington, D.C.: Smithsonian Institution Press.

Bhabha, Homi. 1984. Of Mimicry and Man: The Ambivalence of Colonial Discourse. *October.*

Birbalsingh, Frank. 1986. Indo-Caribbean Test Cricketers. *Toronto South Asian Review* 5 (1): 105-17.

Bourdieu, Pierre. 1977. *Outline of a Theory of Practice.* Cambridge: Cambridge University Press.

Breckenridge, Carol A. 1988. The Politics and Aesthetics of Colonial Collecting: India at World Fairs. *Comparative Studies in Society and History* 31 (2): 195-216.

Cashman, Richard. 1980. *Patrons, Players and the Crowd: The Phenomenon of Indian Cricket.* New Delhi: Orient Longman.

Clarke, Alan, and John Clarke. 1982. 'Highlights and Action Replays': Ideology, Sport and the Media. In *Sport, Culture and Ideology,* edited by Jennifer Hargreaves, pp. 62-87. London: Routledge and Kegan Paul.

Cohn, Bernard. 1987. The Census, Social Structure and Objectification in South Asia. In *An Anthropologist among the Historians and Other Essays,* pp. 224-54. Delhi: Oxford University Press.

Cooper, Frederick, and Ann L. Stoler. 1989. Tensions of Empire and Visions of Rule. *American Ethnologist* 16 (4): 609-21.

de Mellow, Melville. 1979. *Reaching for Excellence: The Glory and Decay of Sport in India.* New Delhi and Ludhiana: Kalyani.

Diawara, Manthia. 1990. Englishness and Blackness: Cricket as Discourse on Colonialism. *Callaloo* 13 (2).

Dirks, Nicholas B. 1987. *The Hollow Crown: Ethnohistory of an Indian Kingdom.* Cambridge: Cambridge University Press.

Docker, Edward. 1976. *History of Indian Cricket.* Delhi: Macmillan.

Elias, Norbert, and Eric Dunning. 1986. *Quest for Excitement: Sport and Leisure in the Civilizing Process.* Oxford: Basil Blackwell.

Freitag, Sandria. 1989. *Collective Action and Community: Public Arenas in the Emergence of Communalism in North India.* Berkeley: University of California Press.

Hargreaves, Joan, ed. 1982. *Sport, Culture and Ideology.* London: Routledge and Kegan Paul.

Hazare, Vijay. 1976. *Cricket Replayed.* Bombay: Rupa.

———. 1981. *A Long Inning.* Bombay: Rupa.

Huizinga, J. 1950 [1944]. *Homo Ludens: A Study of the Play Element in Culture.* New York: Roy.

Hutchins, Francis G. 1967. *The Illusion of Permanence.* Princeton, N.J.: Princeton University Press.

James, C. L. R. 1963. *Beyond a Boundary.* London: Stanley Paul.

MacAloon, John J., ed. 1984. *Rite, Drama, Festival and Spectacle.* Philadelphia: Institute for the Study of Human Issues.

———. 1990. Steroids and the State: Dubin, Melodrama and the Accomplishment of Innocence. *Public Culture* 2 (2): 41-64.

Marshall, Tyler. 1987. It's Now Cricket to Play Hardball. *This World,* November 22.

Mitra, Ashok. 1986. Cricket Frenzy Unites a Dishevelled Subcontinent. *Far Eastern Economic Review,* July 10, pp. 48-49.

Nandy, Ashis. 1983. *The Intimate Enemy: Loss and Recovery of Self Under Colonialism.* Delhi: Oxford University Press.

———. 1989. *The Tao of Cricket: On Games of Destiny and the Destiny of Games.* New York: Viking.

Pandey, Gyan. 1990. *The Construction of Communalism in Colonial North India.* Delhi: Oxford University Press.

Prakash, Gyan. 1990. *Bonded Histories: Genealogies of Labor Servitude in Colonial India.* Cambridge: Cambridge University Press.

Puri, Narottam. 1982. Sports versus Cricket. *India International Centre Quarterly* 9 (2): 146-54.

Raiji, Vasant. 1976. *L. P. Jai: Memories of a Great Batsman.* Bombay: Tyeby.

Roberts, Michael. 1985. Ethnicity in Riposte at a Cricket Match: The Past for the Present. *Comparative Studies in Society and History* 27: 401-29.

Salve, N. K. P. 1987. *The Story of the Reliance Cup.* New Delhi: Vikas.

Shastri, Ravi, and Sandip Patil. 1982. *Shatak Shatkar* (Marathi). Bombay: Aditya Prakashan.

Shin-Pyo, Kang, John J. MacAloon, and Roberto Da Matta, eds. 1988. *The Olympics and Cultural Exchange.* Seoul: Hanyang Institute for Ethnological Studies.

Tripathi, Salil. 1990. Sharjah: A Crass Carnival. *India Today,* May 31, pp. 88-91.

CHAPTER THREE

Upon the Subdominant

Administering Music on All-India Radio

DAVID LELYVELD

"Good-bye Professor Godbole. . . . It's a shame we never heard you sing."
"I may sing now," he replied, and did.
His thin voice rose, and gave out one sound after another. At times there
seemed rhythm, at times there was the illusion of a Western melody.
But the ear, baffled repeatedly, soon lost any clue, and wandered in a maze
of noises, none harsh or unpleasant, none intelligible. It was the song of
an unknown bird. Only the servants understood it. They began to whisper
to one another. The man who was gathering water chestnuts came naked out
of the tank, his lips parted with delight, disclosing his scarlet tongue.
The sounds continued and ceased after a few moments as casually as they
had begun—apparently half through a bar, and upon the subdominant.
—E. M. Forster, *A Passage to India*

It is characteristic of cultural imperialism to confuse levels of analysis by
claiming universal validity for what is limited to particular historical contexts. "The subdominant" is a technical term in the European musical system that was prevalent during the period of British rule in India. European
musical theory from the late eighteenth century to the early twentieth con-
strued pitch in terms of "natural" harmonic overtones; emerging into pro-
gressions of chords, cadences, themes, and movements, the totality of a musical composition was an exposition of tension, release, and resolution.
While E. M. Forster, bewildered by his experience of Indian music for its fail-

ure to fit his tonal expectations, found refuge in satire, Max Weber, writing on the sociology of music, expressed a growing critique of the ideology of "classical" European tonality. For him such music was an example of the "rationalization" and technological transformations of modernity, the triumph of standardization over spontaneity and variation.[1]

The harmonic effects of European music relied on the development in the eighteenth century of "well-tempered" keyboard instruments in which certain closely related pitches were altered, made identical within an octave of twelve fixed notes. The piano with its adjusted intonation replaced the voice as the prototype and standard for musical performance. Unable to create intermediate pitches, it could reach higher and lower with predictable harmonic effect. The "dominant" and "subdominant," located respectively five steps above and below the "tonic," are compared in one textbook account to "two equidistant weights at either side of a fulcrum."[2] But in the system of "classical" tonality they were not, in fact, evenly balanced; there was a built-in asymmetry in the scale that was believed to give the subdominant the role of weakening or holding back, rather than resolution or emphasis.[3]

But one can imagine another use for the term *subdominant,* one with nonmusical overtones in the analysis of society—as a dissonant combination of *subaltern* and *dominant*.[4] Ranajit Guha has developed Gramsci's ideas about the relation between the coercive power of a ruling class and the shared cultural assumptions of the wider social formation in relation to British rule in India, which he characterizes as "dominance without hegemony." Far more coercion than persuasion, British authority could make only a superficial impression on Indian culture. In the colonial situation, he argues, there was a sharp disjunction between the regime of foreigners and the complex layers of the society over which they ruled.[5] From this point of view, "subdominant" might refer to the subordinate elites of Indian society with their various claims to coercive power and ideological authority.

This play on words between the domains of formal musical analysis and categories of social relations may serve to introduce the politics of Indian music in the twentieth century, in particular its adaptation to radio broadcasting, both as a technology and as an institution, during the last years of British rule and the early years of Indian independence. The social location of music, the economics of performance, who the musicians were and who told them what to play, what it took to be one or to be a member of the audience—these and other matters are all bound up with power, authority, and community as they have changed in modern India.

But beyond context, the actual content of the music and the technical principles of its form are at the heart of how one relates social arrangements to cultural understandings. Although music is more difficult to discuss than literature or the visual arts, let alone explicitly political utterances, one may agree with Lévi-Strauss that it is "the supreme mystery of human knowledge."[6] For Theodor Adorno, probably the major theorist of music as ideology, music exemplifies the theory of mediation, the processes by which consciousness interprets actuality and motivates action. Music, unless it is a deliberate act of dissent, may become part of the common sense of a society, accepted as part of a natural and unalterable condition of being. According to Adorno, to understand the conditions of musical production and appreciation, as well as their inhibiting limitations, one must take on, as total systems, the formal characteristics of music as well as the social context in which it can exist.[7]

In India under British rule, the disjunction of cultural consensus between rulers and subjects is particularly striking in the case of music. Unlike literature, visual art, philosophy, law, and numerous other cultural domains, music was hardly an area of serious cultural encounter. Gauri Viswanathan, for example, has documented the substantial effort made by British authorities to establish English literature as the foundation for ideological consent among strategically chosen Indians.[8] But with the significant exception of military marching bands, one is hard pressed to find any effort to introduce European music to India. Conversely, for all the ambivalence and self-affirming character in British studies and appropriations of Indian literature and visual art, these were nevertheless matters of substantial engagement. Indian music, on the other hand, was largely an unknown territory for the British, the object of a few, well-scattered studies by conscientious British scholars, set against a perpetual drone of disparaging remarks by witty British travelers. These musicological Orientalists tended to view music as a matter of scientific understanding and progressive historical development. Indian music, though worthy of antiquarian interest as a clue to the music of ancient Greece, had failed to "discover" the science of harmony and to develop a system of notation that would make composition, the sustained planning of musical effect and its certain reproducibility, possible. For British listeners, it was thus limited, irrational, and, frequently, extremely unpleasant.[9] But it was only with the establishment of radio broadcasting under official auspices in the 1930s that music became a matter of administrative attention. Technology and its uses suddenly made music not only problematic but also important.

All-India Radio under the British: Time and Place

Despite the enthusiasm of a few businessmen and "village uplift" advocates, both British and Indian, radio broadcasting made a slow, uncertain start in the last decades of imperial rule. In London, politicians and officials at the India Office and the BBC entertained high hopes of a magical device to reach past the nationalist movement to a more malleable rural population, assembled after a hard day's work around the village loudspeaker. Authorities in Delhi, on the other hand, were torn between a notion that radio was either a powerful and potentially dangerous political weapon whose introduction should be delayed as long as possible or that it was simply "entertainment" and therefore "hardly a matter for Government to undertake." There was also a frank admission that government auspices could be the kiss of death in view of the growing popularity of the nationalist cause.[10] Finally, in 1935, after five years of holding in receivership the small broadcasting company that operated in Bombay and Calcutta, the government of India decided that it had better create a broadcast monopoly as a department of the central government, lest it fall into the hands of soon to be elected popular governments in the provinces. To carry out this enterprise Delhi requested the assistance of "experts," an administrator and an engineer, to be sent out from London by the BBC and placed in charge of the new department.[11]

For the British authorities in charge of creating a broadcasting system for India, music was at best a loss leader, a device for getting customers into the store. Worried chiefly about the political content of news and radio talks, they did not give music a great deal of attention except when questions were raised about the language of the lyrics and the religion or caste of the performers. According to Lionel Fielden, the first controller of broadcasting, music was " 'padding' because it does not instruct or inform," even if it made up about seven-eighths of all broadcast time. Certainly it was the responsibility of broadcasters, in India as in Britain, to cultivate good taste, not merely to appease the wishes of the majority. In Fielden's opinion, however, Indian music had no accepted "standards" and the only distinction between "classical" and "light" was in the content of the words, "religious" or "erotic," and the social status of the performer. Interest in the "classical" was in any case limited to a very small audience.[12] Fielden complained:

> It is already obvious that a daily 8-hour programme makes an almost too heavy demand upon its [Indian music's] somewhat limited field. Listeners who complain of monotony in the programmes are attacking not so much the shortcomings of the station's staff as the structure of Indian music itself.[13]

In this view Indian music required substantial reform if it was to serve the purposes of broadcasting. It lacked sufficient variety to command the continuous attention of a large public. Also, it had to be redesigned to fit into a reliable schedule of programs. Both these goals could be served by preparing composed pieces and training musicians who could read musical notation. All-India Radio (AIR) employed two European musicologists, John Fouldes in Delhi and Walter Kaufmann in Bombay, to oversee Western musical programming but also to experiment with a new Indian music. Fouldes, who died in 1939, had a long-standing interest in creating a synthesis of Indian and European systems. It would be based on ensemble playing on Indian instruments of raga-based compositions, but it would also employ counterpoint. Concerned with developing a greater differentiation among instruments liberated from the dominance of vocal music and encouraged to exploit their own particular technical resources, he still wanted to be true to the principles of Indian intonation. It was Fouldes who was responsible for banning the harmonium from the radio, except as incidental music in a drama, because its well-tempered scale did such violence to the microtonic intervals characteristic of Indian music.[14]

Precise scheduling was a major criterion for changing the nature of Indian music. The efficient coordination of salaried employees and performers engaged for a particular event was one consideration; another was the calculation of the needs and desires of different audiences, defined as students in school, urban "educated," rural "uneducated," and, later, urban women and rural women.[15] Each would have separate tastes. Peasants, according to Verrier Elwin, wanted slower talk and faster music.[16] Musical performances of poems such as *ghazals* and *bhajans* were relatively easy to fit into short, scheduled segments. Ever since the early 1920s performers had learned to accept the constraints of the 78 r.p.m. phonograph recording, and these became a staple of radio broadcasting.[17] But the decorum of a more extended performance, the open-ended and improvised exposition of a single raga, was ill-adapted to radio, at least as conceived by its administrators. Fielden and others argued that in any case the slowly developing *alap* was just warming up and not essential to the music. As Narayana Menon, who worked under George Orwell in the Indian service of the BBC during World War II, later put it:

> Broadcasting . . . has given our musicians the quality of precision and economy of statement. The red light on the studio door is a stern disciplinarian. Broadcasting has also given our musicians a sense of proportion and a clearer definition of values that matter in music.[18]

AIR did not have the technical resources to broadcast outside padded studios, so every performance produced for radio, at least until 1952, was a live and unique event. But no attempt was made to broadcast in the presence of an audience, aside from the necessary station personnel. Recruiting musical talent was a function of the location of the broadcasting studio, since AIR was in no position to bring people from any great distance.[19] Access to the performance was a matter of equipment, transmitters and receivers, and the vagaries of radio waves according to time, topography, and weather.

Bringing performer and audience into some relation with each other was a problem in broadcast engineering. Along with Fielden, the BBC had sent out one of its top engineers, H. L. Kirke, who toured India and issued a detailed plan for the location and range of transmitters in 1936. Another, more ambitious and long-range plan, drafted in 1944 and revised over the next two years, was prepared under C. W. Goyder, AIR chief engineer from 1936 to 1946.[20]

Kirke's initial plan, limited by the very modest outlay that the government intended to make, assumed that radio would have to pay its way, as in Britain, out of the annual license fees assessed on every set. It was therefore designed to reach the largest concentrations of the urban middle class with middle-wave transmissions in seven cities. A subsequent modification toward short-wave broadcasts increased the geographic range but at the cost of requiring listeners to purchase more expensive receiving sets. Until the eve of independence, undivided British India had stations in nine cities with about 90,000 license holders, not counting five modest operations in the larger princely states.[21] The location of the nine stations determined in large measure the nature of the people called to the microphone. The fact that one of those cities was Lucknow, rather than Allahabad (though Kirke had proposed the latter), for example, skewed the broadcasting to Urdu and Muslim musicians rather than Hindi and Hindu ones.

The Basic Plan of 1944 aimed to create a service "by which every person in India . . . is provided with a broadcast program in his own language and one, moreover, which he can pick up with an inexpensive receiver." It envisaged 125 stations, a goal that has yet to be reached. Based on a detailed survey of topography, soil types, weather patterns, population densities—and cultural boundaries—the plan demanded that India have a decentralized broadcasting system. With *The Linguistic Survey of India* and the 1931 census to guide the definition of audiences, India was defined as a congeries of microregions. Although British social surveys had somehow neglected to map the distribution of musical systems, the plan noted that these were not necessarily congruent with languages and might require further subdivision of broadcasting circles. The plan called for small-power middle-wave transmissions and raised the possibility of introducing the new FM technology as one particularly suited to India. There would be no need to broadcast in a language or musical style outside its region of origin and little occasion for national programming.

B. V. Keskar: Music as Ideology

"The British have never been known as a very musical people." So at least thought the late Dr. B. V. Keskar, who as minister of information and broadcasting from 1950 to 1962 was the major formulator of the musical ideologies and policies of All-India Radio.[22] Whatever efforts the British made to promote their own literary and visual arts in India and even to study and support those of India among Indians and to some extent at home, music, Keskar observed, was generally a matter of mutual indifference if not distaste. There remained a saving remnant of Indian musicians, thanks to the patronage of a few Maratha princely states such as Gwalior, Indore, Baroda, Kolhapur, and Tanjore; but even this had declined as the interests of the rulers turned to "horse racing and ballroom dancing." Only with national independence and, indeed, primarily through radio broadcasting, Keskar thought, could the musical heritage of India be saved.

The damage done to Indian music, Keskar believed, was the result not only of British imperial neglect and the wandering attention of maharajahs. More fundamentally, Keskar placed the blame on the shoulders of North Indian Muslims, both the rulers of earlier centuries and the Muslim musicians who, in Keskar's view, had appropriated and distorted the ancient art, turning it into the secret craft of exclusive lineages, the *gharanas*, and, ignorant of Sanskrit, divorced it from the religious context of Hindu civilization.[23] Furthermore, they had bifurcated the unity of Indian music by creating a "Hindustani" variant as against the still safely Hindu "Carnatic" one. Just as the British had no great place for music in their scheme of things, neither did Islam. In Muslim hands music was no longer "spiritual"; it had become merely "erotic," the special preserve of "dancing girls, prostitutes and their circle of pimps."[24] Respectable Hindus had turned away from this corruption with understandable disgust.

Only recently, in the decades before independence, had there arisen a movement to recover Indian music and restore it to its rightful place in society. In the early twentieth century Vishnu Narayan Bhatkhande, a pleader in the Bombay High Court, set about systematizing the *sastras* in an effort to formulate a "national music," a unification of Hindustani and Carnatic founded on authentic textual authority. Along with Vishnu Digambar Paluskar he endeavored to bring this knowledge out of the temples, palaces, and pleasure quarters into a new realm of public life by resorting to what were now well-tried methods: schools and voluntary associations. Devoted, in Keskar's words, to "the educated middle class," these were not dependent on a complex set of familial, guru-disciple, or patron-client relations. In fact, they particularly attracted Brahmans, especially in Maharashtra. These appropriate guardians of the *sastras* now stepped forward to reclaim the authority in the realm of music that had passed illegitimately to Muslims.

Keskar, though he received his doctorate in political science from the University of Paris,[25] was among the new generation of Maharashtrian Brahmans that Bhatkhande and Paluskar had ushered into the study of music as a requisite of a good education. At the intersection of a variety of claims to cultural leadership—ritual status, links with the ruling class of pre-British regimes, vanguard of those who had received British-sponsored education—Maharashtrian Brahmans were in the forefront of Indian nationalism, often defined as a reassertion of Hindu culture, as opposed not only to the British but also to Muslims, and as Brahman authority over lower-status communities.[26] "Subdominant" in British India, such groups saw national independence as a matter of restoring their ideological authority over the society at large.

For Keskar music was not just a matter of personal cultivation or even cultural identity; it was "a very vital factor in human society," a matter of serious political import: "Deep down in the roots of the human unconscious, music holds a key position in regulating orderly expression of the primeval emotional forces." Further, music is bound up with the evolution of human society from the primitive to the civilized, just as it differentiates between the high and low "strata" of any given society. The system of music in a given culture would be the same, but the level of abstraction and elaboration would differ: "Simple people living in the villages have simple music and enjoy simple songs. . . . The more developed people, who read and write will have complex feelings and will require a more complex vehicle to express it."[27]

Because music was a matter of such importance in "regulating" emotions and the social order, its cultivation ought properly to be a matter of "systematic effort by society or government."[28] The role of the state in newly independent India was crucial to repairing the damage done under Muslim and British rule and to fighting off the incursions of what Keskar called "the music mob," whether it be the vested interests of the old, disreputable class of performers or the commercial attractions of the film industry. Music was too important to be left to the musicians. Authority should rest with *bahusrut*, ideal listeners educated in the Sanskrit texts, rather than mere performers, and the state should empower them to oversee a program of compulsory music education in the schools as well as the distribution of state patronage.[29]

The Nationalization of Indian Music

When the control of broadcasting passed from BBC "experts" to their Indian successors, many assumptions about the nature of radio broadcasting remained unchallenged. Despite the analysis of the 1936 and 1944 plans, however, the idea of a decentralized and fragmented broadcasting system was as firmly rejected on nationalist grounds as it had been on imperialist ones. Under Vallabhai Patel, who was minister of information and broadcasting as well as home minister in the interim government from 1946, the strategy of radio development was to increase kilowatt power of a few selected stations, recognizing at most the major regional languages. Patel's stature in the first government served as a guarantee that radio would remain a matter of centralized government control. Architect of the integration of the princely states, he took their few radio stations into the system. Eventually some were abolished, notably those of Baroda and Mysore, which were considered redundant when new stations were opened in Ahmedabad and Bangalore.[30]

Broadcasting, though not a matter of prominent attention, developed as part of the sequence of five-year plans that went into effect in 1952. The five-year plans were founded on the concept of a mixed economy with the central government in control as much as possible of the basic industries.[31] All-India Radio's role in the culture industry was to be rather similar: as a central government monopoly it would play a leading role in integrating Indian culture and raising "standards." With regard to music the major concern was to replace the system of princely patronage, now clearly dead, and to counterbalance the sources of commercial music, in particular the films.

Until partition All-India Radio's major political battles had revolved around Hindu-Muslim communal disputes, especially the issue of Hindi versus Urdu versus Hindustani. Under Patel and even more so under Keskar, measures were taken to assure that the "Hindu" side would prevail. One of Patel's first acts was to bar singers and musicians from the courtesan culture—anyone "whose private life was a public scandal."[32] The distinction between amateur and professional was called into question so that greater room could be made for performers who had come out of music schools rather than Muslim-dominated *gharanas*. Keskar's method for doing this was to establish an elaborate audition system on the model of the Public Service Commission and other selection board procedures that had been introduced into Indian life in the 1930s. In the case of musicians and singers a "jury" listened to but did not see the performer. Recordings of the finalists were sent on to the appropriate audition board, either Hindustani or Carnatic, in Delhi. Those selected were then graded A, B, or C on the basis of a brief performance and their response to questions designed to test their knowledge of theory. Some were then hired as full-time "staff artistes"; others were retained on a regular basis as "casuals." After some protest the most famous musicians were allowed to skip the audition, but the overwhelming majority were selected in this way.[33] According to J. C. Mathur, who served as AIR director general under Keskar in the late 1950s, almost ten thousand musicians were employed regularly or part time, including many "from educated and 'respectable' families." This represented a very large proportion, it would seem, of India's musicians.[34]

Keskar took a close personal interest in the details of musical programming, but he also brought into the radio staff the kind of people he considered qualified to make judgments about what should be broadcast, namely, people with a scholarly knowledge of the major texts, often with an academic rather than a professional performing background. Prominent among these was another Maharashtrian, Professor S. N. Ratanjankar, formerly principal of the Marris College of Music in Lucknow, who was very much an heir to the movement for a national music initiated by Bhatkhande. Increasingly, qualification for radio performance entailed certification from recognized music academies.[35]

Keskar was also responsible for introducing prerecorded programming, usually distributed from Delhi to the various stations. This was designed to free these stations from reliance on local talent and, more particularly, to familiarize audiences with musical styles from other parts of the country so that eventually a "national music" might emerge. Similar efforts were made with "folk music," now recognized as a special category that could be adapted and distributed for the uses of radio and feed the total musical culture of India. Such policies were matters of government orders and monthly quotas. Pride of place was given to the National Programme of Music, a ninety-minute concert on Saturday evenings that was instituted in 1950 at the outset of Keskar's regime. Five years later Keskar established the marathon

Radio Sangeet Samelan, involving a series of some twenty concerts before invited audiences, carefully balancing Hindustani and Carnatic styles.[36]

The great enemy in this effort to construct a new music by administrative decree was the increasingly popular new style of film songs. As with the problem of language—films intended for an All-India market used a "Hindi" that was in fact Urdu and avoided the Sanskritic vocabulary one heard on postindependence radio—the cinema offered an opposing style of music that challenged the aims of the national cultural policy. The lyrics, aside from being in Urdu, were generally "erotic," and since the late 1940s there were noticeable infusions of orchestration and to some extent rhythm and melody from Western popular music, which Keskar identified with a lower stage of human evolution.[37] The immediate task was to impose a quota of 10 percent of all program time and to screen the selection of recordings so that the more objectionable would not be given further exposure. In 1954 negotiations with the Film Producers Guild of India for rights to film songs broke down so that for a short time they virtually disappeared from AIR programming—all this while it was easy enough to hear them either from Goa or from the high-power commercial broadcasts of Radio Ceylon.[38]

For Keskar, however, as it was for the BBC, the distinction between "light" and "classical" music was a fact of nature and therefore the creation of an alternative popular form was a pressing need. The idea of "light music to counter-blast bad film music" had been raised as early as 1943, and AIR had looked to the example of Uday Shankar's dance troupe.[39] In 1948 Uday's younger brother, Ravi Shankar, who had become music director for the external services, took up Fouldes's old idea of developing a radio orchestra. Sometimes playing composed versions of a raga "as if it were being improvised" and sometimes turning "one of the light *ragas*" into "romantic, bright, lilting pieces with exciting rhythms and lively melodies . . . [with] a very free kind of counterpoint," he was most pleased with a third alternative based on "the pure folk style, using regional tunes." In 1950 this ensemble, known as Vadya Vrinda or National Orchestra, was enlarged as part of the Home Services and Ravi Shankar was joined by a South Indian so that Carnatic music would also be represented.[40] The orchestra had the advantage of giving staff artists something to do aside from their occasional brief performances.[41]

In 1953 Keskar made a concerted effort to create an alternative popular music by establishing at the various stations "light music units," which employed classical musicians along with poets to compose two songs a week. With film music virtually absent from AIR programs at the time, a survey was said to have been made of listener preferences: out of ten households with licensed radio sets, nine were tuned to Radio Ceylon and the tenth set was broken.[42] In 1957 Keskar essentially capitulated and a special service, Vividh Bharati, was opened with national coverage and a very heavy balance of recorded film songs, all separate from the main program channels. Produced in Delhi, Vividh Bharati was sent out in a great homogenous lump through two high-power transmitters in Bombay and Madras, later supplemented by two dozen smaller ones. Over the following decade, however, the competition with Radio Ceylon remained close, until Sri Lanka's own cultural nationalism won out over the enticements of the Indian market.[43] In 1967, as cheap transistor radios became available to a greatly expanded Indian public, Vividh Bharati took the next step: it started broadcasting commercial advertisements.[44]

Music in the Public Sector

As a "standardized" recording, a performance exists apart from its performers; it can be saved or shipped around the country for rebroadcast as needed. Early in the century Ananda Coomaraswamy had denounced phonograph recordings as a degradation of the musician and the immediacy of the aesthetic encounter. "One great disadvantage of mechanical instruments," he went on, "is the fatal facility they afford to the undisciplined and untrained mind."[45] Walter Benjamin's famous essay "The Work of Art in the Age of Mechanical Reproduction," on the other hand, celebrated this very demystification of music, the stripping away of what he called the "aura" of artistic creation. Technology, Benjamin claimed, would allow the audience to control the conditions of its own experience.[46] For Theodor Adorno, however, the propagation of "standardized musical goods" had as its effect "deconcentration" and "the reduction of people to silence." Radio, to Adorno, was "totalitarian" and radio music a "fetish" perpetrated upon a passively satisfied population.[47]

The centralized administration of music established by Keskar and anticipated by the colonial regime does not appear to justify Benjamin's optimistic vision of an autonomous public released from the trammels of authority. The "subdominant" had succeeded to state power and could now claim an indigenous cultural authority in the name of a nation-state that was itself heir to the colonial system of domination. Despite the consumer revolt against AIR music, the state retained control of a highly centralized, if less earnest, broadcast "service." After Keskar, changes in musical policy were few. Vividh Bharati expanded, and a government commission warned that "AIR should not overdo its educative role."[48] In 1956, Ravi Shankar had left his AIR post to take up the international career that helped to give Indian music a prominence, even in Britain, that it had never before achieved. By that time radio, along with long-playing records and public concerts, had replaced private gatherings as the main settings for playing and hearing music. If composed music has achieved its only successes in the very film music that AIR set out to combat, recordings and the performance of brief stereotyped segments could serve some of the same purposes: fitting schedules and interchangeability. One of the achievements that broadcast authorities took credit for was the detachment of ragas from particular times in the day or night; one need not wait for dawn to hear someone play Lalita.[49] For most people, performers and audiences, music was no longer a face-to-face transaction, an interaction of presentation and response. For most audiences, in fact, it was experienced as pure sound, removed in time and space from its creator and made available through a complex of technology and administrative arrangement, from another time and another place, difficult to identify or visualize.[50]

Similarly, as Neuman has pointed out, musicians came to learn styles and develop ideas not so much in a close and diffuse relation with a teacher, or even in an accredited music academy, but by listening to records and tape recordings of a small group of internationally recognized masters such as Ravi Shankar, Ali Akbar Khan, and Vilayat Khan—or for that matter the pervasive "play-back" singers of the films, Lata Mangeshkar and Asha Bhonsle. The changes that were made in music up to that time crystallized; further experiments did not take their place, at least not in India. Some would argue that the music schools and the selection process that provided so many musicians with their livelihood through radio broadcasting led to a narrowing of range and a greater caution. Designed to set and maintain "standards," they discouraged that special, sometimes "disreputable," individuality that had characterized the famous musicians of the previous generation.[51] One might speculate that this earlier, better time, if that is what it was, may have been only a brief interval of relative liberation between the constraints of the princely court and those of the bureaucracy. Yet "classical" and "folk" music pretend to represent a more intimate past; only the electronic melange of film music confesses, very occasionally, the violent disjunction and discord of its origins.

Since the late 1970s there have been significant changes that call for separate analysis. Cassette tapes and two-in-ones (portable radio and tape player combinations) have further detached the music from its point of origin, and the simultaneous promotion of television with the videocassette recorder has only reinforced the status of a performance as a reproducible commodity. Such developments also mean that people are continually enveloped in this electronically reproduced music so that all music becomes the same background sound, something assumed as a condition of life.[52] Listening to music in this way does not command attention to detail or to how the details fit together, the very things a performer or listener would communicate with a gesture or a word in the intimacy of a *mahfil*. It invites neither appreciation nor criticism. As both Coomaraswamy and Adorno anticipated, music presented in this way serves to obscure the social arrangements that are the condition of its production.

But it would be an error, comparable to the fallacies of imperialism, to attribute to modern technology and organization the power to determine universal cultural transformations. Appadurai and Breckenridge have wisely pointed our attention to the ways in which changing cultural terrains create occasions for difference and contestation.[53] The limited success of the All-India Radio music agenda shows that the establishment of a national cultural hegemony was no easier for the formerly "subdominant" than for the colonial regime they replaced. Until the 1980s the overwhelming majority of India's population lived far beyond the reach of the national broadcasting system. By that time the projects of people like Keskar and Ravi Shankar had been overwhelmed by the countervailing force of commercial film music. Bureaucratic broadcasting and capitalistic cinema both sought in their different ways to organize and subsume the varieties of Indian musical experience. Since the 1970s, however, new technologies, particularly cassette recorders, have undermined the dominance of broadcasting and cinema and made it possible for hundreds of production units, legal and illegal, and often highly localized, to create new audiences and settings for a far more various and decentralized musical culture.[54]

Notes

1. Max Weber, *The Rational and Social Foundations of Music*, trans. and ed. Don Martindale, Johanes Riedel, and Gertrude Neuwirth (Carbondale: Southern Illinois University Press, 1958 [1921, from a 1911 ms.]), especially pp. 94, 103, 120-24.

2. Walter Piston, *Harmony*, rev. ed. (New York: Norton, 1948), p. 31.

3. Paul Hindemith, *Traditional Harmony* (New York: Associated Music Publishers, 1943), p. 99.

4. Antonio Gramsci, "Notes on Italian History," in *Selections from the Prison Notebooks*, trans. and ed. Quinton Hoare and Geoffrey Nowell Smith (New York: International, 1971), pp. 52-60; but note translators' footnotes about the difficulty of interpreting Gramsci's terminology.

5. Ranajit Guha, "Dominance without Hegemony and its Historiography," in *Subaltern Studies VI*, ed. Ranajit Guha (Delhi: Oxford University Press, 1989), pp. 210-309. My develop-

ment of this point, as well as much else in this paper, is indebted to a fruitful misunderstanding of an earlier version by Carol Breckenridge and Arjun Appadurai.

6. Quoted in Edmund Leach, *Claude Lévi-Strauss* (New York: Viking, 1970), p. 125.

7. Theodor W. Adorno, *Introduction to the Sociology of Music,* trans. E. B. Ashton (New York: Seabury, 1976), pp. 194-209. In many respects Adorno was anticipated by Max Weber in *Rational and Social Foundations.* See also Janet Wolff, "The Ideology of Autonomous Art," in *Music and Society: The Politics of Composition, Performance and Reception,* ed. Richard Leppert and Susan McClary (Cambridge: Cambridge University Press, 1987), pp. 1-12. For a bold effort at ideological analysis of musical form, see McClary, "The Blasphemy of Talking Politics during Bach Year," ibid., pp. 13-62.

8. Gauri Viswanathan, *Masks of Conquest: Literary Study and British Rule in India* (New York: Columbia University Press, 1989).

9. Early British studies of Indian music, starting with that of William Jones in 1784, were collected in Sourindro Mohun Tagore, ed., *Hindu Music from Various Authors* (1875; reprinted Varanasi: Chowkhanba Sanskrit Series Office, 1965). The other major works by British authors are C. R. Day, *The Music and Musical Instruments of South India and the Deccan* (London and New York: Novello, Ewer 1891), and A. H. Fox Strangways, *The Music of Hindostan* (1914; reprinted New Delhi: Oriental Books Reprint, 1975). For a discussion of how European musical theory served to reinforce the colonial distances of cultural encounter, see Richard Leppert, "Music, Domestic Life and Cultural Chauvinism," in Leppert and McClary, *Music and Society,* pp. 63-104. For the ultimate example of British travelogue commentary on music, see Beverley Nichols, *Verdict on India* (London: Jonathan Cape, 1944), pp. 122-36, which was passed on to me, for better or worse, by Philip Oldenburg.

10. "Note on broadcasting by the Director of Wireless" (P. J. Edmunds), July 1, 1927; Home-Political 217/1927, National Archives of India (NAI). For related proceedings in London, see India Office Library (IOL), L/PO/3/1. My research in these collections was funded by the American Institute of Indian Studies and the National Endowment for the Humanities.

11. For a fuller discussion, see my "Transmitters and Culture: The Colonial Roots of Indian Broadcasting," *South Asia Research* 10, no. 1 (Spring 1990). H. R. Luthra, *Indian Broadcasting* (New Delhi: Publications Division, 1986), is the best, and virtually the only, general history of Indian broadcasting. G. C. Awasthy, *Broadcasting in India* (Bombay: Allied, 1965), is another useful, if more polemical, book.

12. [Lionel Fielden], *Report on the Progress of Broadcasting in India up to the 31st March 1939* (Delhi: Manager of Publications, 1940), pp. 21-24.

13. [Lionel Fielden], *Indian Listener* 1, no. 14 (July 7, 1936); *Report on the Progress of Broadcasting,* pp. 21-24.

14. John Fouldes, "The Harmonium," *Indian Listener* 3, no. 13 (June 22, 1938); bimonthly report to the secretary of state for India, Department of Industry and Labour, May 5, 1937 (Home-Political 52/1/37, NAI); *Report on the Progress of Broadcasting,* pp. 23-24.

15. Luthra, *Indian Broadcasting,* pp. 324-45.

16. [Fielden], *Indian Listener* 1, no. 14 (July 7, 1936).

17. See G. N. Joshi, "A Concise History of the Phonograph Industry in India," *Popular Music* 7, no. 2 (1988): 147-56.

18. Jon B. Higgins, "From Prince to Populace: Patronage as a Determinant of Change in South Indian (Karnatak) Music," *Asian Music,* no. 7 (1976): 23-24. Higgins disagreed, arguing that the musical performance is likely to be perfunctory.

19. It was difficult enough to get some of them to come into the studio. In Delhi a special truck had to be fitted out to bring Mustari Bai, a famous singer who was too large to fit into an automobile (personal communication from Mr. Barakat Ahmad, an AIR employee of the early 1940s).

20. H. L. Kirke, *Report on the Proposed Development of Broadcasting Stations in India* (New Delhi: Government of India Press, 1936) [India Office Library/L/PJ/8/118]; Director-General of All-India Radio, *Basic Plan for the Development of Broadcasting in India* (first draft November 1944, revised September 1945) [IOL/L/I/968]; *Report on the Progress of Broadcasting*, pp. 85-136; Luthra, *Indian Broadcasting*, pp. 80-88.

21. Kirke, *Basic Plan*, p. 1.

22. B. V. Keskar, *Indian Music: Problems and Prospects* (Bombay: Popular Prakashan, 1967), p. 7.

23. Cf. Qazi Zahur ul-Haqq, *Rahnumah-i Mausiqi* (Islamabad: Pakistan National Council of the Arts, 1975), pp. 33-41. On *gharanas*, see Daniel M. Neuman, *The Life of Music in North India* (Detroit: Wayne State University Press, 1980), pp. 85-167; Brian Silver, "On Becoming an Ustad: Six Life Sketches in the Evolution of a Gharana," *Asian Music*, no. 7 (1976): 27-28; Joan L. Erdman, "The Maharaja's Musicians: The Organization of Cultural Performances at Jaipur," in *American Studies in the Anthropology of India*, ed. Sylvia Vatuk (New Delhi: Manohar, 1978), pp. 342-67.

24. Keskar, *Indian Music*, p. 7.

25. In the late 1930s, with a certificate in international relations, with the help of a private stipend from Jawaharlal Nehru; see correspondence between Keskar and Nehru, 1936-38, in Nehru papers, Nehru Library, New Delhi.

26. There is a considerable literature on Maharashtrian Brahmans during the British period, for example, D. D. Karve with Ellen E. McDonald, eds., *The New Brahmans: Five Maharashtrian Families* (Berkeley: University of California Press, 1963); see also Gordon Johnson, "Chitpavan Brahmans and Politics in Western India in the Late Nineteenth and Early Twentieth Centuries," in *Elites in South Asia*, ed. Edmund Leach and S. N. Mukherjee (Cambridge: Cambridge University Press, 1970), pp. 95-118; Richard I. Cashman, *The Myth of the Lokmanya: Tilak and Mass Politics in Maharashtra* (Berkeley: University of California Press, 1975), pp. 17-44; Rosalind O'Hanlon, *Caste, Conflict and Ideology: Mahatma Jotirao Phule and Low Caste Protest in Nineteenth-Century Western India* (Cambridge: Cambridge University Press, 1985), pp. 24-41.

27. Keskar, *Indian Music*, pp. 1-2.

28. Ibid., p. 9.

29. Ibid., p. 26.

30. Luthra, *Indian Broadcasting*, pp. 164-66; Awasthy, *Broadcasting in India*, pp. 12-15.

31. See A. Vaiyanathan, "The Indian Economy since Independence (1947-70)," in *The Cambridge Economic History of India* vol. 2, edited by Dharma Kumar, pp. 947-59 (Cambridge: Cambridge University Press, 1982).

32. Luthra, *Indian Broadcasting*, p. 105.

33. Ibid., pp. 306-8; Awasthy, *Broadcasting in India*, pp. 40-43; interview with Shertallai R. Gopalan Nair, retired producer of music, Trivandrum, July 16, 1987.

34. J. C. Mathur, *New Lamps for Aladdin* (Bombay: Orient Longmans, 1965), p. 127; cited in Neuman, *Life of Music*, which has a rich discussion of the social milieu of musicians at the Delhi headquarters of All-India Radio and its implications for the changing nature of Indian music pp. 172-86.

35. See Awasthy, *Broadcasting in India*, p. 41 for critical remarks about Ratanjankar; interview with Shertallai.

36. Luthra, *Indian Broadcasting*, pp. 311-13.

37. On the evolution of film music in India, see Ashok D. Ranade, *On the Music and Musicians of Hindoostan* (New Delhi: Promila, 1984), pp. 68-78; Peter Manual, "Popular Music in India: 1901-86," *Popular Music* 7, no. 2 (1988): 157-76; Alison Arnold, "Popular Film Song in India: A Case of Mass-Market Eclecticism," ibid.: 177-88.

38. *Indian Radio Times* 9, no. 9 (September 1954); Erik Barnouw and S. Krishnaswamy, *Indian Film*, 2d ed. (New York: Oxford University Press, 1980), pp. 207-14.

39. PM-1/43-II (1943), All-India Radio Directorate-General, New Delhi.

40. Ravi Shankar, *My Music, My Life* (New York: Simon and Schuster, 1968), pp. 82-83; Narayana Menon, "Broadcasting and Music," *Indian Radio Times* 9, no. 3 (March 1954).

41. Neuman, *Life of Music*, p. 175.

42. Awasthy, *Broadcasting in India*, pp. 53-54.

43. [Chanda Commission] *Report of the Commission on Broadcasting and Information Media* (New Delhi: Ministry of Information and Broadcasting, 1965), pp. 73-76; for a Sri Lankan point of view, see Sarath Amunugama, "The Indian Love Call," in his *Notes on Sinhala Culture* (Colombo: Gunasena, 1980), pp. 67-71, for which I am indebted to Peter Manuel.

44. Luthra, *Indian Broadcasting*, p. 369, though he does not make the connection with transistors.

45. "Gramophones—and Why Not?" in Ananda K. Coomaraswamy, *Essays in National Idealism* (Bombay: Central Book Depot, n.d.), pp. 201-6. I am indebted to Carol Breckenridge for providing me with this and other Coomaraswamy essays on music from the same collection.

46. *Illuminations*, ed. Hannah Arendt, trans. Harry Zohn (Glasgow: Fontana/Collins, 1973), pp. 220-53. The essay was first published in 1936.

47. "On the Fetish-Character in Music and the Regression of Listening" [1938], in Andrew Arato and Eike Gebhardt, *The Essential Frankfurt School Reader* (New York: Urizen, 1978), pp. 270-99; see also Adorno's essay "A Social Critique of Radio Music," *Kenyon Review* 8, no. 2 (Spring 1945): 208-17; Philip Rosen, "Adorno and Film Music: Theoretical Notes on *Composing for the Films*," *Yale French Studies*, no. 60 (1980): 157-82.

48. Chanda Commission report, p. 70.

49. Keskar, *Indian Music*, p. 15.

50. Neuman, *Life of Music*, pp. 223-29.

51. Interview with Shertallai.

52. See Alain Danielou (in collaboration with Jacques Brunet), *La musique et sa communité: La situation de la musique et des musiciens dans les pays d'orient* (Florence: Leo S. Olschki, 1971), p. 115.

53. Arjun Appadurai and Carol A. Breckenridge, "Why Public Culture?" *Public Culture* 1, no. 1 (Fall 1988): 5-9.

54. Peter Manuel, "The Cassette Industry and Popular Music in North India," *Popular Music* 10, no. 2 (1991): 189-204.

CHAPTER FOUR

The Indian Princes as Fantasy

Palace Hotels, Palace Museums, and Palace on Wheels

BARBARA N. RAMUSACK

India has long been the destination of intrepid travelers and writers who sought to explore worlds and cultures different from their own. From at least the Hellenic period (witness the account of Herodotus), people from Western Asia and Europe have portrayed India as exotic and other. In subsequent centuries travelers to India from Western Asia, East Asia, and eventually Europe have written extensively about what they saw in India, and their accounts have been the object of scholarly attention. In a highly influential analysis, Edward Said has given some attention to the role of nineteenth-century English and French sojourners to the Orient of Western Asia in creating the phenomenon of Orientalism. Finding a distinction between "British realities and French fantasies," Said has claimed that for the British, "the room available for imaginative play was limited by the realities of administration, territorial legality, and executive power," while "the French pilgrim was imbued with a sense of acute loss in the Orient," and so they "planned and projected for, imagined, ruminated about places that were principally *in their minds.*"[1] One popular representation of this contrast in travelers is found in *Around the World in Eighty Days*. Its French author, Jules Verne, contrasts the imperturbable, disinterested English hero, Phineas Fogg, with his inquiring servant, Passepartout, whose curiosity creates problems. The scope of British imaginative play in South Asia, however, calls for some modification of Said's portrayal of the British that is based on their colonial experience in Western Asia. Bernard Cohn has subtly delineated how the British imagined the Indian princes to be a loyal feudal aristocracy and then orchestrated princely participation in the elaborate 1876 Imperial Assemblage in Delhi that the Prince of Wales crowned with his presence.[2]

Beyond the political sphere, the British, and later North Americans and Indians themselves, imagined the Indian princes, especially those in Rajputana, to represent a world of fantasy in which international tourists might sample elements of an aristocratic way of life that was becoming increasingly remote from daily social reality. The projection of the capitals of princely states as underexplored yet desirable destinations for travelers began during the 1870s and 1880s, continued throughout the era of colonial rule, and intensified after India became an independent democratic republic.

The princes of Rajasthan would be particularly attractive candidates for this transformation from political leaders into eccentric preservers of a dramatic past for cultural as well as technological, geographical, and political reasons. First, prior to the sixteenth century their heroic defiance of Muslim invaders and the sultanate at Delhi invested several Rajput princes with an aura of audacious valor. Rajput bards and some British officers—most notably James Tod in his *Annals and Antiquities of Rajasthan,* published in 1829 and 1831 and frequently reprinted—retold, elaborated, and preserved constructions of Rajput chivalry and heroism. Second, expanding transportation networks, initially roads and railways and then airplanes, would foster the inclusion of Rajput princes in the tourist circuit. Third, the transfer of the British imperial capital to Delhi in 1911 would once again bring the Rajput princes close to the center of political power as they had been during the Mughal era, when the imperial capitals were at Agra and Delhi. It is ironic that this gradual development of Rajputana as a site for a touristic experience of an aristocratic lifestyle would quicken after the establishment of India as a democratic republic. But a burgeoning travel industry that utilized advertising and popular journalism demanded more and more exotic sites for its consumers. As Appadurai and Breckenridge remind us in their introduction to this volume, the media, consumption, and global cultural flows have spawned new forms of travel that constitute one arena among many that create the transnational public culture of the late twentieth century. Several erstwhile Rajput states in Rajasthan have become major sites for the creation of a fantasy world for tourists.

During the late nineteenth century, new means of mass transportation such as steamships and railways, construction projects (especially the Suez

Canal), and new forms of travel (most crucially the conducted tour as developed by Thomas Cook and Son), enabled greater numbers of people to explore the exotic Orient and India in particular. The impact of these physical, technological, and organizational innovations on the accelerating pace of travel was vividly portrayed in *Around the World in Eighty Days*. Published in 1872 in *Le Temps* but soon available in English and in England, where it became very popular, this novel celebrated speed. In order to win a gentlemanly wager, Phineas Fogg seeks to demonstrate how technological innovations such as the Suez Canal, the Great Peninsula Railway in India, and the Central Pacific and Union Pacific Railways in the United States contracted the world. In the process he becomes the precursor of the globe-trotting tourist who collects visas to prove he or she has been somewhere but makes little effort to interact with foreign cultures or peoples.

Much scholarship has viewed the tourist as a cultural phenomenon of the second half of the twentieth century. Daniel Boorstin has characterized the traveler as active, adventurous, and working at something (noting that travel comes from the French *travail,* meaning "work") and the tourist as passive, "expecting interesting things to happen to him," pleasure-seeking, and generally isolated from the landscape and society that he or she traverses.[3] Paul Fussell placed the explorer, the traveler, and the tourist on a continuum:

> All three make journeys, but the explorer seeks the undiscovered, the traveler that which has been discovered by the mind working in history, the tourist that which has been discovered by entrepreneurship and prepared for him by the arts of mass publicity. . . . [The tourist's motives are] to raise social status at home and to ally social anxiety; to realize fantasies of erotic freedom; and most important, to derive secret pleasure from posing momentarily as a member of a social class superior to one's own, to play the role of a 'shopper' and spender whose life becomes significant and exciting only when one is exercising power by choosing what to buy.[4]

Tourism represents the antithesis of the adventure and discomfort of travel, and for Boorstin, Fussell, and other commentators tourism is one more product of the democratic revolutions of the nineteenth and twentieth centuries. In the preceding centuries, especially the eighteenth, travel was generally the prerogative of the aristocratic elite; now, with the proliferation of paid vacations, vehicles that need large numbers of passengers to be economical, especially jumbo jets, and relatively inexpensive package tours, the masses could become tourists.

Tourism began to attract scholarly analysis during the 1960s but achieved the academic respectability marked by a scholarly journal, dissertations, international conferences, and collective volumes of essays only during the 1970s.[5] Some scholars have defined tourism as a "leisured migration" that has occurred at least since ancient Greece but has "become a pervasive social phenomenon" only in modern industrial societies with a "level of productivity sufficient to sustain leisure" for larger numbers of people.[6] The study of tourism has been the preserve of anthropologists, sociologists, and economists who have focused on the functions of travel and vacations in the lives of individual tourists or have described the economic, social, and political impact of tourists on the area or host country where they have traveled. For India, Linda Richter and others have analyzed the formation and implementation of governmental policies.[7] Until the Appadurai-Breckenridge project on public culture, however, relatively little scholarly attention has been given to the cultural aspects of tourism in India.[8]

My ultimate objective is to understand how certain princes and their states have been transformed into a world of fantasy in independent, republican India. This metamorphosis has occurred in many ways: by featuring the lifestyle and objects associated with the princes in art exhibits that purport to focus on India;[9] by using the palaces of Indian princes as physical settings for both Indian and foreign films such as *Shakespeare Wallah*, *The Guru*, *Heat and Dust*, and *Octopussy*;[10] and by packaging princely India for tourists. This essay explores how the princes of India emerged as a distinct category for foreign and, more recently, Indian tourists and the factors that facilitated the evolution of the Rajput princes, in particular, into the quintessential Indian princes for the touristic gaze.

Travel and Tourism in India

Although there were individual European travelers to India from Marco Polo onward, significant numbers began to arrive only in the early decades of the nineteenth century. Many of these travelers came because they had contacts with local British officials and missionaries or in order to earn a living. Their travel arrangements were based on individual initiative and the willingness of Britishers resident in India to provide hospitality for those who had letters of introduction from mutual acquaintances. By the second half of the nineteenth century some travelers visited princely states at the invitation of the Indian princes, such as Maharaja Sayaji Rao of Baroda, whom they met in Europe on holiday or in England during imperial ceremonies.[11] As the physical means of travel to India improved during the closing decades of the nineteenth century, more formalized arrangements were necessary if

larger numbers of tourists were to be accommodated. Thomas Cook under-
took his first conducted round-the-world tour in 1872-73 and in India traveled 2,300 miles establishing a network of agents.[12] Cook's promotional efforts might have benefited from the example of the Prince of Wales, later
Edward VII, who toured India in 1876-77.[13]

The press and popular books chronicled the royal adventures in 1876 and
in 1905 when the next Prince of Wales, the future George V, also visited
India,[14] and lent the allure of aristocratic participation to touring in India.
Travel guides were soon available to help the growing upper class in England
plan an Indian tour. In 1859 John Murray began to publish *A Handbook for
Travellers in India,* which covered the Bombay, Madras, and Bengal Presidencies in three separate volumes, adding a fourth on Punjab and the area
now contained in Uttar Pradesh in 1883. Captain E. B. Eastwick, a member
of Parliament, had made numerous trips to India from the 1850s to the
1870s to gather the basic material for these initial volumes. Over the suc-
ceeding decades British officials such as George W. Forrest, then keeper of
records for the government of India, consolidated the multiple volumes into
one handbook by 1892 and expanded the coverage to include the princely
states. The *Handbook* went through at least nineteen editions, the latest
appearing in 1962, and it has remained a compendium of historical descriptions of places of interest organized according to tour plans with information on mileage; type of train service and quality of roads; and the availability of *dak* bungalows (travelers' rest houses), accommodations within the
train stations, and private hotels. Its Victorian origin is reflected in the nineteenth edition, which continues to offer information on sea voyages from
England to India, instructions for hiring servants, and injunctions on what
to anticipate when staying in *dak* bungalows as well as the advisability of
carrying tinned beans and sausages in certain areas.[15] Another anachronism
in the 1962 edition is the omission of any information on costs of accommodation or on shopping, two major elements of most travel guides published from the 1960s onward and intended to appeal to societies oriented
toward consumption.

A more comprehensive work was W. S. Caine's *Picturesque India: A
Handbook for European Travellers,* which sought "to interest holiday people
in our greatest dependency and its two hundred millions of our fellow subjects."[16] This guide covered fewer places, but it was handsomely illustrated
(see fig. 4.1.), had more extensive descriptions of each site, discussed local
society and culture including the presence of Christian missionaries, and included information on local handicrafts and where they might be pur-

Figure 4.1. Jaipur. The Hall of the Winds (Hawa Mahal).
From W. S. Caine, *Picturesque India* (1891).

chased. Caine was particularly keen on the enameled and the garnet jewelry of Jaipur.[17] These handbooks were complemented by many accounts written by individual travelers about their personal experiences and impressions. Fussell would characterize these works as travel books since they represented the impact of places visited upon the author within the context of a recognizable physical description of the sites.

In a random sample of over a dozen such works published between 1870 and 1920, tours generally followed one of three circuits. The traveler usually arrived by sea at Bombay and then visited sites in Western India, most notably Ajanta and Ellora, proceeded either to Madras, with stays perhaps at Mysore and Hyderabad, or to Delhi followed by stops at Agra, Lucknow, and Benares before ending up at Calcutta. One might alternatively journey to Calcutta from Bombay and then move up the Gangetic Valley to Delhi before returning to Bombay. Railway lines appear to have been the principal physical factor influencing travel plans. Mary Carpenter, an English social reformer from Bristol who went to India in 1866 to promote education for Indian girls, provides a graphic example of the crucial importance of the railway for both unofficial and official British travelers. Carpenter had landed in Bombay and then wanted to proceed to Calcutta to lobby the governor general. An English official in Calcutta advised her, based on recent experience, that the land route between Calcutta and Bombay via Lahore was very difficult and unpleasant. Carpenter subsequently related that

> every one who had practical knowledge on the subject informed us that the best, and indeed the only satisfactory route, was by steamer to Calicut, by rail across the country from Beypoor to Madras, and then by steamer to Calcutta.[18]

This circuitous route was even taken by an official going from Bombay to Lahore.

Princely States as Destinations in the Nineteenth Century

What were travelers and, later, tourists seeking in India? Nelson H. H. Graburn has defined two categories of tourism: culture tourism includes exploring historical sites and seeing different ethnic peoples; nature tourism ranges from ethnic to ecological to environmental, which subsumed recreational and hunting and gathering activities.[19] The princely states offered something in both categories. Which princely states were on the itineraries of nineteenth-century tourists? First, it should be remembered that the distinctions between princely states and British Indian provinces were fluid prior to 1857. Thus Awadh had been a leading example of the luxurious princely state, and its capital at Lucknow was a major stopping place until its annexation in 1856. Thereafter, British travelers tended to pay homage at the memorials to the "mutiny" at Kanpur and Lucknow and to tour Muslim sites in Lucknow but had to look further afield for the Indian prince who was now declared an endangered species to be preserved as an ally of the imperial Raj. The late-nineteenth-century sojourners who published travel books tended to focus on the southern states of Mysore and Hyderabad, on Gwalior and perhaps Baroda among the Maratha-ruled states, occasionally on Jammu and Kashmir, which were difficult to reach, and gradually on the Rajputana states.

Hyderabad was universally acclaimed as the premier princely state. Travelers commented on the opulent lifestyle of the *nizam*, the fort at Golconda, the newly opened Salar Jung Museum, and the glories of Ajanta and Ellora, which were then in the dominions of the *nizam*. History and nature tourism were available further south. Mysore had long been a destination for patriotic Britishers who wished to visit the scene of the British victory over Tipu Sultan and the tomb of this dreaded adversary. In 1881 the British returned

Mysore to the direct rule of Maharaja Chamrajendra Wadiyar, who enjoyed European society and was known for his lavish entertainment of European visitors. The distinctive trademark of a visit to Mysore was the *keddah,* a great elephant hunt, which was held annually or would be organized specially for British nobility, as it was for the duke of Clarence and Avondale in 1887.[20]

During the closing decades of the nineteenth century, the princes emerged as the primary providers of nature tourism in India for important Europeans. Elephant hunts were only one form of blood sport available in the princely states. When the Prince of Wales visited Baroda in 1876-77, the main attraction was a series of staged fights between animals ranging from elephants to rams. The rams were allowed to fight until they killed each other since

> the sight of blood [was] by no means distasteful to the gentleman [the recently deposed Gaekwar Malhar Rao] who was accused of having attempted to kill Col. Phayre. But more human days have dawned, and in the presence of the prince, at least, no very desperate encounter was allowed.[21]

The journalist who made these comments saw no incongruity in the fact that the humane Prince of Wales participated in hunting deer with cheetah, and then with guns in Baroda, and ended his tour of India with three weeks of tiger shooting in Nepal.

Elaborate hunting expeditions became a major component of a visit to an Indian state since their princely organizers enabled the foreign participants to taste adventure in a setting of comfort and frequently of luxury. They orchestrated the excitement of the chase, usually with an assured catch contrived at great expense, the safety of shooting from raised platforms called *machans,* elaborate meals in jungly settings, and high-status souvenirs such as animal skins and photographs of the prince and the hunter with a foot on the slain prey.[22] The tiger hunts of Gwalior and Jaipur became legendary, and even liberal British politicians such as Edwin S. Montagu relished invitations to these extravaganzas. Britons who would otherwise disdain social relations with Indians made an exception for princes since, as Robert Byron, possibly the most influential writer of travel books in the 1920s and 1930s, has remarked, "acquaintance with a Maharajah or Nawab means tigers."[23] Maharaja Ganga Singh of Bikaner organized imperial sand grouse hunts in the Rajasthan desert—a highly prized twentieth-century addition to the winter schedule of foreign dignitaries and tourists.[24]

Besides their attractions for hunters, the Rajput states also offered history packaged in different formats, the opportunity to see "primitive" peoples, and, for those concerned about British political responsibilities, even some evidence of the modernizing capacity of Indian rulers. The Prince of Wales visited Jaipur, which J. Drew Gay, a special correspondent of the London *Daily Telegraph,* claimed was justifiably labeled the Paris of the East. This journalist, who was usually critical of Indian cities, noted that

> in 1728 Jey Singh made Jeypore a handsomer spot than our metropolis of to-day, and . . . for a hundred and fifty years the city of Rajpootana has had wider thoroughfares and better drainage, prettier houses and larger gardens, than any rival in civilised Europe.[25]

Val Prinsep, an artist who was in India during the prince's tour, thought that because of its size and regularity Jaipur "lacked the charm and picturesqueness of many Indian places,"[26] but the majority of travelers thought that Jaipur was the leading Rajput and even the "finest of modern Hindu cities."[27] Most commentators, then and now, seem amazed that any Indian had the ability to plan a city with a grid pattern of streets.

Besides its acclaimed modern appearance, Jaipur had other attractions that helped it to achieve the prominence it has never lost among tourists to Rajasthan. The ease of the railway connection was the major physical factor drawing tourists to Jaipur. Then the rose-colored city whose streets were "crowded with a stalwart race of men, superior in every way to the poor, ill-fed people of so many districts of Bengal or Bombay"[28] provided the backdrop for a living tableau of handsome Rajputs wearing boldly colored clothing—what some have labeled the ethnic attraction of primitive peoples. History could be seen at the ancient fort of Amber and the marble cenotaphs of earlier princes. Finally, Jaipur either already possessed or soon acquired the facilities through which tourists increasingly came to experience other cultures.[29] They ranged from the Jaipur Museum opened by Maharaja Madho Singh in 1881 in the Albert Hall[30] to a public garden and zoological collection that included nine tigers of varying ferocity for vicarious hunters. Jaipur also produced a wide array of indigenous crafts, particularly jewelry, marble work, and dyed textiles that were available for purchase as souvenirs. For British subjects who were responding negatively to the machine age, W. S. Caine lauded the souvenirs of Jaipur "where everything is made by hand, machinery practically unknown, and where the methods and process have been virtually the same for a thousand years."[31]

Other Rajput states were soon added to the circuit. Some—such as Jodhpur, which was soon touted as one of the the most picturesque towns in India—became accessible by railway. Others, most notably Udaipur, could be reached over newly constructed roads connecting the state capital to a railway station. Udaipur was commended for providing an opportunity "to see something of country life in districts remote from railways and Europeans." Furthermore, the maharana of Udaipur, who was judged, "like all Indian princes . . . politeness itself," would usually provide boats for visitors to tour the artificial lake on which Udaipur city is located, although the main attraction was the nearby site of Chitor.[32] In contrast, Alwar is mentioned by some because it could be visited en route from Jaipur to Delhi.

During the twentieth century the numbers of foreign tourists to India increased, but definite statistics are not yet available. Those who published accounts of their tours continued to visit the princely states. Baroda now was praised for progressive policies such as universal, compulsory education, its Maharaja's College, and its state museum, opened in 1894.[33] Mysore was viewed as another prime example of the dramatic modernization possible under personal autocratic rule. In 1936 Basil Mathews, a Christian theologian seeking to discover India, found in Mysore that "the children were plumper and better fed and the villages in general in cleaner trim than in any other part of India that I saw," that "the cheapest and most comfortable homes for depressed class workers" were in this state, and that it was a leader in using hydroelectric power for villages as well as cities.[34] So visitors saw some Indian states as models of what enlightened Indian rulers and administrators could accomplish.

At the opposite end of the spectrum, other princely states were promoted as refuges of romantic but embattled traditions and loyalties. In 1933 C. W. Waddington, a former principal of princely colleges at Rajkot and Ajmer, produced *Indian India*, a coffee-table-sized book complete with twenty-nine sketches by the author of the leading attractions of states in Rajputana and Central India. This work was designed to provide those who had never visited India "some inducement to exchange a winter in Egypt or on the Riviera for the exhilarating climate of the Land of Princes."[35] This appeal represents a shift toward the market of affluent tourists interested in recreational tourism in sunny climes in some combination with culture, especially historical and ethnic, tourism. Beginning in the late nineteenth century, Paul Fussell has argued, this trend lured many British writers away from England in the interwar years.[36] Waddington's itinerary included the usual triad of Jaipur, Udaipur, and Jodhpur but also extended to Bikaner; to Bundi and Kotah, ruled by members of the Hara Rajput clan, a branch of the Chauhans that included Prithviraj, the last Hindu ruler of Delhi; to the Jhala Rajput state of Jhalawar; to the Rajput-ruled states of Jhansi, Orchha, and Panna in Bundelkhand; to the Jat-ruled state of Bharatpur, which would soon become a standard stop on the road between Agra and Jaipur; as well as to Gwalior. His choice reflected the whereabouts of personal acquaintances, the extension of the railway, and the political prominence of rulers such as Maharaja Ganga Singh of Bikaner or their prime ministers in the concurrent negotiations over federation in London.

Rajput States as Royal India for Middle-Class Tourists

In the aftermath of World War II, independent India became the destination of new types and numbers of tourists. Much of the increase in foreign tourists is probably a result of the growing accessibility of air travel to more groups in society. Airplanes also shifted travel patterns within India: Bombay remains a major port of entry, but Western air travelers increasingly disembark in Delhi, thereby bypassing both Calcutta and Madras. Meanwhile, Madras becomes a point of entry for Tamilians and other travelers from Singapore and Southeast Asia. Since air travel enabled them to reach India more quickly, tourists could now come for shorter tours. India had to be packaged into discreet, comprehensive units. Three main foci emerged: Mughal India as seen in Delhi and Agra; Hindu India, viewed in Benaras and Khajuraho;[37] and princely India, concentrated on the Rajput trio of Jaipur, Udaipur, and Jodhpur with more recent extensions to Bikaner and Jaisalmer.

Since 1950 the princely states of Rajasthan have been defined as the quintessential princely states. In *India in Luxury: A Practical Guide for the Discerning Traveller,* Louise Nicholson opened her chapter on Rajasthan by proclaiming, "Rajasthan is classic fantasy India at its best."[38] Hyderabad, Mysore, and Baroda have been eliminated from the category of princely state. Now tourists do not come to India seeking examples of modernization in the Third World; they do not want to tour the petrochemical complexes of Baroda-Vadodra or the electronic industry of Bangalore (Mysore). They seek culture and nature tourism, and the Rajput princes and the state government have been ready to provide it.

In 1958 Maharaja Man Singh II of Jaipur became the first prince to convert a palace into a hotel, citing reasons such as his financial inability to maintain it as a residence, his lack of need for such facilities now that he was no longer *rajpramukh* or governor of Rajasthan, and the balancing need for a good hotel in Jaipur.[39] It is fitting that his selection was the Rambagh Palace, constructed about 1850 as a guest house for European visitors, enlarged three decades later by Swinton Jacob, then in the 1930s extensively remodeled as a residence for Man Singh and eventually for his third wife, the glamorous,

Western-educated Gayatri Devi of Cooch Behar.[40] Rambagh Palace reverted to its original role as a lodging for Europeans—now tourists rather than travelers or British officials. Five years later Maharana Bhagwat Singh of Udaipur converted a summer palace in Lake Pichola into the Lake Palace Hotel, assisted by a 6 percent loan and a five-year tax holiday from the government of India.[41] During the 1970s other princes, most notably Maharaja Gaj Singh II of Jodhpur, opened their palaces and were joined by several of their nobles.

The slower rate of economic development in Rajasthan increased the sense of its distinctiveness from modern India, and the sparse distribution of its population partially mitigated the stereotypes of Indian poverty. Tourists sought historical fantasy, and Rajput princes have been packaged to satisfy this quest. Writing in 1985 in *Connoisseur,* a glossy Western magazine devoted to consumption and collection, Gita Mehta, the author of *Karma Cola* and of *Raj,* a novel about princely India told from the perspective of a nationalist princess, emphasizes the attraction of the lack of economic development in Rajasthan. She contends that:

> Today it is that absence of homogeneity that makes the harsh and barren land of Rajasthan the perfect introduction to an India where peasant women still travel in curtained bullock carts, camel caravans still cross the desert, elephants wait in front of palace forts, tigers drink water from artificial lakes of out which rise pillared pleasure pavilions.[42]

What are the attractions of Rajput princes for foreign tourists? A selection of articles from Western travel magazines demonstrates the latest stage in the creation of the fantasy of the Indian princes. In *MD,* a popular medical journal, a 1986 article by Sooni Taraporevala entitled "The Royal Treatment" begins thus: "In India's palace hotels, ordinary mortals can live like maharajas."[43] The author, a photojournalist and a screenwriter for *Salaam Bombay* and *Mississippi Masala,* is quick to stress that there is modern hotel management at the Rambagh Palace in Jaipur, the Umaid Bhawan in Jodhpur, and the Lake Palace and the Shiv Niwas Palace in Udaipur. There is also a contemporary appeal to aristocratic pretensions with the aside that Shiv Niwas "was originally the maharaja's personal guesthouse, where he was host to Queen Elizabeth, Jackie Kennedy, and the Shah of Iran."[44] Thus one can momentarily be transported to the glorious past of Rajput history and live like modern-day royalty. All for a mere three hundred dollars per day in 1985, which apparently was deemed not a deterrent to affluent American physicians.

Gita Mehta begins "Royal India" with this revealing appeal: "You have heard of the discomforts of India. Now try the pleasures of legendary Rajasthan." Sounding as if she has read Nelson Graburn's influential article "Tourism: The Sacred Journey," Mehta relates that ancient Indian scriptures "regard travel as a form of worship" and recommends that modern worshippers who wish "to ride an elephant through the great gateways of ancient citadels by day and buy miniature paintings in polo bars by night" visit Rajasthan, "the heart of royal India."[45]

There follows a list of the opportunities for the acquisition of souvenirs, mainly jewelry, textiles, items inlaid with semiprecious stones, and carved doors, produced by craftsmen whose forebears were kept alive by the patronage of Rajput princes. Here Mehta continues the tradition begun by Caine a century earlier of recommending to tourists from industrialized states mementos of a distant past portrayed as primitive yet desirable because of its simplicity. These souvenirs not only help to create a past out of the present, they also function as trophies. As Susan Stewart has so incisively argued:

> Removed from its context, the exotic souvenir is a sign of survival, not its
> own survival, but the survival of the possessor outside his or her own context
> of familiarity. Its otherness speaks to the possessor's capacity for otherness; it
> is the possessor, not the souvenir, which is ultimately the curiosity.[46]

At the same time, shopping for souvenirs represents one of the few personal encounters that the tourist will have with local society, since package tours, travel agents, reservations, and guides eliminate many of the negotiations that a traveler used to undertake.[47]

Mehta is more adventureous than most travel writers in her projected fourteen-day itinerary that recommends more exclusive places such as Samode, seat of one of the principal *jagirdars* or nobles of Jaipur, which Stuart Cary Welch praised with stunning photographs in a 1986 issue of *House and Garden*;[48] Jaisalmer, the remote fortress of golden sandstone that lacks a regular air connection;[49] the more easterly trio of Bundi, Kotah, and Jhalawar; as well as the original western triangle of Jaipur, Jodhpur, and Udaipur.

In a 1982 article on Jodhpur and Jaisalmer, Eliot Weinberger underscores the accessibility of the palace hotels to middle-class tourists: "Even such a decidedly unregal visitor such as myself could now spend a few days living in a style to which few are accustomed,"[50] he begins, and continues: "Our ignominious arrival at the Palace in a broken-down auto-rickshaw was greeted by half a dozen servants." When it is time to move on to Jaisalmer, he confesses that, "spoiled almost to a state of somnambulism by life in the palace, I could think of only one way to leave Jodhpur: on the maharaja's private train."[51] While he was living in the maharaja's sleeping car in the Jaisalmer railway station, this student-poet met some musicians brought in to entertain a visiting Indian dignitary, "so in princely fashion we seized the opportunity and hired five of these musicians for [a] private concert" on the rippled sandhills at Som.[52] One can stay in princely palaces and travel in princely trains and even act as a princely patron, enjoying private concerts in a remote and romantic setting.

A 1989 photo article in Condé Nast Traveler, "The Essence of Regal India," conflates advertising with reporting. The Umaid Bhawan Palace at Jodhpur and some undifferentiated sites at Udaipur (by now Rajput palaces are as interchangeable as Gothic cathedrals) are backdrops for Western-designed clothes that have appropriated styles and motifs from India. Suede jodhpurs by the Paris fashion house of Lanvin are photographed under a tiger skin in the lobby of the Umaid Bhawan Palace Hotel, and a sari "skirt" by an American designer, Norma Kamali, is situated next to a statue of Queen Victoria in the public library at Udaipur.[53] Consumerism has been carried to a new level as one is now tempted to buy a high-priced wardrobe—Indian designs filtered through Western manufacturers—in which one could play at being princess or prince for a few days and nights in the palace hotels of Rajasthan. In the same issue there is an article on saris and one entitled "Living Like a Maharaja."[54]

The opportunity to travel in princely railway carriages was expanded in 1982 with the introduction of the palace on wheels. Authentic railway cars specially built for various Indian princes were combined to form a train that offered a three-day tour of Agra, Bharatpur, and Jaipur and a longer run to Jaipur, Jodhpur, and Udaipur. Newspaper articles stress its affordability for Western tourists, the abundance of service personnel, and the luxurious furnishings in the cars.[55] By 1991 a replica palace on wheels was built since the original cars became increasingly unserviceable.

Princes as Fantasy

Why do I think that certain Indian princes and their erstwhile states have been transformed into a world of fantasy? First, the emergence of the Rajput princes as the sole representation of princely India denies the diversity that existed among the hundred or so princes who exercised internal sovereignty during the last century of the British Raj. The present emphasis on Rajasthan reduces that variety to one type. Indian princes come to be viewed as chivalrous rulers who sought to maintain "traditional" societies against Muslim invaders and British officials and to prevent the encroachment of economic and

social modernization. The maharanas of Mewar who resisted giving daugh-
ters in marriage to Mughal emperors and thought that British honors were fit
for their horses become the generalized image of Indian princes. Princely capitals are also reimagined. Jaipur is no longer seen as the "Paris of the East" or a
modern Hindu city but is evoked for its indigenous, traditional aspects: the
Amber Fort, its pink-hued buildings, its colorfully attired inhabitants, and its
abundance of handmade crafts. Since there is relatively little foreign tourism
to most other erstwhile princely capitals such as Baroda, Gwalior, and Hyderabad, these images are not contradicted by other experiences.

Second, the Rajput palace hotels and palace on wheels are stages on
which middle-class foreign and, increasingly, Indian tourists can play at being prince or princess for a day. Many scholars writing on tourism emphasize that tourists seek an inversion of their usual daily routine. Alma Gottlieb
has explored the phenomenon of American tourists who seek to live some
combination of queen for a day and peasant for a day on their vacations; she
sets peasant and queen at opposite ends of a continuum and places most
tourists at some intermediate point. Gottlieb mentions the vogue to stay
overnight in actual castles in Europe but does not consider India.[56] More
broadly, Arjun Appadurai has argued:

> More persons throughout the world see their lives through the prisms of the
> possible lives offered by mass media in all their forms. That is, fantasy is now
> a social practice; it enters in a host of ways into the fabrication of social lives
> for many people in many societies.[57]

Thus tourists are able to construct multiple lives for themselves in places
that make concrete the possibilities and images purveyed by the mass media.

Travel books, Indian and foreign journalists writing for leisure magazines, and foreign movies disseminate exotic images that tourists find that
they can experience in facilities orchestrated by Rajput princes and made
available by government airlines and railways as well as a late-capitalist
tourist industry. In Rajasthan there are unparalleled opportunities to mix
with peasants during the day and to retreat to royal accommodations at
night. If a tourist wishes to have accommodations at both ends of the spectrum, a Rajput *thakur* or noble family at Mandawa in northern Rajasthan
(about 150 miles from New Delhi) in 1991 completed construction of a
mud-walled desert village complete with a swimming pool and modern
bathrooms in each cottage.[58] A few days later one may retreat to a palace
hotel with even more luxurious conveniences, where the erstwhile ruler may
make an occasional appearance. Although it has not been possible to obtain
adequate documentation, there is a general impression that upper-middle-

class Indian tourists are beginning to frequent the Indian palace hotels and to expect the same level of fantasy as their foreign counterparts. Anecdotal accounts suggest that the palace on wheels has been a less successful tourist attraction than the palace hotels. The limited space of train cars makes it difficult to provide all the amenities such as American-style plumbing that Western tourists, who want to live their fantasies in comfort, demand.

A third way in which the Rajput princes have supplied materials for the imaginative creation of fantasy by tourists is through their establishment of museums that encapsulate culture within objects. As I noted earlier, the princes were pioneers in founding museums in their states. After the integration of the princely states into the Indian Union in 1947-48, the princes discovered the benefits of organizing museums as repositories for their personal collections to avoid disputes over ownership of paintings, jewelry, arms, and furnishings that might have been purchased with state revenues. Jaipur has museums from both phases of Indian history. It now boasts three major museums: the nineteenth-century one at Albert Hall; the City Palace Museum, which was opened by Maharaja Man Singh II in 1958 to house the personal collections of the princely family; and the Fort Museum, which opened in the 1980s to display weapons and other items related to warfare.[59] Rajasthan enjoys perhaps the greatest concentration of such museums with major ones at Alwar, Bharatpur, Bikaner, Jaisalmer, Jhalawar, Jodhpur, Kotah, and Udaipur as well as Jaipur.[60] Finally, it should be noted that many of these museums are housed in forts and palaces and approximate country house and chateau museums in England and France. These institutions, with their emphasis on portraying the material culture of the daily lives of princes, present a more romantic view of objects than do modern museums in major urban cities, where objects are displayed in the sterile environment of climate-controlled glass cases. Princely palace museums provide something for tourists to "see" and offer access to the princely lifestyle for those who cannot afford to stay at the palace hotels.

Fantasy, Empire, and Late Capitalism

From at least the sixteenth century, European explorers went to India to experience, to trade with, and to report on the exotic and the other. By the late nineteenth century the English had created a political structure and a constructed landscape in several areas of India that incorporated their ideas about themselves as well as what they thought was appropriate to an imperial power in India. As the British Empire entered its "golden age" during the last quarter of the nineteenth century, material factors such as the Suez Canal, steamships, and railways enabled increased numbers of Britons to travel to India. Those who wrote about their experiences expressed, first, their pride in the glory of the British Empire, of which India was the "jewel in the crown," through their remarks on Bombay, Calcutta, and Madras, the great port cities created by the British but peopled by Indians, and on the sites of British military and supposedly moral superiority, Lucknow, Kanpur, and Kashmiri Gate in Delhi. Second, they toured Agra and Delhi and described the glory of the Mughal predecessors whose accomplishments they thought the British Empire expanded and integrated with modern social responsibilities. These two categories of observations support Edward Said's emphasis on the British realities that left limited room for imagination, but I would argue that British travelers and tourists still wanted to enjoy an imaginary world of exoticism and that they sought it in what increasingly became known as Indian India, the area ruled by internally autonomous Indian princes.

The ambivalent attitudes of British travelers and, indeed, officials are mirrored in their visits to Baroda and Mysore as well as to Hyderabad and the Rajput states. In Baroda and Mysore they could laud examples of Indian progressiveness and the benefits of good administration that substantiated their own efforts to extend social benefits in an autocractic manner in British India. In Hyderabad and the Rajput states they imagined or fantasized about an extravagant life unlike their own in either British-ruled India or in Britain itself.

Fantasy is one of those broad concepts that frequently remain undefined. In literature it is usually opposed to realism or naturalism and as a category includes a spectrum of forms ranging from the fairy tale to science fiction. In psychology fantasy can imply the effort to achieve wish fulfilment. In the travel literature on India during the late nineteenth century, writers chose the fairy tale that places characters in a timeless, mythical space to describe what they saw in Hyderabad, Jaipur, and eventually Udaipur. The reference to fairy tales was appropriate since these writers and many British officials portrayed life in these princely states, especially the Rajput ones, as unchanging for centuries and even millennia. They described the subjects of princely states as happy children who would suffer the autocracy of a prince in return for his benevolent concern and the power of his rituals. In some ways these ideas validated the efficacy of British treatment of the Indian people: the British acted autocratically and used rituals such as the Imperial Assemblage of 1876 to inspire awe and loyalty.

Travelers in the late nineteenth century stood at various places on the continuum from explorer to traveler to tourist. The explorers tramped across the Himalayan borderlands and through Central Asia. The travelers still traversed India alone or with one or two companions and a collection of letters of introduction to British officials, Christian missionaries, and Indian princes. The tourists took the guided tours organized by Thomas Cook or had their arrangements carefully confirmed before they arrived in India. World War I drastically reduced the opportunities for exploration and travel. During the 1920s Europeans and some Americans arrived seeking culture tourism in a sunny environment. Although Fussell has described the interwar decades as the epitome of travel writing, Britons like Robert Byron who visited and wrote about India tended to fulfill Edward Said's later conception of the British as being concerned with the realities of administration. Byron and others devoted more space to analyses of the pros and cons of the Indian demand for self-government than to the fairy tales of the princely states.[61] Travelers and tourists continued to visit the princely states and now found some princes such as Maharaja Ganga Singh of Bikaner and Nawab Hamidullah of Bhopal to be effective modern politicians.[62] Even C. W. Waddington, who produced the most fanciful book on the princely states during the interwar period, recorded material progress in the Rajput states. Mentioning a modern enterprise, the Bundi Hydraulic Lime and Cement Company, Waddington noted that "happily it is remote from the city."[63]

The end of World War II and the achievement of Indian independence that terminated the political power of the princes coincided with the expansion of tourism. As the princes lost their political power, they became even more acceptable as images of the exotic and the other. There is a shift in the rhetoric of travel writers from fairy tale to fantasy. Fairy tale implies a childhood innocence in which death and violence occur but are ultimately resolved in a happy ending. There was no happy ending for most of the princes, and the destruction of World War II reduced the public's willingness to believe in fairy tales and to use that rhetoric. People still sought escape, but now a more generalized and more temporary fantasy became the goal. One could retreat incongruously and evanescently by jet airplane to the world of French counts, English lords, and—most exclusively because they are most distant—Indian princes.

As the late-capitalist combination of tour packages, advertising agencies, airlines, and governments needing foreign exchange coupled with the increased affluence of an expanding middle class, especially in the United States, brought more tourists to India, Indian princes entered a second wave of political transition. They were losing their offices as *rajpramukhs* or governors and having to confront the economic realities of living on a fixed income in a time of growing inflation. One wonders whether, when Maharaja Man Singh II of Jaipur, a leading member of the so-called jet set, turned his palace into a hotel he was, besides seeking extra income, also trying to avoid having to provide complimentary hospitality to acquaintances he met in England and the United States, now more likely to arrive on his doorstep expecting a princely welcome. Furthermore, the City Palace Museum in Jaipur could preserve his patrimony from the clutches of a republican Indian government as well as provide a "tourist attraction" for guests in the Rambagh Palace Hotel.

The third stage in the political evolution of the princes from rulers to citizens occurred in 1971, when the constitution ceased to recognize them as princes and their privy purses, titles, and special privileges were abolished. During the 1970s more princely hotels were opened and older ones such as the Rambagh and the Lake Palace were affiliated with professional hotel companies, apparently to maximize profits and possibly to improve services. The princes took the initiative in providing a royal setting for ordinary tourists as well as movie actors and actresses and were supported by contemporary Indian capitalists. The Taj Hotel Group, which manages the Rambagh and Lake Palace Hotels, helped to further the mystique of the princes by assisting in the production of *Lives of the Indian Princes,* a lavishly illustrated survey by Charles Allen, the author of *Plain Tales from the Raj,* and Sharada Dwivedi. Their efforts were extended by the government, aspiring to package India for the quick trippers, and by travel agents seeking profits. The government provided air connections, a scarce resource, to Udaipur, Jodhpur, and other sites, and travel agents smoothed the way.

As tourism increased and the world shrunk, new sites were needed in order to play the game of who has traveled to the most unusual place. For the 1950s Europe would do for both Americans and Britishers who had not been able to travel on the Continent during the 1940s, first because of war and then because of scarcities. The 1960s demanded exotic locales, and Jacqueline Kennedy's visit to Jaipur in 1962 gave travel to the princely states much the same royal aura as did the visits by the Princes of Wales in 1876-77 and 1905. By the 1980s consumer-oriented travel magazines and evocative advertisements by the Government of India Tourist Office reinforced the cultural attraction of the Rajput princely states as well as their physical proximity to Delhi (see fig. 4.2). The next stage should probably be conference centers in the princely states, since delegates to a conference supposedly spend three and a half times more than an average tourist.[64]

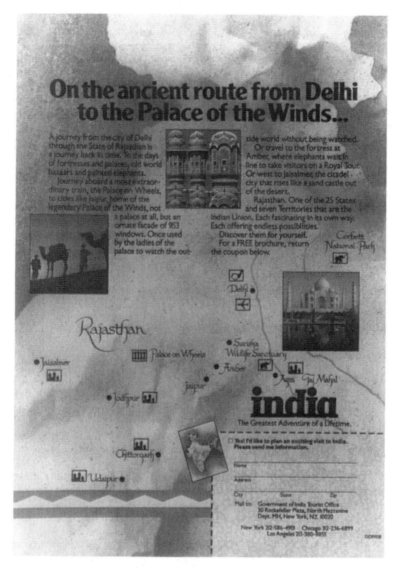

Figure 4.2. Government of India Tourist Office advertisement.
From *Gourmet* magazine, October 1988, by permission.

Notes

This essay was first presented at the sixteenth annual Wisconsin Conference on South Asia on November 7, 1987, at a panel entitled "Taste, Fantasy and Spectacle" that was the first part of a group of papers entitled "The Making of Public Culture in India." Since then I have considerably revised it and have benefited from the critical comments of Carol Breckenridge, Arjun Appadurai, and the Department of History Faculty Seminar at the University of Cincinnati. Another version, entitled "Tourism and Icons: The Packaging of the Princely States of Rajasthan," was presented at the Perceptions of India's Past conference at the American Institute of Indian Studies Center for Art and Archaeology in Varanasi in December 1989. That work will be published in a volume of conference papers edited by Catherine Asher and Thomas Metcalf.

I am most grateful for a 1986-87 fellowship from the National Endowment for the Humanities at the National Humanities Center. There my participation in a seminar entitled "The Other" provided the intellectual stimulation for the conceptual framework of this paper, and the center's extensive library network and able librarians allowed me to pursue the research in published primary sources on which this essay is based. When I was working on the final revision of this essay during the summer of 1992, I benefited from a lively discussion of the Research Triangle South Asia Seminar during which John Richards made the insightful recommendation that I compare my analysis to the adventures related in Verne's *Around the World in Eighty Days*.

1. Edward W. Said, *Orientalism* (New York: Vintage, 1979), pp. 169-70.

2. Bernard S. Cohn, "Representing Authority in Victorian India," in *The Invention of Tradition*, ed. Eric Hobsbawm and Terence Ranger (Cambridge: University of Cambridge Press, 1983).

3. Daniel J. Boorstin, *The Image; or, What Happened to the American Dream* (New York: Atheneum, 1962), pp. 77-117, especially p. 85.

4. Paul Fussell, *Abroad: British Literary Traveling between the Wars* (New York: Oxford University Press, 1980), pp. 39, 42.

5. The acknowledged first article is T. A. Nunez, "Tourism, Tradition and Acculturation: Weekendismo in a Mexican Village," *Ethnology* 3, no. 2 (1963): 347-52. *Annals of Tourism Research* was founded in 1973, and *Hosts and Guests: The Anthropology of Tourism*, ed. Valene L. Smith (Philadelphia: University of Pennsylvania Press, 1977), was generated at the first national symposium on this subject, held in Mexico City in 1974.

6. Dennison Nash, "Tourism as a Form of Imperialism," in Smith, *Hosts and Guests*, p. 35.

7. Linda K. Richter, *The Politics of Tourism* (Honolulu: University of Hawaii Press, 1989), pp. 102-33.

8. Besides Carol Appadurai Breckenridge, "Travel in Late 20th Century India," *India Magazine*, no. 8 (December 1987): 36-45, 50, there is Niloufer Ichaporia, "Tourism at Khajuraho: An Indian Enigma?" *Annals of Tourism Research* 10, no. 1 (1983): 75-92.

9. One example of how the princes are equated with Indian culture is a *Chicago Tribune* article on the exhibit *Costumes of Royal India* at the Metropolitan Museum of Art in 1985-86. The article begins, "Kipling was right: Past maharajahs' riches provide *a passage* to Indian spectacle" (italics added).

10. *Autobiography of a Princess: Also Being the Adventures of an American Film Director in the Land of the Maharajas*, compiled by James Ivory (New York: Harper & Row, 1975), especially "Palaces as Sets: Alwar and Bikaner," pp. 105-29.

11. Oscar Browning, *Impressions of Indian Travel* (London: Hodder and Stoughton, 1903), pp. 189-90.

12. Edmund Swinglehurst, *Cook's Tours: The Story of Popular Travel* (Poole, Dorset: Blandford, 1982), pp. 69-70.

13. Bernard Cohn has discussed how the Prince of Wales's visit was carefully constructed "to excite" the loyalty of the princes and to reaffirm their role in the maintenance of the British Em-

pire in India ("Cloth, Clothes and Colonialism: India in the 19th Century," paper presented at Wenner-Gren Symposium no. 93, 1983, p. 43).

14. Eustace Reynolds-Ball, *The Tourist's India* (London: Swan Sonnenschein, 1907), pp. vii–viii.

15. A brief history of the publication of this book in *A Handbook for Travellers in India, Pakistan, Burma and Ceylon*, 19th ed. (London: John Murray, 1962), pp. v–vii. *Murray's Handbooks for Travellers* were reprinted in a microfiche edition by University Publications of America in 1990 and thus formally enshrined as historical sources. No traveler or tourist would be able to use a microfiche edition in the field.

16. W. S. Caine, *Picturesque India: A Handbook for European Travellers* (London: George Routledge and Sons, 1891), p. ix. A more compact guide with more details about accommodation and railway connections is G. Hutton-Taylor, *Illustrated Guide to India and Indian Hotels* (Calcutta: Thacker, Spink [1900?]).

17. Caine, *Picturesque India*, pp. 111–13.

18. Mary Carpenter, *Six Months in India*, vol. 1 (London: Longmans, Green, 1868), pp. 126–27.

19. Nelson H. H. Graburn, "Tourism: The Sacred Journey," in Smith, *Hosts and Guests*, pp. 26–28.

20. Donald A. Gustafson, "Mysore 1881-1902: The Making of a Model State," unpublished Ph.D. dissertation, University of Wisconsin, 1969, pp. 109–10, and John D. Rees, *Duke of Clarence and Avondale in Southern India with a Narrative of Elephant Catching in Mysore* (London: Kegan Paul, Trench, Trubner, 1891), pp. 78–140.

21. J. Drew Gay, *The Prince of Wales in India; or, From Pall Mall to the Punjaub* (New York: H. Worthington, 1877), p. 90. Gay was billed as a special correspondent of the London *Daily Telegraph.*

22. Although the viceroy would not qualify as a tourist, an exemplary photograph of Lord and Lady Curzon, the viceroy and vicereine of India from 1899 to 1905, standing next to their tiger during a visit with the nizam of Hyderabad in 1902 serves as the frontispiece in Ray Desmond, *Victorian India in Focus: A Selection of Early Photographs from the Collection in the India Office Library and Records* (London: Her Majesty's Stationery Office, 1982). A photograph of the Prince of Wales, an imperial tourist, and his tiger trophy in 1905 in Gwalior and a miniature painting from Patiala of a British "sportsman" shooting a tiger are in Charles Allen and Sharada Dwivedi, *Lives of the Indian Princes* (London: Century, 1984), pp. 142, 262. It is important to note that this latter volume was published in association with the Taj Hotel Group of India. Other instances of photographs of hunters in the princely states with their trophies are in Clark Worswick, *Princely India: Photographs by Raja Deen Dayal 1884-1910* (New York: Pennwick/Agrinde and Knopf, 1980), pp. 52–55.

23. Robert Byron, *An Essay on India* (London: George Routledge, 1931), p. 163.

24. Allen and Dwivedi, *Lives of the Indian Princes*, pp. 135–45, and Naveen Patnaik, *A Desert Kingdom: The Rajputs of Bikaner* (London: Weidenfeld and Nicolson, 1990), pp. 66–77. Another twentieth-century innovation was hunting deer from cars in Patiala, described in E. Alexander Powell, *The Last Home of Mystery* (Garden City, N.Y.: Garden City Publishing, 1929), pp. 262–65.

25. Gay, *Prince of Wales*, p. 307.

26. Val C. Prinsep, *Imperial India: An Artist's Journal* (London: Chapman and Hall [1877?]), p. 88.

27. Caine, *Picturesque India*, p. 95.

28. Ibid., p. 97.

29. This synthesis is based on, besides the sources already cited, Mary Thorn Carpenter, *A Girl's Winter in India* (New York: Anson D. F. Randolph [1892?]), pp. 220–38; André Chevrillon,

In India, translated from the French by William Marchant (New York: Henry Holt, 1896), pp. 191-212; Perceval Landon, *Under the Sun: Impressions of Indian Cities* (London: Hurst & Blackett, 1906), pp. 37-48; Reynolds-Ball, *The Tourist's India*, pp. 75-82; and Michael Myers Shoemaker, *Indian Pages and Pictures: Rajputana, Sikkim, the Punjab, and Kashmir* (New York: G. P. Putnam's Sons, Knickerbocker Press, 1912), pp. 62-74.

30. Thomas Holbein Hendley, *Handbook to the Jeypore Museum* (Calcutta: Calcutta Central Press Co. 1895). This work, clearly intended for the use of foreign tourists, even included information on services at the Church of England and the Roman Catholic chapel as well as more mundane matters of hotels, hospital, and jewelers. Insightful analysis of the architecture and cultural functions of the Jaipur Museum is in Thomas R. Metcalf, *An Imperial Vision: Indian Architecture and Britain's Raj* (Berkeley: University of California Press, 1989), pp. 133-35, and Thomas R. Metcalf, "Architecture and the Representation of Empire: India, 1860-1910," *Representations*, no. 6 (Spring 1984): 50.

31. Caine, *Picturesque India*, p. 113.

32. Ibid., pp. 87-92.

33. One example is found in Browning, *Impressions of Indian Travel*, pp. 189-200.

34. Basil Mathews, *India Reveals Herself* (London: Oxford University Press, 1937), pp. 145-47.

35. C. W. Waddington, *Indian India: As Seen by a Guest in Rajputana* (London: Jarrolds, 1933), pp. 16-17.

36. Fussell, *Abroad*, pp. 137-41.

37. Ichaporia, "Tourism at Khajuraho."

38. Louise Nicholson, *India in Luxury: A Practical Guide for the Discerning Traveller* (London: Century, 1985), p. 77. This guide is one of the most thorough, practical, and informative of its genre currently available.

39. Gayatri Devi of Jaipur and Santha Rama Rau, *A Princess Remembers: The Memoirs of the Maharani of Jaipur* (Philadelphia: Lippincott, 1976), pp. 243-44.

40. Metcalf, *An Imperial Vision*, p. 137.

41. William Davenport, *India: A Personal Guide* (Garden City, N.Y.: Doubleday, 1964), p. 376. The decorator was Delia Contractor, an American from Taos, New Mexico, who was married to a Gujarati engineer whom she had met when she was teaching art at the University of Colorado.

42. Gita Mehta, "Royal India," *Connoisseur*, September 1985, p. 85.

43. Sooni Taraporevala, "The Royal Treatment," *MD*, January 1986, p. 42.

44. Ibid., p. 47.

45. Mehta, "Royal India," p. 85.

46. Susan Stewart, *On Longing: Narratives of the Miniature, the Gigantic, the Souvenir, the Collection* (Baltimore: Johns Hopkins University Press, 1984), p. 148.

47. Boorstin, *The Image*, p. 92.

48. Stuart Cary Welch, "Stronghold of Splendor," *House and Garden*, January 1986, pp. 142-49, 175.

49. Rahul Singh, "Desert Outpost Retains India's Artistic Glory," *New York Times*, January 9, 1983, travel section pp. 20-21.

50. Eliot Weinberger, "Shades of Princely India," *Destinations*, Spring 1982, p. 31.

51. Ibid., p. 33.

52. Ibid., p. 37.

53. Marie-Paule Pelle, "The Essence of Regal India," *Condé Nast Traveler*, May 1989, pp. 100-109.

54. Alison Lurie, "The Language of the Sari," and Louise Nicholson, "Living like a Maharaja," *Condé Nast Traveler*, May 1989, pp. 110-11, 154-56, 178-79.

55. M. M. Kaye, "Rajasthan: Glitter of a Princely Past," *New York Times*, September 26, 1982, travel section pp. 15-16. "Indian Tourist Train Boasts Passenger Cars Built for Maharajahs," *Wall Street Journal*, April 18, 1983, pp. 1, 10. "A Maharajah's Rail Journey in Rajasthan," *New York Times*, June 28, 1987, travel section.

56. Alma Gottlieb, "Americans' Vacations," *Annals of Tourism Research* 9, no. 2 (1982): 165-87.

57. Arjun Appadurai, "Global Ethnoscapes: Notes and Queries for a Transnational Anthropology," in *Recapturing Anthropology*, ed. Richard Fox (Santa Fe: School of American Research, 1991), p. 198.

58. Barbara Crossette, "A Taste of the Desert in India," *New York Times*, March 3, 1991, travel section p. 3.

59. Gayatri Devi and Rau, *A Princess Remembers*, pp. 248-50, and Quentin Crewe, *The Last Maharaja: A Biography of Sawai Man Singh II Maharaja of Jaipur* (London: Michael Joseph, 1985), pp. 205-6.

60. Grace Morley, "Museums of India," *Museum* 18, no. 4 (1965): 234-35. A helpful description of these museums for the contemporary tourist is in Nicholson, *India in Luxury*, pp. 77-107.

61. Byron, *An Essay on India*, especially pp. 66-80, which focus on the political status and options of the princes.

62. Powell praised Bhopal in *Last Home of Mystery*, pp. 240-46, 273-79.

63. Waddington, *Indian India*, p. 133.

64. Surajeet Dasgupta, "Playing Host: India Lures Foreigners," *India Today*, February 15, 1988, p. 85.

CHAPTER FIVE

Dining Out in Bombay

FRANK F. CONLON

Bombay as a City and Site of Public Culture

Although many Indian and foreign observers might regard India as one of those world societies that may be best described as "traditional," in fact India has developed one or more modern sectors that are in some ways coextensive with those of the West while retaining a distinctively Indian flavor.[1] Arjun Appadurai and Carol Breckenridge, concerned that students of Indian culture come to terms with this development, have argued that this process in contemporary India may be best understood within a distinctive new domain of cosmopolitan "public culture." They propose that characteristic institutions of this public culture (cinema, sport, tourism, museums, restaurants) are keys to understanding that which is "modern" in contemporary Indian life.[2] Although much of India's society remains rural or poor or both, it may be argued that the expansion of an educated middle class and the emergence of a new urban-centered public culture have begun, and will continue, to shape and condition Indian social and cultural expectations for the foreseeable future. Nowhere is this more evident than in emergent changes in Indian foodways, most particularly in the growth and elaboration of the institution of the restaurant.

This essay, stimulated by the Appadurai/Breckenridge thesis, explores the history of restaurants and public dining in Bombay and describes aspects of that city's contemporary restaurant scene associated with an emerging cosmopolitan culture. The selection of restaurants for analysis reflects acceptance of the view that they are an element central to the making of public culture in India. Restaurants reflect, permit, and promote the introduction of a wide variety of changes in modern Indian life, including modifications of urban budgets and work schedules, entry of women into the middle-class workforce, new patterns of sociability, and, perhaps, growth of new ways to enjoy wealth through conspicuous consumption. These changes have been accompanied by "very important shifts in ideas about commensality, cuisine, ethnicity, and sociality in India."[3]

The choice of Bombay as locale of the study reflects both earlier and continuing research on the history of that city's social and economic life.[4] Furthermore, Bombay's phenomenal role of being at once India's New York and its Hollywood has guaranteed the city a special place in the modern Indian imagination.[5] Bombay is, in Gillian Tindall's words, "a mecca for incoming peoples, seeking work, seeking money, seeking life itself."[6] Bombay is perhaps the most cosmopolitan city of India, attracting and holding the attention, ambitions, and energies of people from almost every Indian region. In the view of one native son, "Bombay is a gritty, impossible, unforgettable place."[7] Khwaja Ahmad Abbas, himself a long-ago migrant to the city, gloried in its dynamism:

> Some tens of thousands come here to make their future. Some make it, others don't. But the struggle goes on. That struggle is called Bombay. The struggle, the vitality, hope, the aspiration to be something, anything, is called Bombay.[8]

As India's predominant commercial, film, and advertising center, Bombay has, for better or for worse, been a prominent staging ground for India's acceptance of ideas, images, and institutions from abroad. But if Bombay absorbs foreign elements, it transforms them in a process of domestication or digestion that will soon appear on a wider subcontinental stage.

Indian foodway patterns have not been much studied or analyzed by scholars.[9] This is not unusual, for relatively little scholarly attention has been given to food in other regions of the world. It has been only recently that historians and anthropologists have chronicled the growth of the restaurants and related high cuisines in European and Chinese cultures.[10] Research on food in Indian culture has remained largely in the domain of anthropology.[11] It is appropriate therefore to offer a brief sketch of what is known of the historical contexts of public dining in India.

Food and Public Dining in Indian Tradition

Traditional India possessed no enduring tradition of restaurants or public dining, although food played a central role in the life and culture of Indians of all religious communities, social strata, and geographical regions. P. V. Kane, the great authority on Hindu law, observed that in the myriad *dharmashastra* texts the rules regarding the subject of taking meals, *bhojana*, were second in importance only to those of marriage.[12] In the Hindu and Muslim cultures of India, food and its consumption have represented at once a medium of exchange and rank and a reflection of personal moral identity and of social relationship. The norms of social life discouraged the institution of restaurants, that is, commercial establishments for public dining. Although one early source, Kautilya's *Arthashastra,* makes reference to various kinds of public eating houses, the practice of dining out did not find a congenial niche within the traditional values of Hindu orthodoxy.[13] Beyond questions of purity of food preparation, brahmanical tradition further emphasized that because consumption of food in a public place could leave the diner vulnerable to evil influences, "one must take one's meals in private in a place screened from public view."[14]

Hindu ideological concerns for commensality and purity thus contributed to anxiety regarding the provenance and purity of food for consumption—matters that are not subjects of inherent certainty in places of public dining.[15] It has been suggested that there might also exist a "more subtle cultural desire to insulate commercial dealings and food transactions from each other . . . [because of] the Hindu view of food as central to the links between men and gods."[16] Perhaps because of this, throughout the history of the subcontinent down to the present century, the problem of obtaining food prepared outside the domestic hearth was principally faced by travelers, whether merchants or pilgrims. On the road, it was likely to be necessary to provide one's own food. The Buddha made an explicit allowance for his followers to carry food while journeying.[17]

A limited facility for public dining by travelers existed during the Mughal raj within the institution of the caravanserai (or *khan*), which had been introduced into India from Iran by medieval Islamic conquerors, and which was frequently noticed by visitors in cities and towns.[18] The Venetian traveler Niccolao Manucci recorded that Sher Shah had ordered creation of a chain of serais along the main routes with servants appointed to provide both food and drink to travelers.[19] While some serais were large and substantial, particularly in capital cities, elsewhere many of these lodging places were nothing more than "an enclosed yard with chambers round it" for travelers and "their pack animals."[20] An eighteenth-century traveler in Gujarat reported that even for "anyone of consideration," the most that could be hoped for upon entering a village on his journey would be a presentation of food, wood, and pots for preparation of a meal.[21]

In the great cities given shape by Muslim power, culture cookshops and "public bakeries, where almost every variety of cooked food and uncooked victuals could be bought at a reasonable price" flourished as long as the cities prospered.[22] In 1641, when Sebastien Manrique visited Shah Jahan's temporary capital at Lahore, the city teemed with both wealth and people. Manrique found on the outskirts of Lahore a vast market of tents and stalls "filled with delicious and appetizing eatables" with "money-seeking vendors . . . informing strangers, and all who lacked kitchens, where ready-cooked and tasty food could be obtained."[23] Declining urban fortunes appear to have diminished the quantity and quality of such establishments, and in the countryside accommodation remained meager. More than one European traveler in Mughal India complained about a lack of inns and difficulties in obtaining food.[24] Meals might be available from a *bhatiyar-khana* ("cooking house"), a low-status inn of uncertain quality, and in some caravanserais women prepared food for visitors, but often travelers had to have with them a servant who would cook food obtained from local bazaars.[25] In a few instances, travelers' accounts do speak of availability of inexpensive and varied food. While Manrique praised the cookshops on the outskirts of Lahore for their inexpensive variety of vegetarian and nonvegetarian cuisine, he was describing what were in fact temporary stalls, and it is unclear whether they actually served meals or simply sold food to be consumed elsewhere.[26] Events of public dining that did receive notice generally were limited to contexts of public or semipublic ritual functions—a royal feast or food distribution, a charitable distribution of food to pilgrims, or a celebratory feast of a wedding or other rite of passage.

The establishment of British rule in India did not hasten a widespread introduction of European-style hotels and restaurants even for the use of Europeans. To some degree this may have reflected the relative pace at which lodging and dining facilities were developing in Europe itself. The number of nonofficial European visitors to India in the late eighteenth and early nineteenth centuries was not large, however, and scarcely could have stimulated much demand for such establishments. Even in the 1840s a German visitor remarked:

> As there are no inns whatever, the traveler in India is compelled to have re-
> course to the hospitality of the English. . . . Everywhere, even without letters
> of recommendation, you find the most hearty welcome, and the most
> hospitable reception."[27]

The British Raj's hoary custom of giving departing travelers letters of introduction to friends elsewhere who might offer hospitality was a practical necessity for Europeans in India in the days before widespread construction of
the *dak* (postal) or Public Works Department bungalows. One chronicler
observed that hospitality to fellow Europeans had inspired a proverb "that
no hotel could succeed while people were so hospitable."[28] As late as 1909,
Maud Diver wrote of this tradition "in the land of the Open Door."[29]

Visitors to the larger towns might hope to fare better. At least by 1843,
Calcutta possessed "four large hotels," but it was said that during the first
four decades of the nineteenth century Bombay "contained no hotel worthy
of the name."[30] When the veteran "lady traveler" Miss Emma Roberts visited
Bombay in 1839, she bemoaned the absence of adequate accommodation,
noting that some European visitors lacking invitations at private homes were
compelled to rent tents on the Esplanade during the cold weather for want of
decent hotel quarters.[31] Bombay obtained a first-class European-style hotel
only in the late 1860s, when Watson's Esplanade Hotel was constructed on
some ground cleared by the destruction of the Fort walls.[32]

It appears that Indian travelers similarly continued to rely upon kinship
connections when feasible, staying otherwise at remaining caravanserais or
religious pilgrim resthouses such as *dharmshalas* and *choultries*. Indian visitors to Bombay, however, also found limited prospects for accommodation.
In 1863, a Bombay paper commented on the inadequate number of caravanserais or *dharmshalas* in the city for Indian visitors.[33]

While moving through the Indian countryside, European travelers might
find a means of obtaining a meal prepared by a *dak* bungalow cook, but
Leopold von Orloch observed that it was necessary for travelers to carry
along their own tea, sugar, wine, and bread. Occasionally a European visitor
would praise meals obtained at wayside "taverns" or "inns." Bishop Reginald
Heber, on tour in 1825 at Panwell, opposite the harbor from Bombay, encountered "two taverns, one kept by a Portuguese, the other by a Parsee, the
latter of whom, at very short notice, procured us a dinner at least as well got
up, as cleanly and as good, as could have been expected at a country inn in
England."[34] The bishop proves to be a lonely witness, however. Finding satisfactory public dining facilities remained a practical problem for virtually all
subcontinent travelers until at least the middle of the nineteenth century.[35]

Dining in Colonial Bombay

The prospects of public dining for visitors were limited in Bombay as well. Emma Roberts observed that respectable folk could not contemplate with equanimity dining at the rough and ready "taverns" of the town. She did report seeing in the "native town" "*caravanserais* and *cafes* where the country and religion of the owner may be known by the guests congregated about his gate," but Miss Roberts did not visit these establishments and offered no further comment upon them.[36]

Accommodation for visitors—both European and Indian—in Bombay remained problematic during the middle years of the nineteenth century. The opening of Watson's Hotel, with both a "restaurant with a billiard room attached" and a "dining saloon" for guests, provided a solution for well-to-do European visitors, but European Bombay did not see a proliferation of independent dining establishments intended for residents of the city. One exception was the provision of "tiffins" or luncheons for men who worked at offices in the central Fort district. Here, some competition did arise. Jewanjee's Exchange at Meadow and Hummam Streets offered "Hot chops, Steaks and Oysters" in their "First Class Tiffin and Billiard Rooms," while nearby at Forbes Street and Rampart Row, the Jerusalem Tiffin and Billiard Rooms also boasted a reading room with all the latest English papers and proclaimed itself to be "the only European House in the Fort."[37] These establishments in their cuisine and facilities appropriated the styles set by more exclusive private clubs in order to serve the European merchants and tradesmen of the city.

At a time when restaurants were burgeoning in London as public places for the "respectable" elements of society, Bombay's "respectable" European society continued to prefer dining "at home" or "at club."[38] Private entertainments with invited guests continued to bring the city's British elites together. Lady Falkland observed that during her husband's tenure as governor of Bombay, "dinners, balls, occasional picnics and two or three days of races [were] the only amusements."[39] Three decades later little had changed. During the later nineteenth century well-to-do European society might dine out at "special occasion" banquets for visiting royalty or politicians and departing viceroys, governors, and other dignitaries. These were often all-male affairs, and strictly European, usually held within the privatizing premises of a racially exclusive European club.[40] Gatherings of "old boys" from various British public schools provided another occasion for special dinners in the European clubs of Bombay. The tradition of such "public dinners" at the Byculla Club, for example, was supplemented by the arrangement of "private dinners" given by members of the club, including, with the permission of the managing committee, speeches and ceremonials associated with the club-sponsored events. It appears that the occurrence of these feasts peaked in the 1890s and that they grew less common in the early years of the new century.[41] It is not possible to establish definitively why this change occurred, but it appears that the social styles of London were gradually penetrating Bombay European society, leading to a gradual shift of such celebrations and of smaller group events of "dining out" in the city center to hotel dining rooms, which had emerged in response to a gradual growth of European tourism.[42]

Racial exclusivity appears to have been maintained in the policy of hotel dining facilities in establishments that sought primarily a European clientele. Indians might be admitted as room guests, but it was not expected that they would enter the dining hall. This pattern changed significantly in 1904 when the great Parsi merchant Jamsetji Tata's Taj Mahal Palace Hotel was opened. Tata's rule was clear: no Indian would be denied dining-room service, although the prices then, as now, guaranteed that access would be limited to the well-to-do.[43]

Even as late as the 1920s, the limited number of restaurants in Bombay was remarked upon and seemed to require explanation. In an unusual guide to the city, written as a narrative story, a British visitor from Shanghai asks: "How is it that Bombay has no restaurants such as we find in European cities?"[44] His host, a European living in Bombay, explains:

> Such an establishment may not pay here. The communities likely to patronize such a place are not large enough. . . . You must remember that Bombay is, properly speaking, a typical native city. The majority of its inhabitants are Hindus and Mahomedans, who do not eat European food."[45]

The host might have explained further, had he known, that "respectable" members of that Indian majority generally refrained from much public dining regardless of cuisine. For most Indian householders the principal occasions of public dining were special festive events: wedding dinners, caste feasts, and, among Parsis, the confirmatory rite of passage, the *navjot* ceremonies. These events for the most part involved no significant dietary or commensal frontiers—the meals reflected caste or community dietary strictures and were presumably prepared under ritually appropriate circumstances. In the Parsi community, the tradition of well-to-do families sponsoring charitable feasts for the entire community led to the emergence of a new catering profession that has continued to the present day to serve distinctive meals for weddings and *navjot* ceremonies held in community halls.[46]

Restaurant dining was further encouraged by gradual changes in the timing of meals.[47] Many Indian merchants as well as clerical office workers of Bombay's "educated middle class" could, if they dwelt with their families in the city, avoid eating outside their domicile. This was made possible by the scheduling of office hours. In Bombay up until the past forty or fifty years, the conventional opening hour of many public and private offices was 10:30 or 11:00 a.m. This allowed clerical employees to eat a large meal at midmorning at home or in an eating house before going to the office.[48]

Restructuring of office hours and the physical expansion of Bombay city reduced the possibility that most clerical workers could consume all meals at home. When the aforementioned visitor from Shanghai wondered "how do people who work in the Fort manage for their lunch," his Bombay host replied:

> They do as best they can. Generally their meals are sent to their offices; some of them find some kind of meals or other in eating-houses; the poorer classes patronize the Irani shops, which style themselves restaurants, but are mostly filthy dens where poisonous stuffs are sold.[49]

Mention of meals being brought to the office points to one unique Bombay institution that has provided a luncheon alternative to restaurants in the city for more than half a century. Many office workers depend for their midday meal upon the *dabbawallas*, lunch- or "tiffin"-box carriers, who collect home-prepared food from residences and, following an elaborate network of exchanges, deliver it to the very individual for whom it is intended in, for example, the offices in the Fort business district, and correctly return the empty *dabbas* to the appropriate homes in the afternoon.[50] This service offers an inexpensive, convenient, and "homely" alternative to taking lunch in a restaurant by providing home-prepared food to suit each client's palate.[51] Luncheon costs are incorporated in the household food budget, and the perennial labor surplus in the city appears to keep the *dabbawallas'* charges within the means of middle-class clients. The service may also be seen to offer status-conscious office workers escape from the non-middle-class image of carrying a lunch pail to the office. It is my impression, however, that as *dabbawalla* charges rise, more office workers will resort for lunch to restaurants or footpath food vendors, a phenomenon discussed later in this essay.

Utilitarian Public Dining

Not all of Bombay's people were truly householders. The city was a magnet in both industrial and commercial spheres for large numbers of itinerant male workers who came to the city solely for employment, living away from their villages and families.[52] Whether they were bachelors or married with family elsewhere, whether they worked in offices or industries, a significant proportion of the city's male population was required by circumstances to make its own arrangements for eating meals. The city's sex ratio consistently underscored this phenomenon: in 1872 the census revealed that Bombay contained 612 women per 1,000 men; by 1931 this gender gap had reached a proportion of 554 per 1,000.[53]

These "hearthless" men usually were residents of *chawls*, single- or multi-storied rows of one-room tenements. There they might share collective cooking chores with male caste-fellows, but many relied instead on the tradition of the *khanaval*.

Khanavals (Marathi: "board, cost of eating"[54]—or *jevanavals*) were formal or informal public or semipublic eating houses for Indians in Bombay city. Occasionally the traditional term, *bhatiyarkhana*, apparently was used, particularly to identify inns or eating houses run by and for Muslims.[55] It has been impossible to document precisely the earliest appearance of a *khanaval* in Bombay. Indirect evidence suggests that the institution arose sometime after 1830. Molesworth's monumental Marathi dictionary, in referring to the alternative terms *jevanaval* and *jevanaghar*, reports that the first term was an "eating house or ordinary table (*table d'hôte)*" in "a new sense and appropriate to Bombay," and that the second was being "applied by some to the Eating houses (for Natives) *lately set up in Bombay*."[56] Historical dating aside, it may be observed that the growth of the *khanavals* was a response to the growth of Bombay as a market for rural labor and the consequent pattern of migration to the city by male workers. Most of these workers sought to minimize expenses in order to be able to send money home to their villages, so the *khanaval* food had to be inexpensive. Informal *khanavals* sometimes were formed if one male worker, having managed to bring his wife along to the city, then balanced the family budget by having her shop and prepare meals for other men who paid a weekly boarding fee. In some instances these men would also rent sleeping space in the *chawl* room. Because of the social proximity involved, in many cases such a *khanaval* served men of the same village and caste—a pattern that has continued to the present day.[57]

In other instances, the *khanaval* would be run as a business by a widow whose cuisine and clientele would generally be delineated by religion and region of origin. The British authorities considered many of these eating establishments to be grossly unsanitary.[58] Nevertheless, the migration of male laborers to Bombay attracted from their villages and towns by the employment prospects in the city's growing industrial and commercial activity guaranteed a continuing demand for a means of providing suitable, inexpensive meals within religiously and regionally specific diets such as South Indian Brahman, Gujarati Hindu, Sindhi Muslim, Maharashtrian Brahman, or Maratha. If the *khanaval bais* (woman cooks) provided inexpensive food that was squarely within the dietary restrictions of their customers, it was rarely compared favorably to "home cooking." A recent researcher reported that most men complained of "the monotony and tastelessness of the food."[59] For the laboring men of Bombay, "dining out" was not a special treat but a matter of survival in the city.[60]

It should be added that given the limited leisure-time facilities available to most of these "hearthless" working- and clerical-class men, it followed that in the evenings and on holidays they could, within their limited budgetary resources, also seek out places of public refreshment: tea stalls, drink shops, and the newest arrival on the Bombay scene, the Irani cafés.[61]

The Irani Cafés and Growth of Public Dining

"The Irani" has been a venerable Bombay institution. These cafés and provision stores were operated by immigrants from Persia, including Persian Zoroastrians, Muslims, and some Baha'is. A visitor to the city in, say, 1960 might easily assume that Irani cafés were an ancient fixture of the city's culinary history, but in fact they had commenced their rise to prominence only at the beginning of this century. Their entry into the Bombay world of public dining came at a particularly strategic time of development in the city. Bombay city was recovering from the socioeconomic dislocations brought on by the plague outbreaks of 1896 and subsequent years. Economic activity and population both were increasing, stimulating a new potential market for inexpensive restaurant facilities. Furthermore, the Bombay Improvement Trust's urban renewal activities were cutting new roads through the congested parts of the city, creating new commercial frontages where Irani shopkeepers could find profitable opportunities.

The first Irani café-store in Bombay cannot be identified with certainty.[62] One of the Irani pioneers was the Bombay A-1 Restaurant, which opened near the Grant Road Station in 1905. This successful enterprise combined food, services, and decor that became standard throughout the city over the next five decades.[63] Many Irani restaurants began as tea stalls and snack purveyors, featuring aerated waters, Persian breads, sweets, and omelettes ("tomato sauce no extra charge"). Some, such as the Ideal Restaurant at Flora Fountain, remained faithful to that menu to the end; Behram Contractor recalls it as "strictly a tea and bread pudding place."[64] The A-1, on the other hand, soon became well known as a source of a distinctive Parsi cuisine including the green chutney *patra* fish and the rich, multipulse curry *dhanshak*. The A-1 also baked Christmas cakes that were a favorite of middle-class families of all communities.[65]

Irani cafés with their high ceilings, bright lights, mirrors, marble-top tables, and bentwood chairs quickly became social gathering places, earning the title "poor man's parlor," although the city's truly poor would be financially excluded. One Goan immigrant student found it less costly to travel from St. Xavier's High School to eat lunch at his sister's home near Grant Road Station and then go back—a distance of three miles—than to eat out: "I couldn't afford a meal at the Irani restaurant, though it cost less than two annas."[66] Many customers came only for a cup of tea or a snack. Muslim-owned Iranis were predominant in the areas of the city dominated by the Muslim population, while the Zoroastrian shops tended to be situated in localities where they would cater to Parsis and Hindus, but most shops advertised that members of all religions were welcome.[67] Many Iranis stocked some canned goods and biscuits and other items, functioning as a neighborhood general store for "Westernized" goods and foodstuffs.

Although the largest of these establishments were found along the main roads of the southern portion of Bombay, they spread throughout the urbanized parts of the island. Apart from the attractions of their food and drink, these cafés permitted, if not promoted, new models of sociability in Bombay. Given the densely crowded residential quarters with which much of the city's population had to cope, a café could serve as a leisure-time destination, and with the introduction of the jukebox holding an adequate supply of "filmi" songs, the Irani cafés became even more a social resort for Bombay's male population.[68] As time passed these restaurants also played some role in enabling women to participate in dining out as a custom of family enjoyment. Most Irani cafés incorporated "family cabins," wooden and translucent-glass partitioned areas where genteel, respectable groups could dine without being exposed to public gaze. The availability of unexposed dining areas allowed entire family groups, including women, to partake of a meal, or at least tea and snacks. By 1939 the Ideal made a point in advertisements of offering "special accommodation for Ladies."[69] Other customers, perhaps not so genteel, could employ these "cabins" or "family rooms" at other times for liaisons that required discretion.[70]

The Iranis' food and clientele might vary slightly with neighborhood, but the style was uniform, even to the didactic wall notices that the Bombay poet Nissim Ezekiel immortalized in his "Irani Restaurant Instructions":

> Do not write letter
> Without order refreshment
> Do not comb
> Hair is spoiling floor
> Do not make mischiefs in cabin
> Our waiter is reporting
> Come again
> All are welcome whatever caste
> If not satisfied tell us
> Otherwise tell others
> God is great.[71]

These new popular restaurants collectively were, like the *khanavals*, regarded by authorities as a menace to public health. Health and sanitation concerns led in 1916 to an amendment of the Bombay Municipal Act for licensing all eating houses. The city's chief health officer, citing the "very large number of eating houses in Bombay," made the point directly:

> These places play an important part in the lives of the poorer working classes, and the low-paid and unmarried populace, for whom these houses for the most part cater, have to rely on them for their daily food. This fact alone is sufficient justification for demanding that a certain minimum standard of sanitation in regard to these eating houses should be compulsory.[72]

The perception that the eating houses and cafés were problematic extended to their reputation as congregating spots for "antisocial elements." When in 1913 the police recommended that such establishments close by 9:00 p.m., the conservative Parsi paper *Jam-e-Jamshed* objected that as there were no fixed closing hours for offices and factories, there were many who had to work later than 9:00 p.m.:

> The eating houses of Bombay may be the haunts of the *badmash* [bad character] and the ruffian. [However] they feed practically half Bombay. . . . It would suffice to remind the authorities once again, of the fact that a vast majority of the labouring population of Bombay, and together with them the mechanics, craftsmen, petty traders, clerks, office assistants and the rest, are to a certain extent, dependent on these eating houses for the supply of their daily food.[73]

The proposed curtailment of eating house hours was quietly dropped, although the idea resurfaced recently.[74]

While the extent and frequency of public food encounters for most Bombay citizens might have been limited, it seems plausible that once a person had taken tea and *samosas* at an Irani café, the psychological and moral obstacles to public dining, if not the economic ones, would be eroded. Furthermore, it has been suggested that while the *khanavals* and other public eating places were dominated by a sometimes frantic functional concern for eating quickly and without distraction, the Iranis offered a chance for variety and a more leisurely enjoyment of inexpensive meals. Without offering the exotic consumption opportunities that later came to characterize new Bombay restaurants, the Irani cafés represented a transition toward the "meal as experience"—an essential component for the evolution of a restaurant culture.[75]

As in premodern India, travelers outside cities continued to have to seek out dining facilities. Although individuals who made railway journeys could patronize new forms of public meal services, cost was a serious constraint for most middle- and working-class Indians. Thus, only a minority in fact had much experience of hotel catering, refreshment rooms at railway stations, or the dining and buffet railway carriages. It appears that most travelers carried food from home or survived on light snacks and tea. Even into the 1930s, outside the context of travel, the practice of families going out to a restaurant specifically for the purpose of taking a meal and perhaps enjoying the ambience was virtually unknown outside of elite circles.[76]

In Bombay at least, railway catering did provide one avenue to culinary adventure without the necessity of travel. Bombay's Victoria Terminus contained three restaurants, Brandons, Divadkars, and Karims, catering to European, Hindu, and Muslim dietary preferences respectively. For middle-class Hindu young men, it was not the dull certainties of the Hindu refreshment room at Victoria Terminus that was of interest. Rather, it was in Karims' Muslim dining room, where opportunities lay for experiments in eating meat. A Brahman resident of the city, looking back to the 1930s, recalled that while he was growing up in a strictly orthodox vegetarian home, he had been taken by his uncle to Karims' for mutton *biryani*: "It was something I could never have at home, and my uncle was rather a non-conformist."[77]

Still, the world of restaurant dining lay beyond the life of most middle-class Indians of Bombay. The economic crisis of the 1930s severely pinched household budgets. Eating out was identified by some as a major source of economic ills. An influential member of the Chitrapur Saraswat Brahman community—a caste dominated by "middle class" employment and aspirations—carried on a campaign in the pages of the caste journal advising readers to avoid "unnecessary expenses" such as visiting tea stalls or restaurants.[78] One informant who grew up in Bombay, asked to reflect on why middle-class people there had not dined out more in those days, concluded that there were three basic reasons. The most significant was the cost:

> The prices were low, but the wages of clerical workers were very low too. The second thing was that dietary preferences and/or rules meant that at a restaurant you would probably be eating the sort of food that could be had at home where a mother or wife would prepare it better. A third consideration was that dining out was simply not done—people believed that eating houses were not terribly clean, not in terms of ritual pollution, but rather in terms of germs."[79]

Cosmopolitan and European Influences

Meanwhile, the European-centered restaurant trade in Bombay had been developing rather slowly, although not so slowly as to be nonexistent, as hinted in the visitor-resident dialogue quoted earlier. Restaurants were not only being opened, they were being promoted through the newly emerging art of advertising. A 1900 guidebook published for foreign tourists included advertisement of the Criterion Restaurant. No boasts were made about the food, but a European management was highlighted and the Criterion was reported to be "the only concert hall in Bombay," featuring nightly performances by an "Austrian ladies' string-band."[80] The addition of ballroom dancing after 10:00 p.m. assured the management added revenue and appreciably reduced chances of the appearance of an Indian clientele.

Certain European-style or European-owned restaurants continued to play upon the idea of respectability and exclusivity in their commercial messages. The Italian caterers and confectioners Mongini's advertised in 1931 that they were "an old name in Bombay" and offered a somewhat exaggerated reconnaissance of the dining scene, observing that

> Bombay is inundated with Restaurants, each having its particular clique of patrons and it is from these that the "tone" of a cafe may be fairly judged. Step into *Mongini's* at any hour, day or night, when it is open, and you will not fail to remark that its patrons belong to that exclusive class—true Restaurateurs—men and women who have a natural instinct to be drawn, as a magnet is to a needle, to the cafe-compatible, where every sense is catered for, where nothing jars.[81]

It seems obvious that Mongini's "class" campaign was aimed primarily at Europeans. The prospect of a quiet, refined dinner in a city embroiled with the disruptions of Gandhi's civil disobedience campaign would have had its attractions. A similar advertising strategy offering refinement and avoidance of the mundane was pursued by The Wayside, which had opened in 1920 under the direction of a Mrs. Edwards and which described itself in 1931 as a "pleasing ENGLISH INN which is quiet and exclusive."[82]

The end of the 1930s saw several new developments in restaurants in connection with the first construction of buildings along the new extension of Churchgate Street on land that had been reclaimed from the Back Bay during the 1920s. Although the first eating house to be encountered in approaching from the Fort city center was an Irani shop, the Asiatic Cafe and Stores, a number of ground-floor premises in multistory apartment blocks were taken on lease for first-class restaurants. Included was the new Purohit's Dining Rooms, a vegetarian restaurant that had previously operated in cramped quarters near Victoria Terminus. Now Purohit's sought to establish the idea of a stylish vegetarian meal, replete with silver *thalis* (plates) and drinking cups. A gentleman who was growing up in Bombay at that time recalled:

> We thought Purohit's was too expensive to just go to for a meal, but our family and friends would make wagers, with the understanding that the losers would buy dinner at Purohit's. This made the event even more special, and for a special event, Purohit's was very nice.[83]

The space was organized in the tradition of the "family cabin," with wooden-framed translucent glass panels and swinging doors, assuring respectable families the privilege of dining without public scrutiny. Other restaurants along Churchgate Street (subsequently Vir Nariman Road) offered new cuisines and styles of dining, including the Chinese Kamling and the Continental Gourdon & Company. Later, the opening of the Parisian Dairy and Gaylord's introduced the fashion of the sidewalk café. Other entries to this emergent "restaurant row" were the Cafe Napoli, Bombelli's (a Swiss-Italian restaurant), and, later, Berry's, a Punjabi restaurant.

This growth of restaurants was constrained by the effects of World War II. War-related activities brought increased population to the city and, hence, potential customers and prosperity for the restaurant trade. The introduction of rationing and other restrictions on food, however, created difficulties for restaurant managements and their diners. The postwar partition of the subcontinent brought considerable upheaval to Bombay, as some families departed for Pakistan and a substantial body of Punjabi and Sindhi refugee entrepreneurs flowed in. The city was not only receiving devotees of new cuisines: some of the new arrivals came intending to set up businesses, and more than one Irani café owner, offered what seemed a fabulous sum for his businesses and goodwill by a Punjabi or Sindhi refugee-entrepreneur, gave up his establishment. The apparent prosperity and stability of Iran during the 1960s further led more Iranis to sell off their businesses in Bombay and return to what then appeared to be better prospects at home. The cafés have, for the most part, continued to operate under new ownership, although some Bombay citizens would argue that the change was not an improvement.[84]

The influx of new people into the city also brought new palates. During the early years of independence, it appears that an increasing number of Bombay restaurants began to offer basic Punjabi cooking. The postpartition period also saw the introduction and spread, at the level of popular consumption, of the so-called Udipi restaurants with a concomitant popularization of South Indian vegetarian cuisine.[85]

The evolution of high-quality "middle-class" restaurants continued, although food scarcities in the mid-1960s created some disruptions.[86] By this time, however, restaurants and cuisines available to citizens of Bombay had entered a new phase of development that may be identified with the emergence of the cosmopolitan public culture of the city.

The departure of the British in 1947 and the years thereafter might have been expected to produce enormous changes in the world of exclusive, upper-class public dining. Some old establishments quietly faded away, but many found that the Indian upper classes of Bombay were prepared to take up the slack and indeed to generate an even greater demand for restaurant facilities and services. The historical experience of dining out was already established within Bombay society. Furthermore, as the city continued to attract ambitious persons from the entire nation, the expectations of city life were soon appropriated by the newcomers. It may be hypothesized that the restaurant scenes included in Bombay Hindi films further helped to project upon a broader national consciousness what life in the city might be expected to offer.[87] Among the nonelite, the corner cafés and khanavals continued to meet the traditional needs of new generations of working men who had come to Bombay to try their luck. Public dining had evolved in a little over a century from a novelty to a convention, setting the stage for further expansion and domestication of the restaurant culture of Bombay.

The Burgeoning Restaurant Culture of Bombay

In the 1960s Bombay restaurateurs began to recognize the potential for an expanding market of consumers. There now were in the city an increased number of Indians with sufficient discretionary income to indulge in the habit of dining out not from necessity but from opportunity, and for display.

Bombay had experienced physical growth that had more than doubled its size in the expansion into the suburban areas of Salsette Island. The city also was absorbing an ever increasing number of immigrants from virtually every corner of India. Where today the population of Bombay would be estimated at a little over 10 million people, in 1966 it was estimated at only a little over 4 million. Such expansion could not but be reflected in the restaurant trade. In 1909 Bombay, with a population of 977,822, reportedly had 1,839 eating houses, 43 refreshment rooms, 494 tea and coffee houses, 70 cold-drink shops, 114 boarding and lodging houses, and 36 boarding houses, a total of 2,596 establishments.[88] Not all such dining places were sufficiently prominent to obtain notice in Bombay directories. A 1920 city directory specifies the locations of only 550 eating establishments, including "restaurants," "Irani shops," "refreshment rooms," and "boarding houses" as well as "hotels."[89] This array of facilities served a city of 61 square kilometers with a population of 1,175,914. Six decades later, Bombay had outgrown old neighborhoods and was assimilating thousands of new migrants daily. By 1981, when Bombay's size had reached 428 square kilometers and a population above 8 million, the *Illustrated Weekly of India* reported the existence of 11,520 eating establishments within the city.[90]

While some of this expansion of restaurant facilities is surely a direct reflection of the explosive growth of Greater Bombay, the specific emergence of a number of restaurants of more substantial gastronomic ambitions cries out for a more satisfactory explanation. The growth of wealth in Bombay, with its by-product, discretionary income, might explain the market development to some degree. An additional stimulus may have been the gradual dismantling of prohibition in Bombay over the past two decades. While one result of this policy has been the proliferation of "beer bars," some restaurants also obtained serving licenses. It has long been accepted in the North American restaurant trade that alcohol provides a level of profitability that permits far finer food and service than might otherwise be the case. It is likely that a similar relationship has been at work in the Bombay restaurant trade.

Shaping the Restaurant Culture of Bombay

At this point in the story, my perspective is modified by the fact that I first visited and lived in Bombay from 1965 to 1967 and had considerable opportunity to observe the "restaurant scene." During part of my stay I was able to secure residential quarters as a paying guest with an Indian family. In return for my "rent" I had my own room and took my morning and evening meals with the family. Occasionally some of the younger members of the family and their friends and I would opt out of dinner for an excursion to a cinema, in which event we would generally consume some "snacks" sold near the theater or, in at least one case, on the theater premises.

I might also be invited to join the family in "going out to dinner," perhaps once in a month. On one such evening it was decided that we would all go out for Chinese food, but we had no agreement as to where we ought to dine. I suggested a Chinese establishment on Colaba Causeway that struck me as offering tolerable versions of sweet and sour everything. "No, no, no," said another, "let's go to the Kamling. *It looks so Oriental!*" My first reaction was to point out to my friend that there were in fact those in the West who considered Bombay itself to be quite "Oriental," but he retorted that he meant Oriental as in China—the way all "sensible" people thought. We went on to dinner at the Kamling. It was certainly "Oriental" and the food wasn't bad. My friend's idea that Chinese food was best consumed in an "Oriental" ambience was understandable enough. He had, as it were, been sold the sizzle instead of the steak.[91]

This incident was recalled to mind a few years ago when a new English-language fortnightly periodical *Bombay: The City Magazine* (hereafter *Bombay*) was first produced in 1979 by the publishers of the highly successful newsmagazine *India Today*. *Bombay* functioned as both a chronicle and an advertising vehicle of the city's burgeoning consumer economy and culture. The magazine seemed very much a product of its namesake city; it was an innovative enterprise that existed primarily for making money, a commercial undertaking that survived by selling advertising. Both editorial content and advertising copy targeted an upper-middle-class readership possessed of discretionary income and a willingness to spend it. Where older periodicals that have traditionally catered to "middle class" readers, such as the *Illustrated Weekly of India,* were cluttered with "ads" offering bargains or containing extensive written text promoting products and services that met "practical" needs, many of *Bombay's* advertisers preferred promotion through nuanced image and mood. The city's sophisticated advertising industry was quick to adapt to the rhythms of an international culture of consumption, producing advertising copy akin to that seen in the pages of North American periodicals like the *New Yorker* and the *New York Times Magazine.* (*Bombay* is described here in the past tense because it ceased publication in early 1991, caught between rising production costs and stagnant circulation and advertising revenues. A legacy of style and content survives in other serials and a growth of colored newspaper supplements that carry similar advertisements and articles.)

The images and contents of *Bombay* did not reflect the actualities of most "middle class" citizens, whose horizons of consumption are limited by harsh realities of static income and economic inflation. If India's cosmopolitan public culture is to be the object of scholarly analysis, its essentially elite qualities must be acknowledged. Only a minority of those who absorbed the message of *Bombay*'s advertising may realistically expect to participate fully in the realities of expanded consumption. On the other hand, it may be argued that simply the act of looking at stylish advertising is a form of consumption that subtly informs one's taste, sensibilities, and expectations. As one son of Bombay observed:

> The permissive whisky-and-soda lives of the rich, projected in type-cast imagery through the city's Hindi films and through Bombay's advertising industry, the largest in the country, are of absorbing interest to the whole population.[92]

Early in the career of *Bombay*, an "Eating Out" feature containing reviews of selected local restaurants was introduced. The reportage made it clear that some restaurants in the city were indeed now being promoted in terms of more than simply cuisine. Themes, ambience, and style were offered directly as enticements to potential customers. *Bombay* appeared to be assisting its readers in identifying and sorting the myriad dining options in the city and in making the most of possible adventures in eating. Some "Eating Out" columns offered what amounted to instructions that would encourage or enable middle-class Indians to consume new cuisines and innovative restaurant styles. Here seems to be the juncture between the traditional concern for finding satisfactory food in Bombay and the emergence of a new "public culture." If the majority of *Bombay*'s readers could scarcely afford to patronize some of the upscale establishments, the reviews appear to have found a substantial audience who vicariously experienced the presumed pleasures of the restaurant under discussion. In any case, it certainly appears that restaurateurs who gained a favorable notice from *Bombay*'s columnists welcomed this cachet.

In general, *Bombay*'s coverage of various aspects of the city and its life suggests a modern incarnation of the "in unknown London" style of journalism that provided substantial content for the middle-class press in Victorian Britain. In a restaurant article regarding traditional Muslim "*biriani* factories" in the Mohamadali Road area—not terra incognita for Bombay's well-to-do, but certainly terra infirma—there is a sense of being led to areas that are, frankly, a bit dangerous, yet sanitized by vicarious access.[93] This aspect meant that *Bombay* did not concentrate only on the upscale, trend-setting establishments, but also occasionally ran a feature on college canteens or old-time cafés. In a feature entitled "Off the Eaten Track," the editors noted:

> While the prominent eating places and hotel restaurants draw custom on their own strength, in Bombay it's the little places tucked away in obscure galis and crowded ghettos which really tilt the balance. Eateries in the most basic sense of the word, these restaurants (if they can be called that) have none of the fanciful decor and contrived atmosphere which characterize their more expensive counterparts. Difficult to find, often hard to get to and lacking the graces of larger restaurants, the quality of food in these eateries nevertheless makes the arduous trek worthwhile.[94]

It may have struck some *Bombay* readers that they could not entirely escape "fanciful decor" or "contrived atmosphere" since one of the featured "eateries" was the Aram Kutchi Restaurant, which offered Kutchi cuisine; its "walls [are] done up like a village interior, Kutchi coverlets are used for upholstery, the music is popular Saurashtrian and Kutchi folk, and the waiters are liveried like the shepherds of that arid land."[95] On the other hand, the Radio Restaurant just opposite Crawford Market, which I personally can testify is a genuine dive, did get a write-up that clearly stated that the food was not good but the style was fascinating: "Take your outstation guest and let him soak in the atmosphere. Keep eating down to a minimum."[96]

It seems evident that one pattern of restaurant culture has not changed in the past two decades—a willingness to borrow images and names, if not concepts, from the metropolitan centers of the British Raj. Many of the pre–World War II Irani cafés embraced Raj and royalty in nomenclature, for example the Alfred, Prince Albert, British Flag, Brittania, Coronation Darbar, Edward, George, King George, New Empress, Royal Marine, Royal Good Hope, and Union Jack restaurants. Metropolitan models of a vaguely perceived image of high-class culinary and social status were seen in, among others, the Savoy, the Temple Bar, and the Cecil. A remarkable example of this transmission was the Rustom brothers' Corner House Restaurant, said to be inspired by the original Lyon's Corner Houses of London. The Rustom brothers' locale at the Girgaum-Charni Road junction would not remind a Londoner of the "corner" of Oxford Street and Tottenham Court Road, but the sincerity of the compliment could hardly be doubted. Today the borrowings from the West are not centered entirely upon London, although the top-of-the-scale dining rooms in the five-star hotels have acquired through the channels of international financial connections some specific inspirations, as for example Menage a Trois, a transplant from Knightsbridge to the Taj Mahal Hotel.[97] One recent entry into the market, Bombay Brasserie, takes its name from another London establishment but offers what might be termed an all-India nouvelle cuisine in an elegant setting designed to create "the ambience of the stately home offering gracious hospitality—or even an exclusive club.[98] At the fast-food level, Bombay does not yet have a "Big Mac," as New Delhi does, but a local entrepreneur has opened, without regard to franchising agreements or trademark registration, a Jack in the Box.[99]

New varieties of cuisine have become popular in Bombay restaurants. An innovation from the late 1960s was the introduction of "sizzlers," first at the Excelsior Cinema restaurant, but soon spreading elsewhere; the entrée, on a hot metal plate resting in a wooden platter, arrives at the table in a sizzling cloud of steam. The idea took hold so convincingly that several chefs quickly moved to add "vegetarian sizzlers" to their menus in order to appeal to the widest possible range of customers.[100]

Something like an approach to a "national" cuisine for "crossover" enjoyment may be seen in restaurateurs' attempt to include any item on their menus for which it is perceived there may be a market.[101] For example, the Bristol Grill, now owned by the Madras hotel Dasaprakash, offers a South Indian vegetarian buffet to which has been added Gujarati fare, while at Status, a Punjabi vegetarian restaurant operated by the Kamat family chain, the management has introduced a Gujarati *thali* "cooked by experts from Surat."[102] Accommodating the varying dietary expectations of multigeneration family parties has required Bombay restaurants to be both responsive and innovative.

How to explore new cuisines in comfort while holding on to one's dignity in specialty restaurants is a challenge in any society. Many of Bombay's middle- and upper-class consumers, having limited experience of such cuisines, might feel diffident about culinary adventures. From time to time, *Bombay* offered guidance to its readers about what to do and how to behave in certain settings; if the writing seems to the knowledgable reader to be tongue-in-cheek, it nonetheless provided useful, usable hints to a neophyte. At the Lobster Pot in the Sea Rock Hotel, described as "the ideal place to impress your girlfriend or make your guest from Marseilles feel at home," for example, the *Langouste Newbourg* was

carefully presented with a signature garnish of lightly cooked carrots, beans and ladyfingers [and] has succulent morsels of lobsters. Prepared before your table—like most of the other dishes—the lobster is heated in paprika and butter and flamed with cognac. With cream added, the concoction is then reduced and seasoned with lobster butter and flavoured with sherry as a large flourish.[103]

But while all this is happening, how is one supposed to behave? *Bombay* offered succinct instructions:

The rule of thumb, while all this elaborate culinary expertise is put on display, is to look appreciative (but not overwhelmed) and nod benignly when the food is finally placed before you. And in case your dish is prepared in a white sauce, *make sure to tell the captain whether you want it done bland or spicy to cater to your Indian palate.*[104]

It might be noted that the "family cabin," now called a "private dining room," exists at this elegant restaurant, thus preserving a tradition from the old Irani cafés, although at Lobster Pot prices no one anticipates that they are more often for discreet liaisons than for "family dining."

Some restaurant innovators, finding themselves unable to wait for the customers to be educated, simply impose some order. The Saladero opened what was reported to be Bombay's first serious salad bar. Salads, which are an exotic culinary item in India, have not had much success in Bombay, being offered at high prices for small portions of basically uninteresting fare. The Saladero's manager, noting that the salad dips and dressings were not understood by patrons who mixed them up in ways that were "disastrous," saw much utility in telling customers exactly what they should eat and with what. *Bombay*'s only comment was that "in a city where interesting meals are getting either increasingly rare or increasingly expensive" the salad bar offered hope.[105]

Innovative angles and explorations of ethnicity seem to meet in restaurant revivals. Gaylord's at Churchgate was an established restaurant that added a new decor and Turkish cuisine in a bid to strengthen an eroding trade. Like those of most Indian restaurants, however, its management is sensitive to the unwillingness of some of its customers to experiment. Hence the Gaylord continues to offer "a smattering of most cuisines, Indian, European and Chinese—all adapted to a basic Punjabi palate," but nonetheless one may now also find at Gaylord a "Turkish Adventure."[106]

Bombay restaurant marketing has promoted innovations in decor, particularly in the five-star hotels that ostensibly cater to foreign tourists (as often from Arab countries as from the West) but whose major custom has been drawn from Bombay's well-to-do elites. After the Hotel President was taken over by the Taj Mahal group, the old-style dining room, Mayfair, was made over into an elegant Indian restaurant, Gulzar. There were complaints, however, that "in the time-tested tradition of the Taj Mahal hotels the Gulzar combines high prices with steadily diminishing servings."[107] Perhaps catering to an affluent Sindhi residential enclave in its vicinity, the Gulzar included regional specialities of Sindh. Recent changes in taxation policies—a luxury tax and a surcharge on hotel restaurant services—may reduce the market shares of these establishments, yet it is also likely that in attempting to draw in customers at higher prices, they may create even more innovative cuisines and settings.[108]

Foreign cuisines have to some extent been domesticated in Bombay. Some Bombay restaurants promoted this transition even before 1947. Italian fare was popularized by Mongini's in the Fort and Vianelli's at Chaupati. Subsequently, Chinese cuisine, or something that might better be termed "Bombay-Cantonese" cooking, became the basis for judging Chinese cooking (I exclude my friend who judged it all by the decor), and several innovative operations became successful in Bombay. A new Chinese restaurant, Chinatown, was described in 1982 as "the most original restaurant to appear on the city scene . . . completely unlike the standard Bombay-Cantonese." Many special dishes and gracious touches were offered, including complimentary cups of a special jasmine tea flown in from Singapore. The old-line Bombay-Cantonese was retained on the menu "for the die-hards and [the] unadventurous."[109] Mention of Chinatown leads to another aspect of Bombay restaurant culture—the connection with celebrities: restaurants encourage and cater to well-known sports and film figures.[110] Chinatown's success, it was said, was in part a result of its popularity with Shashi Kapur and other film-industry personalities.[111] An even more attractive Chinese restaurant, the China Garden, opened to rave reviews that noted its clean modern interior, striking ambience, innovative and high-quality cuisine, and celebrity clientele. The owner employed two "socialite interior designers" to produce "a dream of a restaurant."[112] One local observer says:

> The restaurant scene in Bombay changed with the arrival of Nelson Wang and the China Garden. Before him, the restaurants were over-carpeted, under-lit, with solemn diners talking in hushed voices and background music of the type that Indian Airlines plays before taking off or while landing. Nelson Wang removed the carpets and bared bright marble floors with light and sounds reflecting, people talking at the tops of their voices, greetings across the table, no music.[113]

The Hunan style of Chinese cooking was later introduced in several Bombay restaurants.

Clearly, the upscale restaurants of Bombay offer a wide assortment of cuisines and settings. Among the ethnicities to be explored are those of India itself. For example, in the best tradition of the Festival of India, the Village, an elaborate open-air restaurant, displays curios of rustic India. A potter is employed to make clay pots (and engage the interest of those waiting for their tables). The waiters are, according to *Bombay*, liveried like cowherds and, "speaking impeccable English," give good service; water is poured out of the earthen jars, food is in clayware, "and everything has the distinct aroma of the backwoods."[114] On a less elaborate scale, the Pritam da Dhaba opened in 1985 as a recreation of a roadside *dhaba* that typically would cater to the truck drivers of the Punjab highways. An authentic open kitchen with raised mud *choolahs* produced "mostly good" food, although with more varieties than would be found in a true roadside stall. On the other hand, the authenticity of insisting that customers sit on *charpai* cots created resistance: a two-hour meal offered "a form of torture that only masochists would welcome."[115]

Changes and Continuities

One final comment on Bombay's "dining out" phenomenon must capture the so-called fast foods. As one author put it, "The trend today is to grab a bite." Youngsters are tending to eat out more, for a change from home cooking and to relax in snack bars where they can also listen to recorded popular music, mostly imported Western rock. Hamburgers and pizza have been rather thoroughly domesticated within Bombay's various fast-food outlets. Their popularity seems rooted as much in the ravages of inflation as in the culinary delights of the products. Bombay snack bars have such evocative names as Waikiki, Sundance Cafe, Hard Rock Cafe, Chuck Wagon, and the aforementioned Jack in the Box; the latter has not only the obligatory loud "background" music, but also a video game parlor.[116] A well-known Bombay literary and political figure, Khwaja Ahmad Abbas, complained in 1987:

> Bombay food is found no-where! The old Irani Restaurants are gone, the vegetarian restaurants are gone, the Rice Plate for six Annas is gone, now the fast food—Chicken in plastic *thalli* for Rs. 25/- with Ice Cream for kids at Rs. 5/- each. You eat from card-board plates and plastic spoons, because there is no time to eat and relish your food. Fast-fast-faster-fastest goes the rhythm of eating. What you get is peptic ulcers in the bargain."[117]

Perhaps Abbas's distaste arose within that indulgently austere aesthetic of plain living and high thinking associated with devotees of both Gandhian and socialist ideals. If so, the distaste may be misapplied since the new phenomena in fact represent an evolution of popular consumption practice that has grown among a large percentage of Bombay's population. Fast-food restaurants ought not to be seen as merely an innovative adaptation of foreign models by Bombay's public-dining industry. Another source is rooted in older agencies—the street-corner vendors and handcart food sellers of the city. Footpath food vendors have long been plying their trade in Bombay, to the delight of the citizens and the anxiety of the municipal health authorities. The *bhelpuriwallas* at Chaupati beach have become as much a part of a visit as the hot dog vendors of New York's Coney Island.[118] Elsewhere in the city, the variety of street food has remained immense despite problems of storage, water supply, weather, and police harassment. Street vendors' overhead is low, and business can flourish provided "that they provide something that is cheap, tasty, seductive."[119] An extension of this tradition is found on the skyscraper-lined streets of Bombay's Nariman Point. There the rental cost of building space is so prohibitive that very few restaurant owners have been able to afford a lease. (In *Topsy Turvy*, a satirical revue of life in Bombay produced by actor/impresario Sylvester da Cunha, one sketch is about finding a reasonably priced lunch at Nariman Point.)[120] Each day at the lunch hour, thousands of office workers literally descend upon the virtually permanent stalls and vans of street vendors. Here too new cuisines are encapsulated within the range of Indian palates. One van owned by a Muslim features "Chinese" lunches cooked by a Maratha Hindu from Jalgaon who adapts his productions to the tastes of his customers. He explained, for example, that Gujaratis "have a sweet tooth so I put in extra sauce for them. Punjabis like *thikha* so I add extra chilli."[121] Asked about this "competition," the manager of Kamling diplomatically responded, "I can't vouch for the authenticity of the food, but it's value for money." As an alternative to the *dabbawala* or as a white-collar parallel to the *khanavals*, these street vendors seem largely to meet the utilitarian dining needs of the officegoers while creating another form of "restaurant" for Bombay.[122]

Conclusions

This essay has been concerned to describe the emergence in contemporary Bombay of a restaurant culture that has become one of the mediators of what Breckenridge and Appadurai have termed India's cosmopolitan public culture. In order to establish the roots of public dining phenomena in Bombay, an extensive historical survey establishes that public dining at the utilitarian level of daily necessity (the *khanaval*) has been a continuous feature of the city's life since it began its growth as a great colonial commercial and industrial center in the early nineteenth century. By contrast, restaurant dining in Bombay as an elite activity for leisure time, whether for European colonial society or for Indians, emerged much more haltingly. While historical evidence does suggest that urban necessities linked to industrial working-class laborers and commercial middle-class office workers significantly eroded traditional cultural imperatives against public dining, wealthy Bombay citizens often appeared to be content to experience public dining only in encapsulated domains of family, caste, or community. Colonial rule seems to have had only a tangential relation to this phenomenon. The growth of restaurant dining in Bombay extends across the political watershed of Indian independence. With the exception of certain establishments and institutions that had been racially exclusive preserves for Europeans, there appears to be no clear break between the colonial and postcolonial period.

A full discussion of nonelite eating possibilities in contemporary Bombay must lie beyond the scope of this essay. Any visitor to the city today will become aware of the extent to which a broad spectrum of the society "dines out," even if it is at humble establishments. Much of the evidence presented may suggest that there always existed a profound dichotomy between the domains of customers, styles, and foods of Bombay's utilitarian eating houses and those of elite restaurants. Observers might be tempted to view the latter merely as interesting, possibly amusing, manifestations of the cultural consumption on the periphery of a Euro-centered world capitalist system. Such a reaction should be resisted insofar as it slips too easily into a comfortable assumption that Indian public culture is merely a derivative, if colorful, form of global modernity. There is no "typical" Bombay dining patron. Viewed synchronically, considerations of class may be seen to align the customers of the two extremes. Certainly an average customer of a textile-mill-neighborhood *khanaval* is unlikely to drop by the Taj Mahal Hotel's Sea Lounge for a cold coffee ice cream, which would cost him the equivalent of one week's meals, even if he brazened his way past the formidable doorman. And, apart from the excursions "Off the Eaten Path" suggested by *Bombay*, few habitués of the expensive restaurants will frequent the tea stalls and lunch homes of Parel. Still, in the complex metropolitan setting of Bombay, a growing "middle class," itself internally differentiated, has occupied a complicated world of consumption between the extremes. It seems likely that in the evolution of India's public cultures this middle ground of consumption will contribute prominently to complex flavors of public taste, even if the more classical forces of economic wealth define the extent of participation.

Placing the analysis in a historical framework, emphasizing the dynamics of change over time, illustrates more clearly that most of Bombay's population has existed between the extremes of great wealth and abject poverty and that at many intermediate levels people have experienced a growth of purchasing power and purchasing incentive. During the twentieth century increments of income and experience have encouraged and enabled an ever widening popular participation in the phenomenon of restaurant dining. Even if the "upscale" restaurants of Bombay have made their mark by catering only to the very rich, that social category in Bombay has always been open to new wealth and ambition, and patronage of such establishments has become a mark of status, as underscored in a recent voyeuristic novel of Bombay "socialite" life.[123] If there has been a marked change in recent years, it may be that the employment of new themes and styles has begun to trickle down into new, less costly restaurants whose custom is drawn more from the city's growing middle classes.

Another consideration must be that these developments have not been limited to Bombay. Although discussions of the city's enormous population growth have centered on migration to Bombay, urban expansion has also entailed both a natural increase and considerable circulation out of the city. Just as Hindi films and national periodicals have projected an image of Bombay's culture to the rest of the subcontinent, so too have the "Bombay-returned" brought to other localities powerful memories and expectations of what it is to be "up to date." All this may be taken as proof that Bombay is on the "edge of India" in more than just geography. The Calcutta editor M. J. Akbar complained:

> Bombay's culture and thinking have simply drifted away from the rest of the country . . . It is not just a question of wearing jeans, or sharing ideas from the West (to which there can be no sensible objection), but of adopting foreign patterns and ideas without question, as a city might when it stopped thinking.[124]

Dom Moraes drew a different perspective, one often favored by Bombay residents, comparing the city to New York: "Like New Yorkers, the citizens of Bombay have some indefinable but perceptible quality that makes them easily identifiable to their countrymen."[125] He might have added "copiable" as well.

And what of the foods offered in the Bombay world of restaurant dining? In an Indian nation of multiple regions and communities, it might be argued that all Indian cuisines represent "ethnic cuisines," at least in the context of a great cosmopolitan metropolis. Ethnic cuisines may reflect the modern functions of ethnicity that work as adaptive self-interest mechanisms.[126] Furthermore, explorations in ethnic-cuisine restaurants may offer a relatively easy means for vicarious experience of another culture.[127] Yet ethnic restaurants face the dilemma of remaining "true to tradition" or of accommodating aspects of the dominant foodways of their locality. Commercial compromises such as offering ethnic cuisines along with familiar Indian regional dishes may diminish "authenticity" to the point where the only "ethnicity" left is in the words printed on the menu.

The evolution and growth of restaurants in Bombay, and in India generally, may be in part linked to the colonial past. The utilitarian, functional public dining facilities of the city were a direct by-product of the pattern of labor recruitment from the countrysides of the subcontinent. Men residing in the city without their families while they worked as mill hands, dock laborers, railwaymen, and office clerks generated a demand for inexpensive, functional meal services that would enable them to save their earnings to send back to their homes. While this phenomenon occurred in a colonial context, there is nothing specifically colonial within it. Colonialism may have had an impact on gastronomic patterns of the Third World,[128] but the emergence of a restaurant culture was consistent with patterns of metropolitan consumption, in this instance in Britain. Similarly, the appropriation of elite consumption patterns of the foreign colonial elites by emergent well-to-do Indians may be interpreted as a subcontinental illustration of consumption mobility characteristic of the developed and developing worlds alike.

In conclusion, one cautionary note is required. Scholarly analysis of public culture must not lose sight of the fact that the abstractions of style and consumption really matter only when living people are experiencing and reacting to them. I am reminded of an interview in connection with this project with two very thoughtful Bombay natives who now live in Seattle. One of them, an academic of broad education and interests, was anxious to think some more about public culture and what it could reveal about the direction of Indian life. He wondered if in looking at ambience, decor, and even cuisine purely in descriptive terms an important point was not missed: the factor of enjoyment. He recalled that "my uncle would come to our house and say, 'Hey, Ramesh, let's go,' and off we'd go. I never asked where. I knew it would be for food. It was always an adventure."[129] My informant's wife added that when she was growing up in Bombay during the 1930s, resources were stretched thin in her middle-class family. When people did go out to dine it was seen as a special occasion: usually the party would include members of two or more families together for a celebration or observance. In part, eating out solved the difficulties of preparing food for large gatherings in Bombay's typically cramped residential quarters. Furthermore, eating out reflected a sense of occasion, whether it be celebration of a high pass on a school exam, a birthday, or an engagement:

> We didn't think of going out except for special occasions. We couldn't afford to but it was always a treat; it was always great fun. I think most of our friends in Bombay still feel that way about it.[130]

Partaking of sustenance together has long been a marker of human community and identity.[131] Thus, scholars of public culture must acknowledge and consider that for many Bombay restaurant patrons "dining out" still represents primarily excitement and celebration. We have to ask whether in constructing a theory of a "restaurant culture" the diners are only to be thought of as an "audience" that consumes the productions of the "producers" of public culture, or if we ought not also to reckon on what role the "audience" may itself have as "producers," even if the production is only an innocent merriment of celebration and adventure.[132]

Notes

1. A preliminary version of this essay was read as a paper in a panel entitled "Public Culture in India" organized by Carol A. Breckenridge at the Wisconsin South Asia Conference in November 1987 and stimulated by several essays concerning the problems and aspects of "public culture" in contemporary India. Some of the research for this paper was accomplished "in the field" during the author's periods of residence in Bombay between 1965 and 1987. Thus, credit must be given to the American Institute of Indian Studies, the U. S. Department of Education, and the Indo-U. S. Subcommission on Education and Culture, who picked up the bill but never told me where to dine. Although some of the evidence must be frankly acknowledged to be impressionistic, I have found that many of my colleagues accept that my opinions carry some weight, so to speak. The critical readings of earlier drafts of this essay by Professors Breckenridge and Appadurai and by members of the University of Washington History Research Group are gratefully acknowledged. The essay was completed in its final revised form in 1990.

2. A theoretical overview is offered by Arjun Appadurai and Carol Breckenridge in their introduction to this volume. Appadurai and Breckenridge also argue that an analysis of public culture challenges and expands the historian's notions of culture, which are predicated on such polarities as high and low, elite and popular. It may be premature to spend much time on the matter of terminology. Appadurai and Breckenridge have rejected the use of the term *popular culture* for reasons that strike me as being reasonable and adequate. I have discovered in discussions with some historians of Europe and America, however, that *public culture* possesses some intellectual luggage, namely, in a vigorous historiography regarding the history of political discourse, most particularly that of early Anglo-American political theory. In J. G. A. Pocock, *Virtue, Commerce and History: Essays on Political Thought and History, Chiefly in the Eighteenth Century* (Cambridge: Cambridge University Press, 1985), public culture is primarily concerned with the development and implications of civic virtue and emergent republican ideologies. My

colleague John E. Toews brought this to my attention in his "Intellectual History after the Linguistic Turn: The Autonomy of Meaning and the Irreducibility of Experience," *American Historical Review* 92 (October 1987): 890-92.

3. Appadurai and Breckenridge, introduction to this volume.

4. Within that work, it has been possible to demonstrate a considerable historical depth for manifestations of the public culture domain extending earlier than the past two decades. Indeed, contrary to a priori assumptions, there is no clearly defined "break" associated with the end of colonial rule, but instead a continuity of development of the restaurant phenomenon culminating in an effloresence of consumption at the present day. This should enhance our understanding of the processes by which modern cosmopolitan culture has emerged. In the example of restaurants in Bombay, historical evidence of a longer-term accumulation of the experience of public dining in Bombay, even in utilitarian settings and circumstances, may help to account for the apparently successful transition of Bombay society toward its contemporary patterns of restaurant "consumption" in the cosmopolitan mode. Furthermore, this has called into question certain bits of "urban folklore" to which many Bombay citizens themselves subscribe regarding the degrees of change that have occurred over the past century in the public life of the city.

5. Frank F. Conlon, "Industrialization and the Housing Problem in Bombay, 1850-1940," in *Changing South Asia: Economy and Society*, ed. Kenneth Ballhatchet and David Taylor (London: School of Oriental and African Studies, University of London; Hong Kong: Asian Research Service, 1984), pp. 153-68, and Conlon, *A Caste in a Changing World: The Chitrapur Saraswat Brahmans, 1700-1935* (Berkeley and Los Angeles: University of California Press, 1977).

6. Gillian Tindall, *City of Gold: The Biography of Bombay* (London: Temple Smith, 1982), p. 19.

7. Dom Moraes and the editors of Time-Life Books, *Bombay* (New York: Time-Life Books, 1979), p. 5.

8. Khwaja Ahmad Abbas, *Bombay, My Bombay! The Love Story of the City* (Delhi: Ajanta, 1987), p. 165.

9. On early India, see Om Prakash, *Food and Drinks in Ancient India from Earliest Times to 1200 A.D.* (Delhi: Munshiram Manoharlal, 1961). Cf. McKim Marriott, "Caste Ranking and Food Transactions," in *Structure and Change in Indian Society*, ed. M. Singer and B. S. Cohn (Chicago: Aldine, 1968), pp. 133-71; R. S. Khare, *The Hindu Hearth and Home* (New Delhi: Vikas, 1976); R. S. Khare, *Culture and Reality: Essays on the Hindu System of Managing Foods* (Simla: Indian Institute of Advanced Study, 1976); and R. S. Khare and M. S. A. Rao, eds., *Food, Society and Culture* (Durham, N.C.: Carolina Academic Press, 1986). One historical essay noted is Carol A. Breckenridge, "Food, Politics and Pilgrimage in South India, 1350-1650 A.D.," in Khare and Rao, *Food*, pp. 21-53.

10. Most studies comprehend those phenomena as expressions of newly emergent social formations and aspects of the development of "taste." See, for example, Stephen Mennell, *All Manners of Food: Eating and Taste in England and France from the Middle Ages to the Present* (Oxford: Basil Blackwell, 1985); Gerard Brett, *Dinner Is Served: A Study in Manners* (Hamden, Conn.: Archon, 1969); Reay Tannahill, *Food in History* (New York: Stein and Day, 1973). At least one survey of Victorian London includes a fair amount of information on that city's dining establishments: Donald J. Olsen, *The Growth of Victorian London* (Harmondsworth: Penguin, 1979), esp. pp. 102-11. Cf. Jack Goody, *Cooking, Cuisine and Class: A Study in Comparative Sociology* (Cambridge: Cambridge University Press, 1982), pp. 97ff., and Robert Forster and Orest Ranum, eds. *Food and Drink in History: Selections from the Annales Economies, Sociétés, Civilisations*, vol. 5 (Baltimore: Johns Hopkins University Press, 1979). The extended historical tradition of restaurants in Chinese culture was first given extended attention when a pioneering symposium on food in China was published as K. C. Chang, ed., *Food in Chinese Culture: An-*

thropological and Historical Perspectives (New Haven, Conn.: Yale University Press, 1977), and has been further advanced in E. N. Anderson, *The Food of China* (New Haven, Conn.: Yale University Press, 1988).

11. Cf. Khare, *Hindu Hearth and Home*, pp. 264-73, which touches, at least tangentially, upon the place of restaurants and other public dining places in changing patterns of commensality. Another aspect of food research is seen in Mahadev L. Apte and Judit Katona-Apte, "The Left and Right Sides of a Banana Leaf: Ethnography of Food Arrangement in India," a paper presented to the American Anthropological Association in December 1975. Arjun Appadurai has described the contemporary phenomenon of cookbook publication in India and the creation of a "national cuisine" among those whom he identifies as the "spatially mobile class of professionals, along with their more stable class peers in [urban] . . . India" (Arjun Appadurai, "How to Make a National Cuisine: Cookbooks in Contemporary India," *Comparative Studies in Society and History* 30 [January 1988]: 3-24 at 6). Appadurai speculates on culinary logic paralleling the world of cookbooks in the growing restaurant industry (p. 9).

12. Pandurang V. Kane, *History of Dharmasastra*, 2d ed., vol. 2, part 2 (Poona: Bhandarkar Oriental Research Institute, 1974), pp. 757 and 757-800 generally. Some general insights on classical Islamic views on food preparation and consumption are provided by Maxime Rodinson, "Ghidha," *Encyclopaedia of Islam*, new ed., vol 2. (Leiden: Brill; London: Luzac, 1965), pp. 1057-72.

13. R. P. Kangle, *The Kautilya Arthasastra, Part III: A Study* (Bombay: University of Bombay, 1965), p. 161.

14. Kane, *Dharmasastra*, p. 759: "One should take food in privacy, for one who does so is endowed with wealth and one who eats his meals in public becomes bereft of wealth." It must be acknowledged that isolated evidence suggests that in early South India, at least, public food shops offered cooked rice and meats for sale; see A. L. Basham, *The Wonder That Was India* (New York: Grove, 1954), p. 204.

15. Khare, *Hindu Hearth*, pp. 264-73.

16. Appadurai and Breckenridge, introduction to this volume.

17. Om Prakash, *Food and Drinks*, p. 85.

18. Hameeda K. Naqvi, *Urban Centers and Industries in Upper India, 1550-1803* (London: Asia Publishing House, 1968), pp. 79-81. On caravanserais, see N. Elisseeff, "Khan," *Encyclopaedia of Islam*, new ed., vol. 4, pp. 1010-17.

19. Niccolao Manucci, *Storia do Mogor or Mogul India, 1653-1708*, vol. 1, trans. W. Irvine (Calcutta: Editions India, 1965), p. 115. There are references to Akbar's practice of opening houses to feed poor Muslims and Hindus, but these appear to have been entirely charitable in plan and do not meet a definition of public restaurant. Cf. Abu Fazl Allami, *Ain-i Akbari*, vol. 1, trans. H. Blochmann (Calcutta: Royal Asiatic Society of Bengal, 1939), pp. 210-11, 285-86.

20. Henry Yule and A. C. Burnell, *Hobson-Jobson: A Glossary of Colloquial Anglo-Indian Words and Phrases*, new ed., ed. William Crooke (London: John Murray, 1903), p. 162. Thus, a Mughal capital city, Agra, said to have 660,000 inhabitants in 1640-41, was reported to have ninety caravanserais for the accommodation of strangers (*Travels of Fray Sebastien Manrique, 1629-1643*, vol. 2 [Oxford: Hakluyt Society, 1927], p. 152. Cf. Naqvi, *Urban Centers and Industries*, pp. 124-25, on accommodation at Patna and Benaras.

21. James Forbes, *Oriental Memoirs: A Narrative of Seventeen Years Residence in India*, 2d ed., vol. 2 (London: Richard Bentley, 1834), p. 40. Forbes did report that Mughal rule had produced *serais* in the countryside along the principal roads, noting that well-to-do travelers carried along provisions and the poor found some modest local provisions (p. 195).

22. K. M. Ashraf, *Life and Conditions of the People of Hindustan*, 2d ed. (New Delhi: Munshiram Manoharlal, 1970), p. 220.

23. F. S. Manrique, *Travels of Manrique, 1629-43*, vol. 2, ed. E. Lenard and H. Hosten (Ox-

ford: Hakluyt Society, 1927), p. 186. Manrique reports that some cookshops offered roast meats, others fowl and birds; still others provided Persian-style *pilaos*. Hindu dietary preferences apparently were also addressed, for Manrique noted "the simple foods of the native and superstitious Pagan . . . dishes made of rice, herbs, and vegetables" (p. 187).

24. Surendranath Sen, in the introduction to *Indian Travels of Thevenot and Careri* (New Delhi: National Archives of India, 1949), pp. lvi-lvii, cites several specific seventeenth- and eighteenth-century travel accounts.

25. One significant variation is found in the account by the Russian Athanasius Nikitin of his travels in the Deccan during the fifteenth century A.D.: "In the land of India it is the custom for foreign traders to stop at inns; there the food is cooked for the guests by the landlady, who also makes the bed and sleeps with the stranger" (R. H. Major, ed., *India in the Fifteenth Century, Being a Collection of Narratives of Voyages to India*, part 3 [London: Hakluyt Society, 1857], p. 10). Cf. comments by Manucci, *Storia*, vol. 1, p. 115.

26. Manrique, *Travels of Manrique*, vol. 2, pp. 186-88.

27. Leopold von Orloch, *Travels in India, Including Sinde and the Punjab*, vol. 2, trans. H. Evans Lloyd (London: Longman, Brown, Green, and Longmans, 1845), p. 38.

28. James Douglas, *Bombay and Western India*, vol. 1 (London: Sampson, Low and Marston, 1893), p. 187.

29. Maud Diver, *The Englishwoman in India* (1909), quoted in Charles Allen, *Plain Tales from the Raj* (London: Andre Deutsch, 1975), p. 91.

30. S. M. Edwardes, *Gazetteer of Bombay City and Island*, vol. 3 (Bombay: Times Press, 1910), p. 299. Edwardes makes reference to the opening in 1837 at Mazagaon of a European-style hotel, the Hope Hall, but in 1810 the existence of an institution by that name was noted as the place where Englishmen returning from a day of riding would pause for a dinner; see Samuel T. Sheppard, *Bombay* (Bombay: Times of India Press, 1932), p. 143, citing the *Bombay Courier*.

31. Emma Roberts, *Notes of an Overland Journey through France and Egypt to Bombay* (London: Wm. H. Allen, 1841), p. 257. A German visitor in 1842 stayed at the Victoria Hotel in the Fort, which he described as "the only inn in this place, which much resembles our German post-houses, while the charges are on the scale of the first-class hotel in London"; he did, however, obtain "a good supper" (Orloch, *Travels in India*, vol. 1, p. 30). Another option open to European male visitors was temporary membership in the Byculla Club or the Bombay Club; see Samuel T. Sheppard, *The Byculla Club, 1833-1916* (Bombay: Bennett, Coleman, 1916), pp. 146-47, 138n.

32. The Esplanade Hotel advertised itself as "the only one in Bombay that is conducted entirely by Europeans" (*Bombay Gazette*, March 3, 1871, p. 4).

33. *Chabuk*, quoted in *Bombay Gazette*, October 30, 1863, p. 3. Further facilities were built during the 1860s.

34. Reginald Heber, *Narrative of a Journey through the Upper Provinces of India, from Calcutta to Bombay, 1824-1825*, vol. 3 (London: John Murray, 1828), p. 105.

35. It would be imprudent to take at face value the comparisons of food service facilities in India and Europe in the early nineteenth century, if only because the implicit comparisons of an observer like Emma Roberts suggest a far more widespread knowledge of and sympathy for restaurants. Brett, in *Dinner Is Served*, p. 14, makes the point that modern European food habits were "enabled" in part by economic change, most especially the gradual increase of population and of volume of imported food and the general rise of living standards, all contributing to an improvement of quantity and quality of food consumed. Brett somewhat arbitrarily defines the essential feature of a "restaurant" to have been "the large number and variety of the dishes it offers. The restaurant of today has forerunners, most notable among them being the inn, the chop house and the Ordinary, but it has no ancestors. It seems to have grown out of the eighteenth

century interest in prepared food for invalids . . . and in the shops which dispensed such foods. The word *restaurant* first appeared in France, but not earlier than about 1765."

36. Ibid., p. 233. Cf. Edwardes, *Gazetteer*, 3:299-300.

37. *Bombay Gazette*, January 3, 1871, p. 1; *Bombay Gazette*, March 3, 1871, p. 4.

38. As late as 1890 notice was given to the opportunity for "well accredited travellers," that is, British visitors with introductions, who could obtain rooms at the Byculla or the Bombay Club. Furthermore, temporary membership in the racially exclusive Royal Yacht Club gave access to "an excellent restaurant" (W. S. Caine, *Picturesque India* [London: George Routledge, 1890], pp. 2-4).

39. Viscountess Falkland, *Chow-Chow: Being Selections from a Journal Kept in India, Egypt and Syria*, 2d ed. (London: Hurst and Blackett, 1857), p. 52.

40. Sheppard, *Byculla Club*, pp. 132-44. One Bombay editor made a semifacetious suggestion that the government pass a "Burra Khanna Act" to regulate "the plethoric dinner," which "begins too late and lasts too long, leaving but little time for conversation and music; it injures the average human being by imposing a greater strain on his interior organs than they should be called on to bear, at least in this country" (*Bombay Gazette Overland Summary*, January 7, 1871, p. 5).

41. Sheppard, *Byculla Club*, pp. 76-77.

42. See Barbara N. Ramusack, "The Indian Princes as Fantasy: Palace Hotels, Palace Museums and Palace on Wheels," in this volume.

43. S. K. Kooka, "Times Past, Times Remembered," *Taj Magazine* 11, no. 2 (1982): n.p. There is an undocumented tradition of Bombay urban folklore that Tata once had been turned away by the dining room at Watson's Esplanade Hotel and had decided to build a greater establishment where such discrimination would not exist; Tata's official biographer, however, attributes the Taj Mahal to Tata's "patriotic" view that the growth of Bombay required a monumental first-class hotel (Frank Harris, *Jamsetji Nusserwanji Tata: A Chronicle of His Life* [Bombay: Blackie, 1958], pp. 72-73). A recent survey of this class of hotel in the colonial East is Martin Meade et al., *Grand Oriental Hotels* (London?: Vendome, n.d.[c.1989].

44. Ben Diqui, *A Visit to Bombay* (London: Watts, 1927), p. 28.

45. Ibid., pp. 28-29.

46. Shirin Bahadurji, "Jamva Chalo Ji," *Bombay* 6, no. 7 (November 22-December 6, 1984): pp. 56-60. In contemporary Bombay catering of weddings and other functions for persons of all communities has become a substantial industry with some two thousand active firms ("Cooking Up Millions," *Bombay* 10, no. 24 [August 7-21, 1989]: 39-43).

47. Cf., for Britain, Arnold Palmer, *Moveable Feasts* (London: Oxford University Press, 1952).

48. Edwardes, *Bombay City and Island Gazetteer* 1:243, noted this in the first decade of the twentieth century in describing the routines of the middle-class Prabhu community. The late-morning openings remained the dominant model in later years (*Labour Gazette* [Bombay], May 1926, pp. 860-61). It must be conceded that not all clerical staff enjoyed such hours — certainly retail shop assistants and ordinary copyists worked far longer hours and were thus not permitted such adjustments of dining to working hours.

49. Diqui, *Visit*, pp. 28-29.

50. The institution of the *dabbawallas* and their complex network of collection and distribution of lunch containers merits study within the context of distinctive aspects of urban geography in Bombay. The work of the Bombay Tiffinbox Suppliers Association, as they are called, is, however, tangential in the present context of a concern with public dining as it appears to exist as an adaptation by Indian families to avoid resort to restaurants during office lunch hours. Bachi J. Karkaria, in "The Incredible Dabba Connection," *Taj Magazine* 11, no. 2 (1982): n.p., credits the tradition to British invention. Carriers also take factory and mill laborers meal

boxes containing food prepared at home or at a *khanaval* (Hemalata C. Dandekar, *Men to Bombay, Women at Home: Urban Influence on Sugao Village, Deccan Maharashtra, India, 1942-1982* [Ann Arbor: University of Michigan Center for South and Southeast Asian Studies, 1986], pp. 247-48).

51. Laxmi Hiremath, "Zesty Indian Luncheons: The Miracle of Bombay's Dabba System," *India Currents*, May 1988, p. 36.

52. K. C. Zachariah, *Migrants in Greater Bombay* (Bombay: Asia Publishing House, 1968), pp.113-15.

53. Census of India, 1931, vol. 9: *Cities of the Bombay Presidency* (Bombay: Government Central Press, 1933), p. 31. Even in 1971, it was reported that the ratio had reached only 717 per 1,000 (Ashish Bose, *Studies in India's Urbanization, 1901-1971* [New Delhi: Tata-McGraw-Hill, 1974], p. 397).

54. James T. Molesworth, *Marathi-English Dictionary*, 2d ed. (Bombay: Bombay Education Society, 1857), p. 203.

55. Thomas Candy's completion of J. T. Molesworth's *Dictionary: English and Marathi* (Bombay: American Marathi Mission Press, 1847), pp. 355 and 219, offers *bhatarakhana* for both "inn" and "eating house," while *khanaval* is cited only as "cost of eating" under the English term "board" (p. 80). Molesworth, *Marathi-English Dictionary*, p. 600, specifies *bhatarakhana* as "an inn or eating house (esp. a Musalman hotel or cookshop)," adding that the term was used to invoke "a tumultuous and disorderly intermixture, at feasts and entertainments, of the purified and the impure or common."

56. Molesworth, *Marathi-English Dictionary*, p. 323 (emphasis added).

57. Dandekar, *Men to Bombay*, pp. 249-50.

58. A. R. Burnett-Hurst, *Labour and Housing in Bombay: A Study in the Economic Conditions of the Wage-earning Classes in Bombay* (London: P. S. King & Son, 1925), p. 64. Burnett-Hurst tends to run together references to *khanavals* and Irani cafés.

59. Dandekar, *Men to Bombay*, p. 249. According to Dandekar, in the early 1980s fewer women were willing to take up the demanding work of a *khanaval*, and consequently the male customers did not air their grievances too loudly since alternatives were hard to find.

60. The place of a *khanaval* and problems of diet for young clerical ("middle class") migrants of the Saraswat Brahman community in Bombay is noted in Conlon, *A Caste in a Changing World*, pp. 119-121, 176.

61. Cf. J. C. Massellos, "Spare Time and Recreation: Changing Behaviour Patterns in Bombay at the Turn of the Nineteenth Century," *South Asia*, n.s. 7 (June 1984): 34-57, concentrates upon the circumstances of a wider, poorer public and offers significant examples of "leisure" activities.

62. Various informants offered conflicting views on this matter. Two stalwart old Irani establishments at Dhobi Talao, Kayanis' and Bastanis, were frequently cited, but the matter must remain unresolved. The Cafe Mazda on Sleater Road near Grant Road Station advertised that it was founded in 1898, but it is not possible to confirm this from another source (H. D. Darukhanawala, *Parsi Lustre on Indian Soil*, vol. 2 [Bombay: G. Claridge, 1939-63], p. lxxxiv).

63. Shalini Ramchandani, "The Last of Irani Restaurants?" *Times of India*, March 6, 1977, p. 11; Busy Bee [Behram Contractor], "Trailing Those Charming Cafes," *Taj Magazine* 11, no. 2 (1982): n.p.; M. G. Moinuddin, "The Poorman's Parlour," *Bombay* 8, no. 8 (December 7-21, 1986): 49-53.

64. Busybee [Behram Contractor], "Thoughts of Glorious Repasts," *Bombay* 11, no. 1 (August 22-September 6, 1989):123.

65. Interview with Ramesh Gangolli, September 16, 1987; Rashmi and Chander Uday Singh, "Flavour of the Past," *Bombay* 4, no. 5 (October 22-November 6, 1982): 96-97.

66. Aloysius Soares, *Down the Corridors of Time: Recollections and Reflections*, vol. 1 (Bom-

bay: author, 1971-73), p. 55. Given the wide range of variables, it is impossible to offer an exact translation of value. Two annas (one-eighth of a rupee) may be understood in terms of approximate purchasing power for a student in 1910-11 as equivalent to 1989 U.S. $1.50 or more, although actual exchange rates would make it worth less in formal terms.

67. Ramchandani, "The Last of Irani Restaurants?" p. 11.

68. Edwardes, *Gazetteer* 1:179 notes a variety of places young men visited for drinks and snacks in Bombay.

69. Advertisement of Ideal Restaurant (Darukhanawala, *Parsi Lustre on Indian Soil*, vol. 1 p. 659).

70. Mennell, *All Manner of Food*, p. 154 notes that in the nineteenth century, while new London restaurants were large and high-ceilinged, the Parisian restaurants now had *cabinets particuliers*—a tradition associated with eighteenth-century coffeehouses and the equivalent of the private "family cabins" of the Bombay restaurant tradition; see Robert Thorne, "Places of Refreshment in the Nineteenth-Century City," in *Buildings and Society: Essays on the Social Development of the Built Environment*, ed. Anthony D. King (London: Routledge & Kegan Paul, 1980), pp. 233-37.

71. Nissim Ezekiel, *Latter-Day Psalms* (Delhi: Oxford University Press, 1982), pp. 24-25.

72. J. A. Turner and B. K. Goldsmith, *Sanitation in India* (Bombay: Times of India, 1922), p. 883. Act I of 1916 added "keeping of eating houses" to the list of trades specified in part IV of Schedule M, Section 394 of the City of Bombay Municipal Act, thus requiring licensing of premises and defining eating house to be: "any premises to which the public are admitted and where any kind of food is prepared or supplied for consumption on the premises for the profit or gain of any person owning or having an interest in or managing such premises." *Oriental Review*, June 30, 1912, called for regulation of boarding houses in Bombay to control the spread of cholera and other diseases (*Bombay Report on Indian Newspapers*, week ending June 29, 1912, para. 61).

73. *Jam-e-Jamshed*, June 17, 1913 (*Bombay Report on Indian Newspapers*, week ending June 21, 1913, para. 29).

74. In 1989, a state government minister suggested closing all restaurants at 12:30 a.m. to reduce the crime rate! Asked how this could have any effect, a police official stated: "We can question everybody at night and they won't be able to escape with the standard answer of going to a restaurant" (*Bombay* 10, no. 15 [March 22-April 6, 1989]: 16).

75. The "functional" eating house par excellence among the Maharashtrian middle-class officegoers was the Madhavashram near the Girgaum Police Court, where the rush for meals before and after office hours meant that those eating in the "first shift" dared not linger over their *thalis* as the "second shift" impatiently stood directly behind their chairs. Interview with R. Gangolli.

76. Interview with S. Nanavati, Bombay, December 26, 1986.

77. Interview with Dr. Gopal Hattiangdi, July 31, 1987. Another informant, Dr. Ramesh Gangolli, noted in our interview that in the 1930s he too would count on his uncle to take him out to snacks in restaurants where he might otherwise have never gone.

78. H. Shankar Rau, "Family Budgets," in *A Chitrapur Saraswat Miscellany* (Bombay: author, 1938), pp. 15-31.

79. Interview with R. Gangolli. With respect to sanitary considerations, see Turner and Goldsmith, *Sanitation*, pp. 883ff., for an alarmingly lengthy list of common hygienic flaws in Bombay restaurants.

80. William Berol, *Tourist Handbook to Bombay* (Bombay: n.p., c.1900), p. 116. The Criterion derived its name from the well-known establishment that had opened at Piccadilly Circus in London (Donald J. Olsen, *The Growth of Victorian London* [Harmondsworth: Penguin, 1979], pp. 108-9).

81. Times of India, *Bombay: Metropolis of the East* (Bombay: Bennett, Coleman, 1931), p. 103.

82. Ibid., p. 56. Mrs. Edwards had just sold the Wayside to a Parsi firm.

83. Interview with R. Gangolli.

84. Ramchandani, "The Last of Irani Restaurants?" p. 11.

85. The term *Udipi* refers to the Krishna temple of Udipi in South Kanara (contemporary Karnataka state), which had a tradition of feeding pilgrims. One of the Shivali Brahman cooks, seeing the potential for providing the traditionally excellent vegetarian fare for profit, opened what became a model of "hotels," i.e., restaurants. The history of the evolution of this blending of brahmanical tradition, entrepreneurship, and good cooking needs study. See S. Krishnan, *Host to the Millions: The Story of Krishna Rao of Woodlands* (Madras: New Woodlands Hotel, 1983).

86. In the winter of 1965-66, Bombay city restaurants and eating houses were restricted from serving food grains on certain days of the week, and eventually all meal service was abolished on one evening each week as a temporary measure.

87. The role of the cinema in the domain of public culture is a subject that requires further research. In the case of restaurant dining, it would be secondary to plots and problems of most films. It is likely, however, that the visual images of urban ways would be assimilated by a wider audience. See Beatrix Pfleiderer and Lothar Lutze, eds. *The Hindi Film: Agent and Re-Agent of Cultural Change* (New Delhi: Manohar, 1985).

88. Edwardes, *Bombay City and Island Gazetteer*, 3:300.

89. Based on analysis of *Times of India, Directory of Bombay City 1920*, pp. 479-711.

90. *Illustrated Weekly of India* 102, no. 23 (July 5, 1981): 61. The figures suggest a possibility that the proportion of eating establishments to population has declined. If this were so, it might be explained by the growth of nuclear families among Bombay's working and middle classes, with a consequent increase in domestic food preparation.

91. I first encountered this phrase in an American manual on improving sales promotions published in the 1940s. I have been unable to confirm the title of this source. The image, however, is entirely appropriate for the following discussion of the "consumption" of restaurants' style and images.

92. Moraes, *Bombay*, p. 156.

93. Rashmi Uday Singh, "Bombay's Biryani Factories," *Bombay* 6, no. 4 (October 7-21, 1984): 114-21.

94. "Off the Eaten Track," *Bombay* 3, no. 14 (March 7-21, 1982): 86-88.

95. *Bombay* 3, no. 14 (March 7-21, 1982): 87.

96. *Bombay* 3, no. 21 (June 22-July 6, 1982): 51.

97. *Bombay* 5, no. 13 (February 22-March 6, 1984): 98-99.

98. "All That Glitters," *Bombay* 10, no. 16 (April 7-21, 1989): 40-41.

99. "Snappy Snacks," *Bombay* 3, no. 11 (January 22-February 6, 1982): 47-48.

100. *Bombay* 5, no. 5 (October 22-November 6, 1983): 103-4.

101. Cf. Appadurai, "National Cuisine," p. 9.

102. *Bombay* 5, no. 12 (February 7-21, 1984): 81-82; *Bombay* 5, no. 7 (November 22-December 6, 1983): 100-101.

103. *Bombay* 4, no. 9 (December 22, 1982-January 6, 1983): 86-87.

104. Ibid., p. 87, emphasis added.

105. "Salad Days," *Bombay* 8, no. 3 (September 22-October 6, 1986): 52-53.

106. "Turkish Adventure," *Bombay* 6, no. 13 (February 22-March 6, 1985): 66-67.

107. *Bombay* 3, no. 22 (July 7-21, 1982): 65-66.

108. *Bombay* 10, no. 16 (April 7-21, 1989): 40-41.

109. *Bombay* 4, no. 1 (August 22-September 6, 1982): 48-50.

110. Cf. "Star Attractions," *Bombay* 9, no. 19 (May 22-June 6, 1988): 45-46.

111. *Bombay* 4, no. 1 (August 22-September 6, 1982): 48-50.

112. "Enchanted Eating," *Bombay* 6, no. 17 (April 22-May 6, 1985): 64-67. Having been taken there to lunch in January 1987, I can avow that China Garden offered food both marvelous and expensive.

113. Busybee, "Glorious Repasts," *Bombay* 11, no. 1 (August 22-September 6, 1989): 114.

114. "A Cut above the Rest," *Bombay* 4, no. 12 (February 7-21, 1982): 64-65.

115. "The Ethnic Taste," *Bombay* 7, no. 4 (October 7-21, 1985): 60-61.

116. Anjali Ewing, "Let's *Not* Eat Out Today," *Illustrated Weekly of India* 102, no. 23 (July 5, 1981): 60-63. Cf. "Snappy Snacks," *Bombay* 3, no. 11 (January 22-February 6, 1982): 47-49.

117. Abbas, *Bombay, My Bombay!*, p. 166.

118. H. Shankar Rau, "The Glories of Bhat," *Kanara Saraswat*, May 1936.

119. Arjun Appadurai, "Street Culture," *India Magazine of People and Culture* 8, no. 1 (December 1987): 20.

120. *Bombay* 10, no. 24 (July 22-August 4, 1989): 41. The satire turns upon the Maharashtra government's setting up a luncheon service in the State Assembly chambers and then enforcing upon the would-be diners the type of myriad bureaucratic requirements associated with any government undertaking.

121. Prakash More, interview, "Noodling Around at Nariman Point," *Bombay* 10, no. 12 (February 7-21, 1989): 38-40.

122. This essay has not addressed directly the question of whether there is a culturally significant distinction in Bombay's public dining between indoor and outdoor settings. The economic aspect of inexpensive food from street vendors may be acknowledged, but the question of aesthetic and cultural comfort for those who have sufficient wealth to exercise a choice remains a question to be researched. Certainly, outdoor "garden" settings as annexes to restaurants have existed for at least three decades, as in the sidewalk cafés of Churchgate, yet my observations suggest that some customers are ambivalent about outdoor settings. Nevertheless, the phenomenon continues to increase and is now found also in provincial towns and cities of India. Bombay's climate—the discomforts of hot-season midday glare and monsoon-season rains and winds—does limit sit-down outdoor restaurant dining.

123. Shobha De, *Socialite Evenings* (New Delhi: Penguin, 1989), features visits by the novel's characters to many of Bombay's elite restaurants as backdrops, but emphasis is on the visit, not the culinary experience.

124. M. J. Akbar, "Delusions of the Prosperous," *Bombay* 8, no. 1 (August 22-September 6, 1986): 128. Akbar's criticism is not leveled at cultural synthesis, but rather at what he believes to be Bombay's inflated sense of importance and "self-created sense of isolation."

125. Moraes, *Bombay*, p. 9.

126. Cf. Abner Cohen, ed. *Urban Ethnicity* (London: Tavistock, 1974) and Charles F. Keyes, ed. *Ethnic Change* (Seattle: University of Washington Press, 1981).

127. Pierre L. van den Berghe, "Ethnic Cuisine: Culture in Nature," *Ethnic and Racial Studies* 7 (July 1984): 393-94.

128. Richard W. Franke, "The Effects of Colonialism and Neocolonialism on the Gastronomic Patterns of the Third World," in *Food and Evolution: Toward a Theory of Human Food Habits*, ed. Marvin Harris and Eric B. Ross (Philadelphia: Temple University Press, 1986), pp.455-479, notes colonialism's impact on diet.

129. Interview with R. Gangolli.

130. Interview with S. Gangolli, September 16, 1987.

131. Wilbur Zelinsky, "The Roving Palate: North America's Ethnic Restaurant Cuisines," *Geoforum* 16 (1985): 51-52n. I must thank my colleague John Findlay for calling this source to my attention.

132. This essay was completed in its final revised form in 1990. Bombay's restaurant scene has continued to evolve, but without the benefit of *Bombay: The City Magazine,* which ceased publication in March 1991. Restaurant reviews now appear in various newspapers and magazines. At least one guide to Bombay restaurants—Diana C. Proeschel and Saroj Merani, *Flavours: A Selective Guide to Eateries in Bombay* (Bombay: Perennial Press, 1988)—has been published.

PART II

The Historical Present

CHAPTER SIX

Consuming Utopia

Film Watching in Tamil Nadu

SARA DICKEY

First-time visitors to South Indian towns and cities are often struck by the overwhelming presence of cinema.[1] What the visitor sees is matched by what South Indians do: more movies are produced and watched per capita in South India than almost anywhere else in the world.[2] Movies not only are watched, they also constitute a pervasive visual and aural presence outside of the theater. Huge, dazzling posters line the main streets, and smaller posters are slapped onto spare wall space. Movie songs blare from horn speakers and cassette players at weddings, puberty rites, and temple and shrine festivals. Coffee stalls play tapes of movie dialogues. Rickshaws and shop boards are painted with movie stars' pictures. Young women and men follow dress and hairstyle fashions copied from the latest films, while younger children trade movie star cards, learn to disco dance like the film heroes, and stage mock battles in imitation of their favorite stars. Fan clubs hold meetings in the streets, boasting about their star and mocking his rivals.

Cinema is public spectacle, inside the theater and out. Most of its consumers belong to the urban poor. In Tamil Nadu, filmgoing is seen—and disparaged, in part as a result of its public and spectacular nature—by all elements of the "public" as a largely lower-class preoccupation, while filmmaking is the province of people who belong almost exclusively to the middle and upper classes. Cinema is one of the main vehicles by which the urban poor, limited by a lack of economic resources, are drawn into the growing public culture of India.[3] Consumption of cinema, and consumption within cinema, also provide access to the luxuries of public culture through the spectacular and utopian fantasies that, I will argue in this essay, are constructed for viewers through films.

None of this is meant to suggest that people of the middle and upper classes do not watch films or go to the cinema hall. They do, utilizing film watching in addition as an occasion for donning fashionable clothes and displaying fine jewelry. More and more, however, wealthier viewers are choosing to avoid the crowded theaters by watching movies on their own videocassette recorders. While video has not yet had the same impact on the South Indian film industry as is lamented in Bombay,[4] it does appear that the most *public* aspect of the act of film watching, that of going to the cinema, is increasingly dominated by the poor.

The people I refer to here as the "urban poor" include skilled and unskilled laborers and very low level office workers, and their household members, who possess or control little in the way of land and other property and endure a general lack of economic security. Almost all have incomes at or near the Indian poverty line; all are by their own standards clearly poor and financially insecure. Although this term includes people who vary widely in such features as occupation and income, it is nonetheless useful for a number of reasons. First, it corresponds to the category of people that Tamils lump at the bottom of the socioeconomic hierarchy, and to the self-ascribed identity of people in this position. Such people refer to themselves as poor people (or as laborers, people who suffer, or people who have nothing), and are referred to by members of higher classes as the lower class or the mass. Second, I have avoided imposing a more precise class label, such as the classical Marxist terms familiar to students of Western capitalist societies, because the application of these categories in India is fraught with difficulties; historical variations in social and economic structures mean that such categories rarely correspond to the most meaningful local divisions in India. Thus I have chosen the phrase "urban poor" because it corresponds to the most prominent local subdivision of people made on a socioeconomic basis, while terms such as "working class" or "proletariat" would not.

One of the most pervasive aspects of the lives of the poor in Madurai is a sense of social and economic insecurity. Jobs are dependent on an employer's whim or on unreliable seasons; house rent can be raised beyond reach at any moment; food and other commodity prices often jump unexpectedly. Insecurity extends to social relations, where uncertainties abound as well.

Grown children neglect to care for their aged parents as they should; husbands may die or abandon wife and children; siblings refuse to honor their responsibilities to one another at children's marriages and other paramount occasions. Madurai residents often complained that life was once easier, and that the social and economic insecurity they now experience is increasing.[5] Taking this insecurity into account is crucial to understanding the appeal of Tamil cinema, which supplies not only an escape from anxiety but also a means to diminish it. The escape is made possible precisely because films echo the basic concerns of viewers' lives.

The purpose of this essay is, in broadest terms, to explore the appeal and significance that films hold for their viewers. Particular attention will be paid to the type of escape constructed in Tamil films and to the process of spectatorship, especially that part of the process involving viewers' reactions to and interaction with film content. Although my research has focused on urban viewers, most of my conclusions are relevant to rural consumption of films as well.

The suggestion that Tamil film can be intimately connected to viewers' lives flies in the face of most previous considerations of Tamil and other Indian cinema, which range from dismissal to excoriation. As Pradip Krishen has pointed out, popular Indian cinema is most frequently regarded by critics as "frivolous escape, or simply, degraded spectacle" (1981: 4). Rosie Thomas, one of the only English-language writers to discuss mainstream Indian cinema in terms of its own canons and attractions, quotes a journalist's complaint similar to many I have read in Indian newspapers and journals that "all that [the films] stand for is exotica, vulgarity and absurdity" (1985: 119). Foreign and Indian critics frequently make unfavorable comparisons with Indian art or parallel cinema, a form that more closely coincides with the canons of European art cinema.

If most critics refuse to discuss popular movies on the films' own terms—instead passing judgment from high-culture perspectives—they betray a similar resistance to viewing the audience's interest in films as anything other than titillation or mindless fantasy. In general, the idea that popular cinema could hold meaning for its audiences or provide insight into their lives is greeted with disdain (see Krishen 1981: 4).[6] (Nor is moral or aesthetic disparagement of films limited to formal critics; popular opinion in Tamil Nadu can be equally denigrating.) These attitudes parallel much of the Western academic criticism of mass and popular culture that has appeared since the Frankfurt school, whose writers largely favored the image of a passive consumer. Other analysts, sparked primarily by the work of Raymond Williams

(1977, 1982), have recently begun to explore consumers' roles in actively responding to and occasionally challenging the content and ideology of expressive cultural forms; but such approaches have had virtually no impact on the analysis of mainstream Indian cinema.[7]

I have addressed this aspect of the passive-active debate elsewhere (Dickey 1989). Here I intend to focus on activity of a different kind, that is, viewers' active search for escape and illusion, and in addition to engaging implicitly with Indian film critics or popular culture analysts, I will pay particular attention to work on the social meaning and function of spectacle, particularly that of Debord (1983). Spectacle—the importance of seeing *and* of being seen—is central to much of public culture.

In turn, Debord argues that at the center of spectacle lies illusion, the separation of image from reality. He contends that, in capitalist societies, all that was once directly experienced "has moved away into a representation" (1983: §1), and spectacle to Debord is nothing if not pure representation. The significance of the image or illusion is twofold: first, it comprises the unilateral communication of the dominant class, and second, it elicits passivity from the subordinate spectator class. The spectacle, that is,

> presents itself as something enormously positive, indisputable and inaccessible . . . The attitude which it demands in principle is passive acceptance
> which in fact it already obtained by its manner of appearing without reply, by
> its monopoly of appearance. (1983: §12)

Before addressing the escape provided by this spectacle, we must examine the broader question of the relationship between cinema and its viewers. To this end, the following three sections address the melodramatic form of cinema, its role in crisis resolution, and viewers' own perceptions of the significance of cinema and its relation to their lives. In the fourth section I move to a detailed discussion of the construction of utopia in Tamil cinema, the relationship between consumption and utopia, and the role of spectacle and illusion in providing escape.

Melodrama and Popular Entertainment

The relationship between Tamil cinema's consumers and its producers, and the impact of this relationship on film content, is much as it is in popular entertainment elsewhere. One of the features of commercial entertainment with the greatest influence on content is the necessity for its producers to respond to a modicum of the entertainment desires, both conscious and unconscious, of their paying audience. Speaking of North Indian movies, Kakar has portrayed popular cinema as "a collective fantasy containing unconscious material and the hidden wishes of a vast number of people" (1981: 12). While the makers of popular cinema may have different "unconscious" desires and needs than their audiences, he argues, they are nonetheless motivated to discover prospective viewers' own needs by the goal of financial success:[8]

> The prospect of financial gain, like the opportunity for sexual liaison, does wonderful things for increasing the perception of the needs and desires of those who hold the key to these gratifications. The quest for the comforting sound of busy cash-registers at the box-office ensures that the film-makers develop a daydream which is not idiosyncratic. They must intuitively appeal to those concerns of the audience which are shared; if they do not, the film's appeal is bound to be disastrously limited. (ibid.: 12-13)

The dependence of filmmakers on healthy financial returns ensures that they will try to fill their movies with the elements that viewers consciously and unconsciously seek from entertainment. The creation of a successful movie does not, however, require satisfying *all* of a viewer's desires; rather, creators of film must simply ensure on the one hand that the movie's content does not clash with any of these desires too strongly, and on the other that a sufficient number of them are met with adequate force. As Dyer points out, while entertainment "responds to real needs *created by society*," it simultaneously defines and delimits "what constitutes the legitimate needs of people in this society" (1985: 228). The felt needs or concerns of the audience are not uniformly represented or expressed in popular movies. Producers and directors avoid some themes that might be of significant interest to audiences while also imposing themes that are peripheral to viewers' interests.

The form and content of Tamil cinema are highly melodramatic. Melodrama—a term that originally referred to a dramatic presentation interspersed with songs and music (a definition that still fits Tamil film)—today is generally regarded as any expressive form characterized by the sensational portrayal of and appeal to heightened emotions. Elsaesser argues that the social functions of melodrama have varied historically according to sociopolitical conditions, with the genre's importance peaking during "periods of intense social and ideological crisis" (1985: 167). Thus, for example, French melodrama prior to the French Revolution had "pointed to the arbitrary way feudal institutions could ruin the individual unprotected by civil rights and liberties," but dramas of the Restoration "functioned more as a means of consolidating an as yet weak and incoherent ideological position." While earlier melodramas were often tragic, those of the Restoration ended happily, reconciling "the suffering individual to his social position, by affirming an 'open' society, where everything was possible" (ibid.: 169).

The happy endings of these Restoration melodramas bear a significant resemblance to Tamil films, whose fortuitous resolutions may indicate an avoidance of the true conditions of most viewers' lives. Tamil cinema as a whole fits the category of reactionary cinema proposed by Wood (1985) in a critique of Western horror movies. Wood differentiates between progressive films—those whose tragic endings deny any possible escape from the confining situation constructed in the movie—and reactionary ones, which are characterized by happy endings and, like the Restoration melodrama, offer hope to viewers. I would concur with Wood to the extent that his perspective suggests that the happy endings of most Tamil films allay the anxieties of poor viewers by implying that the problems and contradictions of their lives can be resolved without effort. Viewers' reactions to such resolution will be discussed later; for the moment let me simply indicate that any overt or covert message along this line would be likely to suit the interests of middle- and upper-class filmmakers, who have a stake in viewers' acceptance of a comforting message that assists in the maintenance of the present social order.

Thus, as Dyer suggests, the selective response of filmmakers to the entertainment needs and desires of their audiences helps to define the category of legitimate viewer needs as dictated and accepted by the dominant class.[9] However, Tamil filmmakers also employ the apparently opposed tactic of portraying crises that resemble the difficulties faced in viewers' own lives. That is, while filmmakers reinforce the current social order by selecting themes that support it or encourage resignation to it, they also appear to challenge it by criticizing certain aspects of society. Films can "present basic social evils" even as they reinforce submission (Elsaesser 1985: 169). Audiences may pick up on criticism on one level as they absorb submissiveness and resignation on another. As Elsaesser points out, there is "a radical ambiguity attached to the melodrama . . . Depending on whether the emphasis fell on the odyssey of suffering or the happy ending . . . melodrama would appear to function either subversively or as escapism" (ibid.).

Whether a film encourages subversion or submission is dependent largely on whether and how the crises it portrays are resolved. The mechanisms of resolution in Tamil cinema are very similar, for example, to those that Elsaesser describes for melodramas of the French Restoration, in which

> complex social processes were simplified either by blaming the evil disposition of individuals or by manipulating the plots and engineering coinci-

dences and other *dei ex machina,* such as the instant conversion of the villain, moved by the plight of his victim, or suddenly struck by Divine Grace on the steps of Notre-Dame. (ibid.)

Such melodramatic conflict resolution, and its resultant happy ending, can be problematic, however. Because melodrama is based to some extent on reality, which is more typically filled with protracted crises than with divine bolts of lightning, the happy endings of most Tamil movies are achieved at the cost of repression—repression of real-life experiences, knowledge, and fears that would contradict the facility of the melodramatic solution (compare Nowell-Smith 1985: 193). Dyer, speaking of American musicals (whose "utopian sensibility" closely resembles that of Tamil films), emphasizes the problems created by the contradictions arising from the genre's tendency to press toward unrepresentative (i.e., "unrealistic") solutions for problems rooted in reality:

> To be effective, the utopian sensibility has to take off from the real experiences of the audience. Yet to do this, to draw attention to the gap between what is and what could be, is, ideologically speaking, playing with fire. What musicals have to do, then (not through any conspiratorial intent, but because it is always easier to take the line of least resistance, i.e., to fit in with prevailing norms), is to work through these contradictions at all levels in such a way as to 'manage' them, to make them seem to disappear. They don't always succeed. (1985: 228)

Because of the conflict between the "what is" in the viewer's experience and the "what could be" outcomes in movies, Tamil melodrama—as always incorporating both the reality and the fantasy—is internally contradictory. Melodrama can be said to do its "work" by successfully glossing over the contradictions, making life appear happy and life's problems easily soluble; it can also create a less soothing cover-up by allowing the contradiction to rupture the smooth surface of the film, either within the movie itself (leading to a tragic ending), or within the eyes of viewers when the attempted reconciliation is so transparent that the conflicts remain visible. While Tamil cinema embodies these contradictory aspects within each filmic text, most Tamil movies are structured such that chance, coincidence, or villainy makes a "true" resolution unnecessary—apparently circumventing the problem of contradiction—so that the contradiction need not be noted by the viewer. Instead, this type of melodrama offers viewers the delusion that the exposed problem is not a problem at all, or at least that it can be solved happily and its unpleasant ramifications avoided. Because filmmakers—who may not be quite as unconspiratorial as Dyer would have it—have crafted their films carefully to avoid creating social and psychological discontent (and, I believe, because they enjoy some viewer collusion in this), Tamil films almost always avoid the potential problems inherent in the mix of realistic concerns with fantastic solutions.

One of the reasons that viewers accept the sugarcoating of real-life problems is that the primary conscious motivation for watching movies is to escape from those very problems. Because of its gripping, absorbing nature, melodrama is particularly suited to offering this escape into another world (see, for example, Elsaesser 1985: 187). Furthermore, as Elsaesser puts it, melodrama steadfastly "refuses to understand social change in other than private contexts and emotional terms" (ibid.: 170). The problems portrayed in Tamil films derive from the real difficulties experienced by many urban poor viewers, as we will see, but are depicted in the very personal terms of individual film characters. This individualizing strategy ignores the social and political aspects and causes of the problems and thus reinforces the tendency of cinematic resolutions to disguise the nature and severity of the crises portrayed.

Here I should point out that in this sense, Tamil cinema typifies not only the "blind" for dominant ideology that numerous earlier analysts have identified in popular culture, but also more specifically typifies the genre of spectacle as Debord defines it. Debord portrays the language of spectacle as "*signs* of the ruling production" that unilaterally communicate the separation of classes (creators and spectators) (1983: §4, 24, 29). Indeed, Tamil cinema carries and communicates the ideology of its upper- and middle-class creators; and escape, of course, is not generally conceded as a revolutionary act. Examination of spectatorship reveals that the process of dialogue is more complex than this, however. I will return to questions of communicators and audiences, as well as to the other process of separation that Debord identifies in spectacle: the substitution of the appearance or image for reality. It is through this illusion that melodrama attracts viewers and provides escape.

Movie Themes and Crisis Resolution

Critics and analysts of melodrama often speak as if we must approach its viewers' motivation in one of two ways. As Filon phrased this dichotomy in 1897, audiences either "go to the theatre to see a representation of life, or to forget life and seek relief from it" (quoted in Elsaesser 1985: 188n). Are Tamil viewers, then, attracted to cinema because they see in it reflections of their own life circumstances, or because they see lives that are fantastically different from their own? In fact, as the preceding discussion suggests, neither realistic representation nor pure fantasy dominates melodrama's appeal; rather, it is based on a resolution of the two—a psychological resolution, that is, of crises deriving from real life that are resolved in exotic settings through unusual and unrealistic events.[10]

Tamil films combine elements of the realistic and the fantastic in settings, plots, and themes. Much of the setting is straight out of Tamils' daily lives—it is so familiar, in fact, as to be unremarkable to the typical viewer. Other elements of the set, however, are pointedly more luxurious or modern than most viewers have experienced in their own lives. Many film characters have cars, fancy furniture, and Western-style clothing, and the locales they move through are often exotic. (Even those movies with supposedly realistic settings, such as recent films shot in villages, are "hyperreal"—as one older English-speaking viewer put it—to the extent that their portrayals are actually romanticized or nostalgic stereotypes rather than accurate representations of most rural or urban environments.)[11] Plots and themes also mix realism and fantasy, thereby extending the surface departure from everyday life through melodramatic stories highly dependent upon coincidence.

Many of the film's events are sparked, and its characters motivated, however, by such familiar concerns as women yearning for children or parents wishing for their children's respect. Thus what we find is a blend of the familiar and the fantastic: while enough of the movies' content comes from the known world to make their scenarios identifiable, there is also sufficient dreamlike luxury and emotional passion for the film to function as an escape from the more oppressive features of that world. Both of these aspects aid in what I see as film's major psychological function—and one of its most appealing, albeit unconscious, attractions: the comfortingly easy dissolution of familiar psychological stresses.

These stresses derive from the economic and social insecurities I described earlier. In examining Tamil movies' central themes, it becomes apparent that they deal largely with social relationships and their psychological implications. Most concern one of two types of relationships: those between men and women, and those among family members. A third and smaller set deals with class identity and class relations. Examples of themes in the first set include the sacrifices and perseverance of a faithful wife; the transformation of a self-centered and erotic woman into a proper Tamil woman; and the dissolution of a happy family of men (or, by extension, the traditional joint family) because of a woman who marries into it. The second set includes such themes as, again, the breakup of the joint family; family members' transgressions of their duties toward one another; tensions between the demands of natal families and marital families; "love" marriages versus arranged marriages; and husbands' adultery. Finally, the third set includes comparisons of the "nature" of the rich and poor, the relative sophistication of each, and the value of their different types of education; tensions arising from interaction between lower-class and upper-class characters also receive some treatment.

Another group of recurrent themes has to do with issues that filmmakers, who explicitly portray themselves as moral guides for the masses, insert as didactic lessons for viewers. These "imposed" themes, as I have called them elsewhere (Dickey 1993a: 103-5), have largely to do with the evils of drugs and alcohol and the goodness of religious minorities. They were rarely mentioned by viewers in their discussions of films, and they have little to do with the most crucial concerns of most viewers' daily lives.

All of the three main sets of themes, however, represent areas about which urban poor Tamils experience some concern during their daily lives. Such anxieties contribute to the pervasive sense that life is insecure, and increasingly so. (While there may actually have been little or no change in the security of such areas as family and class relations in the relevant past, it is the *perception* that social and economic circumstances have become insecure and continue to deteriorate that is most salient to this analysis.) Rather than exacerbating anxiety, however, films ameliorate it by subsequently portraying solutions to the problems raised. But these resolutions are not realistic answers that could be applied in everyday life; instead, they are almost always dependent on a stroke of coincidence that magically wipes out the difficulty, making it appear that the crisis is not really a problem at all—and certainly not a problem worthy of concern or action. I will discuss the implications of this process of resolution, and the relationship between illusion and reality that it implies, after considering the salience that viewers recognize in the major themes of cinema and in the films themselves.

The View from the Audience

Viewers' comments demonstrate active engagement with and response to cinema. Many Tamils hold strong views on cinema, both negative and positive, and movies and actors are frequent topics of conversation among poor Madurai residents. While I found in my research that—thanks in large part to the disdain accorded cinema in public opinion—many people are unwilling to discuss the cinema in any formal context, such as with an unknown interviewer or in the presence of their elders, the subject often comes up in informal conversations.

The attitudes that viewers express in private conversations differ not only from some critics' and filmmakers' opinions but also from general public opinion, which holds cinema to be at best distasteful and at worst depraved. The public that holds this opinion includes all classes. Most poor respondents to a questionnaire administered by my lower-class assistant reported that cinema "makes people go bad." This is the respectable view (even among those who watch movies most frequently), and it is the only one that can be expressed outside of the company of close friends without risk of being accused (with varying degrees of derision) of "cinema madness." As the following discussion demonstrates, however, individual conversations rarely reflected such views.

I was told the stories of many movies while I was in Madurai. Those that were volunteered during the course of conversations or interviews were usually short and often ended with an interpretation of the movie's message or moral (*karuttu*). Those that I solicited were generally much longer in the telling, often taking half an hour to an hour. I asked for the film's "message" at the end of each of these, and most storytellers responded readily. It was clear that perceiving messages in films was a culturally appropriate way of thinking for many poor urban residents. They also had vociferous opinions about the effects of movies on viewers and the reasons for watching them.

My questions about connections between the movies and viewers' own lives, however, were not answered as readily, possibly because the fantasy cloaking events in films hinders such direct comparisons. Nonetheless, while this did not seem to be a subject that most people had given extensive consideration before, many of them did suggest some connections after brief reflection. While a few answered that no connections existed because films never showed ordinary, mundane lives like their own, and others pointed out that films about everyday life would not be exciting enough to make any money, most people identified specific similarities between their lives and the movies.

The details of these answers surprised me somewhat. Since the people in the neighborhoods I worked in often referred to categories such as "poor people like us" or "people who suffer like us," I had expected them to respond in class-related terms—something on the order of "movies do not show suffering people like us." Instead, most people answered in very personal, often role-related terms. A thirty-one-year-old woman of a lower-middle caste, for example, spoke of the film *From Six to Sixty* (*Aariliruntu Arupatu Varai*), whose hero educates and marries off his brothers and sisters at his wife's and children's expense, but is abandoned by the siblings when he becomes impoverished. She compared this to the ingratitude that she and her husband have received from his coresident siblings, whose marriages her husband had arranged and financed but who now refuse to contribute any money to household expenses. Another woman, sixty years old and of an upper-middle caste, told me that the characters of the film *Life* (*Vaazhkai*), who fail to care for their aging parents, are just like her wealthy sons, whom she and her husband had given everything possible but who now lie about their money and refuse to care for their parents. A scheduled-caste (Untouchable) man of about forty-five years, a friend's husband who openly met with his mistress, told me that films reveal that men often go after women other than their wives. This creates trouble at home because the husband spends all his money on another woman and there is no money for the children's care. The films show that there are many consequences to such action, he said, and that the husband and wife should live happily together.

These examples illustrate Tamil filmgoers' tendency to make comparisons between the movies and their own lives in terms of very specific personal relationships. Rather than identify themselves in this case with a larger unit such as a caste or class, these viewers think in terms of the relationships between themselves and a brother, their children, their in-laws, or a wife. Other informants made comparisons to their relationships with husbands and parents. All of these are close family relations, and the reports reflect difficulties and anxieties about them—the same types of concerns reflected in movie themes that address relations between men and women and among family members. If, as I have suggested, such themes do parallel issues in viewers' lives, viewers seem to have some awareness of this connection. Viewers' relatively slow responses to questions about these connections, however, imply that such connections normally remain out of the forefront of consciousness, which may help keep the urgency of conflicts in these relationships from disturbing the pleasure viewers feel in escaping them when watching a film.

These issues, along with those concerning class identity and relations, are also echoed in viewers' reports about the central moral of a movie. One young middle-caste man told me that the theme of the film *The East Side of Amman Temple* (*Amman Koovil Kizhakkaalee*) was "the glory" of the wedding emblem, the *thali,* which was tied violently around the heroine's neck and effected her transition from spoiled brash girl to modest Tamil wife. Emphasizing a wife's duty to persevere in her sacrifices for her husband, a newly married thirty-year-old upper-caste woman described the story of *The Hearts of Two People* (*Iruvar Ullam*). In this instance, she said, a husband changes his bad character after marriage, but his wife refuses to accept that he could change; when he is later (mistakenly?) arrested, she recognizes her error in judgment and admits his good character. The theme of this film, according to the storyteller, was that a patient woman can change her husband's character. This woman's sister, a forty-year-old widow, told me the story of her favorite film, *Honor of the First Order* (*Mutal Mariyaatai*), in which the affection between an older upper-caste man and a young scheduled-caste woman is eventually recognized by the two of them and validated emotionally, if not consummated physically. This film, she said, teaches that "there is no bar or age limit to love."

A middle-aged upper-caste woman described the film *Poems of the Seashore* (*Kataloora Kavitaikal*), explaining that its theme stresses how an educated young woman helps a rough young man even though he is illiterate. After recounting the story—in which the poor Hindu hero and the middle-class Christian heroine have fallen in love while their unknowing parents arrange for each to marry someone of their own community—she commented on the feelings of and social disparity between the two lovers:

> He is her love. She should not leave him. It is not proper to accept the educated and leave the uneducated. In the end there is this theme: an educated girl has loved a rough fellow. Even though he acts badly, she comes to know that he is really good.

Here we see two issues at work. Like the woman who described *Honor of the First Order*, this woman claimed the film teaches that love can occur across such social boundaries as caste and education; moreover, she asserted, once the bond of love has united the lovers, it supersedes the relationships that would normally be socially prescribed. Also noted is the worthiness of the uneducated. She stressed that the uneducated are good *inside*—the true measure of worth—despite a sometimes rough surface or exterior, and that they should be given the same consideration as the educated.

A number of people commented that the film *Illiterate Fellow* (*Patikkaatavan*), whose hero is an uneducated but hardworking and honest young man, had a similar point. One young scheduled-caste man said that "it shows how we poor have good hearts and minds. We are better than the rich people who have cars and fancy clothes." Others emphasized the film's focus on the severing and reconnection of family ties. In this vein, one young man commented:

When the brothers are young, their elder brother's wife beats them in anger and drives them out. But in Madras they are taken in by another man. The love of Rajnikanth [the hero] for his brother is great. Through his own efforts he gives his brother a respectable position, but the brother doesn't respect [what he is given]. He speaks hurtfully to Rajnikanth, that is, like a child who rejects its mother. In the end, all the brothers unite (*ceerntuvaarkal*).

Significantly, no parallel statements were ever made about "imposed" themes such as the dangers of alcohol, whether in discussing movies' morals or their connections with viewers' lives. While viewers never to my knowledge rejected a film because it contained such themes, they clearly did not accept the themes themselves as appealing or of great value.

I should repeat at this point that the majority of statements made by poor urban viewers about movies' morals and the connections with their own lives had to do with personal relationships, many of them criticizing the moral failings of close relatives. A sizable portion of respondents also made some comment on the injustice of the ways in which the poor are treated and portrayed by the rich and argued for the moral superiority of the poor over the rich. Despite deeply felt protests against its effects, however, few if any viewers suggested that the class system itself is immoral. Viewers hoped to improve their position within the hierarchy, or to eradicate negative stereotypes of the poor—wishes that are fulfilled, as we have seen, in some movie themes—but never suggested the eradication of class.

Viewers see the intended purpose of filmgoing as a means of passing time (*pozhutu pookku*) or of escaping (*tappu*) from the boredom or worries of daily life. As a widowed friend put it:

When my husband was alive, we were happy, and we went only to good movies. Now I go when I'm bored. Sitting there for a few hours, my worries get a little smaller (*kavalai koncam kuraivu pookum*). That's why I go. When I'm worried and I go, then I get a little bit happier.

Viewers almost never suggest, for example, that they go to the movies to learn something. Most of them, however, do believe that cinema can serve a purpose, or have effects, other than the immediate and conscious ones that draw viewers to watch the movies. Such effects, they say, can be either positive or negative, depending on the type of movie and the particular viewer's personality.

This interaction of the film and the individual was first expressed explicitly during a conversation with a forty-year-old upper-caste woman. I asked if she thought that films had any influence on the people who watched them:

A: Yes. It makes for hardship in the families. When someone sees a film, they may get a great desire to see more. If the family is in difficulty, they do not have any money, but the person will want to go to movies all the time anyway. This creates hardship because of the desire and because of the money it takes from the family. In another family, the husband and wife may fight because of movies. She wants to go to them, but he says she can't, or maybe he says that she can go only once a month or once a week. If she goes anyway, after he has gone to work, and he finds out, then they will fight.

Someone else can see a family film and see how they should live. They come home and decide that that is how their family should be, that is how they should raise their children, that is how the husband and wife should act. They decide not to fight anymore. But someone else sees a very bad picture, and because of it they act badly. They go bad. They treat their family badly, and their family members won't act well.

Q: How is this?

A: If they see someone [in the movie] with another man's wife, or drinking illicit liquor, or with other bad habits.

Q: Everyone?

A: No—usually good families won't see bad movies. Ninety percent of people see movies and improve. Ten percent see them and go bad. If a good person sees a bad movie, they won't go bad.

I heard many similar statements suggesting that the potential influence of cinema depended on the nature of the person watching it. One of them came from a twenty-nine-year-old middle-caste man, who told me that most movies have a message for one or two people in each family. When I asked him if this meant that these messages or morals would have any influence on filmgoers, he said that they would have some effect on reflective people but none on bad people, who either would not recognize the message or would reject it.

Thus most people saw cinema as having a variable influence dependent on each viewer's innate propensity for good or bad and, perhaps, for self-reflection. It should also be mentioned, however, that a few people rejected the idea of "mixed" effects. While almost no lower-class Tamils ascribed invariably negative effects to films, some saw cinema as having a profoundly positive influence on society. One older scheduled-caste man, for example, claimed that cinema keeps people out of trouble by giving them something to do with their free time. Without cinema, he said, "everyone will be in jail. That's the effect of film. Without cinema, there would be no country (*naatu*), no people (*makkal*)."

Others argued that it was impossible to determine what cinema's influence was, since the audience had as much effect on films as films had on the audience. An upper-caste woman made this point elegantly, explaining: "Directors take from real life and society, then we see the movies and learn from them. It's like adding water to milk—you can't tell which is which." Still others denied that cinema had any influence at all. One of them, a young middle-caste man who reported seeing fifteen films a month, told me that "we cannot say that they [viewers] become bad just by seeing the films. We go bad on our own. Nor can we say that movies improve people.... The filmmakers create their films from watching *us*. We are not going bad from seeing the films."

The comments reported in this section illustrate a number of points concerning the audience's perception of and reaction to cinema that are significant for this analysis. Viewers actively evaluate what they see on screen and reject films or film elements that seem either too realistic or too remote from real-life interests. They seek out the movies as entertainment and as an escape from the difficulties of their lives. This desire for escape does not suggest, however, that they view what goes on in the movies as completely disconnected from their lives. Rather, they see very personal connections between themselves and their relationships, on the one hand, and the characters and relationships shown on the screen on the other. In reporting movie stories they focus on themes that address these relationships and issues of class identity. These poignant issues are central to poor Tamils' lives: they involve among other things the effects of marriage on individuals and families, possibilities for romantic love, the responsibilities of children and siblings, and the disregarded inner virtues of the poor. The films create utopic resolutions of these issues, as we will see. Escape and reality are intimately connected.

Viewers also believe that watching the movies and seeing situations that speak to their own circumstances can have effects on behavior. Many of these effects will be positive, but the nature and occurrence of cinema's behavioral influence depend in the last instance on each viewer's preexisting character. Good people will probably improve; bad people may become worse. Viewers' own statements thus contradict critics' claims that filmgoing has pervasively pernicious effects. Some even argue that going to the cinema is a more personally and socially beneficial activity than most of the other time-filling options available to poor urban residents.[12] In filmgoers' eyes, then, participation in this arena of public culture can have lasting and often positive effects. Clearly there is a discrepancy between what is admitted in informal or intimate contexts to represent viewers' personal feelings and what is recognized to constitute the "proper" attitude toward cinema.

A Taste of Utopia

We have seen that Tamil movies mix elements of fantasy and reality in their sets, plots, and themes. Thematically, they combine representations of familiarly realistic individual and social problems with fantastical resolutions of those problems. Elements of fantasy are also often found in the ways in which familiar problems are portrayed, in that the contexts in which movie crises arise are rarely identical to the actual physical or behavioral environments of lower-class Tamils' lives.

Dyer suggests that popular entertainment offers its consumers a vision of utopia,

> the image of 'something better' to escape into, or something we want deeply that our day-to-day lives don't provide. Alternatives, hopes, wishes—these are the stuff of utopia, the sense that things could be better, that something other than what is can be imagined and maybe realised. (1985: 222)

In order to do this, Dyer maintains, entertainment provides not *models* of utopia but a sense of how utopia would *feel.*

Tamil cinema corroborates this contention. It provides viewers with a sense of utopia in two ways: through a portrayal of luxury that far exceeds the circumstances of most Tamils' lives; and through resolutions of many of viewers' most persistent and deep-seated anxieties, some of which are brought about by the hard physical circumstances of their lives, which contrast so thoroughly with the spectacular abundance of the movies. While on the surface these two routes to utopia may appear distinct, one relying as it does on material setting and the other on emotional resolution, it quickly becomes evident that they cannot be split so clearly. Instead, the momentary vision of abundance is a *part* of the message. Films, that is, do not simply provide their audiences with a momentary experience of luxury and ease— they also suggest that wealth and the comforts it buys are within reach. As Enzensberger has put it, "Consumption as spectacle contains the promise that want will disappear. . . . [It is] the anticipation of a utopian situation" (1982: 61). Movies are not just a three-hour relief from poverty; they also feed hopes that a spectacularly easier life is attainable.

While this would suggest that films encourage people to desire or hope for better lives, albeit without offering the means of active change, the deeper mechanisms of the films—the workings of their story themes, which both incorporate and are embedded in spectacular surroundings—largely act to pacify viewers in their present circumstances. Most themes, as we have seen, allay anxieties and promote a sense that life, free from many of its conflicts and difficulties, is already "utopian." In order to clarify the mechanisms by which problems stemming from daily life are resolved in Tamil movies, I will review this process using some typical themes as illustration.

As I noted earlier, the three most typical categories of film themes involve relations between men and women, relations among family members, and class relations and identity. One of the most frequent themes of the first set (in fact, of Tamil cinema overall) is that of a woman sacrificing her desires or interests for those of a man. It often revolves around a woman's attempts to transform her husband's misbehavior (such as drunkenness or neglect of his family) and win his love and attention. The tension between the woman's sacrifices and desires and the behavior of her husband is typically resolved when the husband reforms (sometimes as a direct result of his wife's selflessness) and returns to the faithful woman to be fully hers.

The image of this ideal woman is also involved in the resolution of another theme: the metamorphosis of a self-centered, arrogant woman into a properly demure Tamil wife. This theme addresses viewers' concerns about the perceived enhancement of women's power relative to that of men, and about issues of female sexuality. The modern, alluring heroine represents the (potential or actual) women that men encounter as a threat to male social and sexual dominance. This woman may be physically desirable but her behavior is frighteningly unfamiliar to most men. Through some external agent—frequently the act of marriage, in which the *thali* (tied by the husband during the marriage ceremony) serves as a central cultural symbol of men's binding control over women's disruptive power and sexuality—the heroine is instantaneously converted into the reassuring form of demure Tamil womanhood.[13]

Women may also be objects of anxious concern to both men and other women when they marry into a family. Often this is realized in films in the form of the wife/sister-in-law who instigates the breakup of a joint family. The power of such women is ultimately overriden by brothers or father or mother, and the film ends with the family reuniting. Such results offer the hope that family bonds, which Tamils perceive to be loosening, will regain their preeminence over extrafamilial concerns and cause family members to accept the responsibilities that they should bear.

Other concerns about the family are also salved by movies. Films may reinforce the ideal that a husband will have preeminence in his wife's eyes over the family she has grown up with, assuage fears that a young man will transfer his feelings and responsibilities from his natal family to his marital household, and promise that adulterous husbands will leave their mistresses and return to their wives and children.

Another issue that links concerns for the family with worries about male-female relationships is the emphasis on "love" marriages rather than the traditional arranged marriages (the latter being overwhelmingly predominant in real life). Unlike most earlier movies, current films usually present positive outcomes for these nonarranged relationships. Successful love relationships appear in almost every current Tamil film. Such depictions may comfort viewers or give them hope in two ways: first, they support the hopes many viewers hold for increased romance in their own lives;[14] and second, for younger viewers they may represent the fulfillment of their rebellion against parental restraints, and possibly of more general individual rebellion against wider societal constraints.

Themes portraying class identity and class relations tend to resolve concerns about discrepancies between rich and poor. They demonstrate the superiority of the inner greatness that characterizes the poor over the "surface" advantages attained through the money of the rich. Thus, a film like *Illiterate Fellow* implies the ultimate "worthiness" of the poor and uneducated through its portrayal of the hero, who is an honest, hardworking, devoted, and finally victorious archetype of the poor. His righteous nature is contrasted with the greed, arrogance, and deceit of the rich. Other films also suggest that the "natural" and often nonformal education of the disadvantaged should be compared favorably to the formal academic learning of the wealthy. Occasionally films also deal specifically with the relations between classes, portraying tensions between rich and poor based on cultural, economic, and moral differences; their lower-class heroes ultimately triumph over the degradations heaped on them by the upper class.

The lesson in these representations of class relations and identity is that despite the apparent advantages of the wealthy, it is the poor who possess true goodness of character. Moreover, wealth may not even be desirable, since its holders are typically short on moral qualities; at the least, the goodness of character of the poor compensates for their lack of luxury and social graces, making them the "better people." Finally, these films show that the poor *will* eventually receive justice (whatever the viewer may construe this to be) because of their truly good nature, and—it is hinted in more than one case—because God is on their side.

I have suggested that these movies correspond to Wood's category of "reactionary" films. By offering a view of society in which viewers' hopes are fulfilled and their problems dissolved, most Tamil films suggest either that life will become better without active struggle on the part of the downtrodden or that the virtues of a life of poverty outweigh its disadvantages. Husbands will reform and children will honor their parents, and riches may appear but are superfluous at any rate because the poor already possess a true wealth of spirit. In the themes of the reactionary film, utopia either will arrive on its own or has already been achieved.[15]

Viewers themselves often reject tragic films and others whose endings leave them feeling dissatisfied. They also say that they do not like to watch movies in which problems are shown "realistically." They criticize these films as uninteresting. Filmmakers are aware of this and portray crises in settings that are exotically removed from most viewers' daily lives. Thus, for example, an independent young woman is more powerful than her suitor because she is much richer; a woman's husband rejects her and takes a mistress who is a beautiful Carnatic singer; a young man is poor because in childhood he ran away from his cruel sister-in-law, and is ridiculed by the younger brother for whom he has provided a college education.[16] Each of these difficulties has its frequent correlates in poor viewers' lives, but virtually never in the glamorized or melodramatic form found in films. Greater realism than this is rejected by most Tamil viewers, for whom fantasy is preferred not only at the level of resolution but also in the portrayal of problems in order for the film to work as an escape from those problems. Escape, as we have seen, is the primary conscious motivation for viewers' attendance at the movies.

Films provide relief from viewers' immediate and long-term worries in several ways. At the very least, a three-hour movie provides physical and emotional separation from the quotidian context of those worries. I have suggested, however, that the relief gained in the cinema hall also persists outside of it, carried into the everyday world. Tamil movies almost always have happy endings. After the villains have been killed or converted, hero and heroine joined in love, and wayward family members reunited in a palatial setting, viewers may leave feeling supported in their hopes for an easier life. Films offer hope that wealth will appear and problems disappear—though there is not *necessarily* a causal link between the two—all without active effort on the viewer's part. Most of all, however, the melodramatic portrayal and resolution of crises in Tamil films allays some of the audience's deepest anxieties—about relationships between men and women or among family members and about the problems of lower-class identity—making life at least temporarily less stressful. This process of resolution also suggests that, since these problems are not truly problems after all and the poor have the best of life, life is already good. Both visions, of abundance to come and of present satisfaction, are utopian.

Because the first formulation suggests that the riches the poor desire will shower down while the other urges an inversion of normal status hierarchies to suggest that the poor are better than the rich and thus that wealth is superfluous, these two utopian visions conflict. This paradox is rarely if ever addressed in films, however, which offer both messages within the same text. The implicit assumption appears to be that the greater the number of sources of comfort the better.

The successful resolution of movie crisis/viewer anxiety is based on a critical balance between fantasy and reality. In order to allow viewers to escape from the insecurities of real life, the concerns dealt with in movies must draw from those very insecurities so that the problems in movies can stand for the real ones in a recognizable way. That they do so is clear from the connections viewers have noted between their own lives and movies. Both the portrayal and the resolution of those problems, however, must be clothed with sufficient fantasy to allow an escape from the insecurities they draw on. Thus the ambiguous status of the image, the illusion that Debord sees at the heart of spectacle: here it must both mimic reality and differ crucially from it if it is to provide escape. Escape is constituted by substituting the image for reality—a process that may be more active than Debord believes, and certainly is more *desired* by spectators than in his portrayal. Modern-day participants in spectacle, including Tamil film watchers, want illusion, enjoy playing with the image. While the resolutions and resultant "escape" provided by illusion do not encourage viewers to achieve their goals through extracinematic effort—corroborating by omission the general belief that effort aimed at removing or modifying the causes of insecurity rarely bears results—and while viewers' comments likewise reflect little challenge to the social order, it is nonetheless clear that, in MacAloon's words, "the image of the passive victim will not now do" (1984: 271).

Similarly, the communication that takes place between audiences and creators of spectacle is in no sense unidirectional. Film themes and viewers' responses to them make it difficult to agree with Debord's contention that in spectacle, "one part of the world *represents itself* to the world and is superior to it" (Debord 1983: §30). Spectacle does objectify, does externalize, does remove the viewer from action, but, in the first place, much of what is objectified is not only what the filmmaker urges on the viewer but also what viewers have demanded as a vision of their *own* lives; and second, as with any other form of expressive culture, what is portrayed becomes a part of the

public sphere, to be discussed, applied, perhaps manipulated back into viewers' lives, potentially effecting change. I have already suggested that participation in spectacle may involve a dual role—that of seeing and being seen—
and it appears that participation may be dual in another way as well: when
the image stands for the self. Spectacle works as escape partly because viewers are watching *themselves*—because they can temporarily replace their real
selves with the image they see. The question of who speaks to whom becomes less clear-cut. In other areas of public culture as well, such as tourism,
consumers may simultaneously become spectators of themselves,[17] and the
line between creator, actor, and spectator blurs.

At the beginning I stated that this essay aimed to explore the significance
of Tamil cinema for its urban poor viewers. While the significance appears
to lie largely in an escape constituted through utopian fantasy, the pleasure
of that escape derives from its roots in real-life social and psychological
stresses and from the soothing of those stresses through melodramatic resolution of crises. This connection between escape and reality also appears in
viewers' ready distillation and application of morals from film stories and in
the concrete connections they see between those stories and their own lives.

The split between image and reality repeats in other aspects of cinema,
and indeed is sufficiently frequent that we may ask whether such a split or
contradiction is central to the pleasure that Tamil and perhaps other cinemas offer. It is found in the contradiction between the privately acknowledged pleasure found in cinema and the publicly espoused disdain for this
low-culture entertainment. The disdain is associated with the ideologically
dominant middle class, and, regardless of whether it is originally adopted
from that source, reflects a conflict between pride in one's own culture and
desire for distance from that culture, a distance achieved by voicing high-
culture tastes (see Bourdieu 1984).[18] This split is identical to that found in
the films' utopian formula, divided between glorification of a present that
needs no transformation and promises to transform the present into a glorious future.[19] Movies suggest that life is fine now, in no need of change since
the poor already possess the best aspects of life (morality and strength of
character), and *simultaneously* that present difficulties will soon be resolved
without effort and will be replaced by abundance (material wealth). Thus we
might say that the image does not so much replace reality as divide itself into
(present) reality and (future) fantasy. Pleasure is here intensified by the understanding that even if the everyday world does not turn out to be perfect,
the future will, and vice versa. Viewers are not urged by film to create a
utopia in the "real" world; rather, in a medium where even the realest reality

is somewhat fantastic, the activity (and pleasure) of the viewer is comprised of seeking out the utopian image of self.

Notes

1. The field research for this essay was carried out primarily in Madurai, a city with a population nearing one million, in the southern state of Tamil Nadu, between October 1985 and January 1987 and in May-June 1990. Brief periods were also spent meeting with film industry members in Madras. I am indebted to Carol Breckenridge, Arjun Appadurai, and F. G. Bailey for their valuable comments on this essay.

2. Most years, India produces more films than any other country (see, for example, Dharap 1985: 626; Thomas 1985: 116), and of the three major centers for film production within India—Madras, Bombay, and Calcutta—the Madras industry is the largest in terms of number of studios, capital investment, gross income, and number of people engaged in production, and it is consistently at or near the top in terms of number of films produced (Hardgrave and Neidhart 1975; Barnouw and Krishnaswamy 1980: 294-95; Guy 1985: 463). It has been reported that one-fourth of all India's cinema houses are in the state of Tamil Nadu (Hardgrave and Neidhart 1975: 27), a figure that industry members told me in 1986 had, if anything, risen. It has also been claimed that film has penetrated Tamil society "more deeply than the society of any other state in India" (Forrester 1976: 288).

3. Other areas in which the poor become involved in public consumption and display, albeit to a limited extent, include tourism (almost always religious pilgrimage) and fashion.

4. One reason for the lower impact of video on the South Indian industry may be the large proportion of the audience made up of members of the lower class, most of whom in the late 1980s still had little access to video.

5. Wiebe has reported similar sentiments among tenement residents in Madras, who state that they are economically worse off than their parents were. They "recall life as being 'easy' in those days," when the cost of living was lower, families were more supportive,"and so on," and now express discontent with their occupations, levels of education, and economic security (Wiebe 1981: 127-29).

6. For a strikingly similar view from a Western social scientist, see Pfleiderer 1985: 108.

7. Among these recent works are Enzensberger 1982; Lombardi-Satriani 1974; Hall and Jefferson 1976; Hebdige 1979; Radway 1984; Ang 1985; Limón 1989; and Walsh 1989. See also de Lauretis 1984 (38). Most of these works skirt the issue of pleasure; Radway and Ang, as well as Mulvey 1975 and 1981, are exceptions. A new turn in the dialectic can be seen in the edited volumes of Modleski (1986) and MacCabe (1986) and the writing of Stam (1988), which argue that some writers have now gone too far in perceiving empowerment in expressive forms. In the field of Indian cinema, the primary exception to the rule is Thomas 1985.

8. Ang (1985: 23-24) makes a similar argument, although without the psychoanalytic emphasis.

9. This point assumes filmmakers' membership—or aspirations to membership—in the dominant class. The assumption is merited in Tamil Nadu. It should be pointed out, however, that dominant class standing does not necessitate that filmmakers support their class and its ideology in their films. The 1960s saw sustained and trenchant social criticism in Tamil cinema—although much if not all of it was made with an eye to attracting audiences who had become enamored of the DMK party and its populist rhetoric.

10. In an analysis of the appeal of the American television series *Dallas* for Dutch audiences, Ang answers this question by arguing that while the program is not "true to life" in "concrete living circumstances," it nonetheless possesses "emotional realism" (1985: 44-45).

11. Roberge has likewise argued that "in conventional [Indian] cinema . . . a sham naturalism masquerades as 'realism'" (1985: 34).

12. Such opinions contrast strongly with those of many directors, who contend that, while filmmakers have a moral responsibility to enlighten the masses, most films nonetheless are filled with violent and sexual elements that corrupt rather than educate viewers (who, in this formulation, are responsible for demanding these titillating elements in the first place; see Dickey 1993a).

13. On the significance of binding symbolism in marriage, see Reynolds 1980.

14. For a discussion of love marriages in films and the importance of romance for Tamil viewers, see Dickey 1993a.

15. Lest it seem that all Tamil movies paint a monolithically rosy picture, I should note that films that could be categorized as "progressive" occasionally appear as well, and can be successful. These include two films that appeared while I was first in the field, *A Wife Is Electricity* (*Camsaaram Atu Minsaaram*) and *Lord of Smiles* (*Punnakai Mannan*). In the first, a joint family splits up and, although its former members become reconciled, they fail to reestablish a joint household as would happen in a more typical Tamil film. In the second movie, the love relationship established in the course of the film ends in the death of the couple. Such endings are rare today, however. The decision to give a story a happy or a tragic ending rests with the filmmaker, who is rarely motivated to suggest that viewers' lives are unsatisfactory or lack hope.

16. These situations appear in the films *The East Side of Amman Temple* (*Amman Koovil Kizhakkaalee*), *Sindhu Bairavi* (*Cintu Pairavi*), and *Illiterate Fellow* (*Patikkaatavan*), respectively, all of which appeared while I was in Madurai in 1985 and 1986.

17. See Carol Breckenridge and Arjun Appadurai's introduction to this volume.

18. Spectacle and illusion may help us to account for the degraded status of cinema in the realm of public culture. MacAloon (1984) has chronicled well the modern disdain for the "purely" or "merely" spectacular. Tamil cinema is gaudy, bawdy, and full of a fantasy based in large part on the consumption so conspicuous within cinema. Cinema is thus seen as superficial, and consumption *of* cinema as wasteful, excessive, and escapist. It is also disparaged purely for its public nature—not only because of the public crowds but also because of the indecent public display made by performers (a display particularly decried, nowadays, for actresses). While the desire for illusion and escape are sufficient to persuade many to partake in the public spectacle, others who can afford separation choose to participate in the spectacle only privately. In examining public culture, we may find that those who enjoy participating in public consumption when consumption is strictly limited by income or other markers of prestige—as, for example, in finer restaurants—will prefer to consume in private when access to the public sphere is not so limited.

19. Similar conflicts between identification with and distancing from the lower class can be seen throughout activities connected with the cinema. The conflict appears, for example, in the attributes praised in movie stars, in fan club service activities for the poor, and in voting preferences for movie star-politicians (see Dickey 1993a, 1993b).

References

Ang, Ien. 1985. *Watching Dallas.* Translated by Della Couling. London: Methuen.

Barnouw, Erik, and S. Krishnaswamy. 1980. *Indian Film.* 2d ed. New York: Oxford University Press.

Bourdieu, Pierre. 1984. *Distinction.* Translated by Richard Nice. Cambridge, Mass.: Harvard University Press.

Debord, Guy. 1983. *The Society of the Spectacle.* Detroit: Red and Black.

de Lauretis, Teresa. 1984. *Alice Doesn't.* Bloomington: Indiana University Press.

Dharap, B. V. 1985. "Facts and Figures about the Industry." In *70 Years of Indian Cinema (1913-1983)*, edited by T. N. Ramachandran, p. 626. Bombay: CINEMA India-International.

Dickey, Sara A. 1989. Accommodation and Resistance: Expression of Working Class Values through Tamil Cinema. *Wide Angle* 11 (3): 26-32.

——. 1993a. *Cinema and the Urban Poor in South India.* Cambridge: Cambridge University Press.

——. 1993b. The Politics of Adulation: Cinema and the Production of Politicians in South India. *Journal of Asian Studies* 52 (2): 340-72.

Dyer, Richard. 1985. "Entertainment and Utopia." In *Movies and Methods: An Anthology,* vol. 2, edited by B. Nichols, pp. 220-32. Berkeley: University of California Press.

Elsaesser, Thomas. 1985. "Tales of Sound and Fury: Observations on the Family Melodrama." In *Movies and Methods: An Anthology,* vol. 2, edited by B. Nichols, pp. 165-89. Berkeley: University of California Press.

Enzensberger, Hans Magnus. 1982. "Constituents of a Theory of the Media." Translated by Stuart Hood. In *Hans Magnus Enzensberger: Critical Essays,* edited by R. Grimm and B. Armstrong, pp. 46-76. New York: Continuum.

Filon, Pierre Marie Augustin. 1897. *The English Stage. Being an Account of the Victorian Drama.* Translated by Frederic Whyte. London: J. Milne.

Forrester, Duncan. 1976. Factions and Filmstars: Tamil Nadu Politics since 1971. *Asian Survey* 16: 283-96.

Guy, Randor. 1985. "Tamil Cinema." In *70 Years of Indian Cinema (1913-1983),* edited by T. N. Ramachandran, pp.462-75. Bombay: CINEMA India-International.

Hall, Stuart, and Tony Jefferson, eds. 1976. *Resistance through Ritual.* London: Hutchinson, in association with the Centre for Contemporary Cultural Studies, University of Birmingham.

Hardgrave, Robert L. Jr., and Anthony C. Neidhart. 1975. Films and Political Consciousness in Tamil Nadu. *Economic and Political Weekly* 10 (1/2): 27-35.

Hebdige, Dick. 1979. *Subculture: The Meaning of Style.* London: Methuen.

Kakar, Sudhir. 1981. The Ties That Bind: Family Relationships in the Mythology of Hindi Cinema. *India International Centre Quarterly* 8 (1): 11-21.

Krishen, Pradip. 1981. Introduction. *India International Centre Quarterly* 8 (1): 3-9.

Limón, Jose. 1989. *Carne, Carnales,* and the Carnivalesque: Bakhtinian *Batos,* Disorder, and Narrative Discourses. *American Ethnologist* 16 (3): 471-86.

Lombardi-Satriani, Luigi. 1974. Folklore as Culture of Contestation. *Journal of the Folklore Institute* 11 (1/2): 99-121.

MacAloon, John J. 1984. "Olympic Games and the Theory of Spectacle in Modern Societies." In *Rite, Drama, Festival, Spectacle,* edited by J. J. MacAloon, pp. 241-80. Philadelphia: ISHI.

MacCabe, Colin, ed. 1986. *High Culture/Low Theory.* New York: St. Martin's.

Modleski, Tania, ed. 1986. *Studies in Entertainment.* Bloomington: Indiana University Press.

Mulvey, Laura. 1975. Visual Pleasure and Narrative Cinema. *Screen* 16 (3).

——. 1981. Afterthoughts on "Visual Pleasure and Narrative Cinema" Inspired by *Duel in the Sun* (King Vidor, 1946). *Framework,* no. 15/16/17.

Nowell-Smith, Geoffrey. 1985. "Minnelli and Melodrama." In *Movies and Methods: An Anthology,* vol. 2, edited by B. Nichols, pp. 190-94. Berkeley: University of California Press.

Pfleiderer, Beatrix. 1985. "An Empirical Study of Urban and Semi-Urban Audience Reactions to Hindi Films." In *The Hindi Film,* edited by B. Pfleiderer and L. Lutze, pp.81-130. New Delhi: Manohar.

Radway, Janice. 1984. *Reading the Romance: Women, Patriarchy, and Popular Literature.* Chapel Hill: University of North Carolina Press.

Reynolds, Holly Baker. 1980. "The Auspicious Married Woman." In *The Powers of Tamil Women,* edited by S. S. Wadley, pp. 35-60. Syracuse, N.Y.: Maxwell School, Syracuse University.

Roberge, Gaston. 1985. *Another Cinema for Another Society.* Calcutta: Seagull.

Stam, Richard. 1988. "Mikhail Bakhtin and Left Cultural Critique." In *Postmodernism and Its Discontents,* edited by E. Ann Kaplan. New York: Verso.

Thomas, Rosie. 1985. Indian Cinema: Pleasures and Popularity. *Screen* 26 (3/4): 116-31.

Walsh, Andrea. 1989. "Life Isn't Yet Over": Older Heroines in American Popular Cinema of the 1930s and 1970s/80s. *Qualitative Sociology* 12 (1): 72-95.

Wiebe, Paul D. 1981. *Tenants and Trustees: A Study of the Poor in Madras.* Delhi: Macmillan India.

Williams, Raymond. 1977. *Marxism and Literature.* Oxford: Oxford University Press.

——. 1982. *The Sociology of Culture.* New York: Schocken.

Wood, Robin. 1985. "An Introduction to the American Horror Film." In *Movies and Methods: An Anthology,* vol. 2, edited by B. Nichols, pp. 195-220. Berkeley: University of California Press.

CHAPTER SEVEN

Melodrama and the Negotiation of Morality in Mainstream Hindi Film

ROSIE THOMAS

Mother is in peril, threatened by a villain who is—unbeknown to him—her own lost son, kidnapped as a child and brought up by villains. He has bound her, gagged her, and hung her from a tree. Should the barrel at her feet begin to roll, she will inevitably be strangled by the rope around her neck. Moreover, the barrel is full of petrol, the hillside is strewn with straw, and the villain has a flaming torch . . .

It is a predictably uncomfortable moment of Hindi cinema: the moral universe is grossly violated and the disorder apparently irresolvable.

In many ways this one image (drawn from a comparatively successful 1979 film, *Kartavya* [Duty; producer and director Mohan Segal]) encapsulates a central dynamic of mainstream Indian cinema as a genre: the still works as a kind of trailer, which is both a condensation of a number of themes—working on many different levels—and the proposal of an enigma or tension that can be resolved only by seeing the film(s). While the image will be discussed in more detail later, it is at present simply relevant to note the coding of good and evil and the implicit moral framework around which notions of "tradition," "modernity," and "Indianness" are articulated. Mother, as usual, wears strictly "traditional" Indian dress: a white sari, *suhaagmala*, and *kangans*.[1] The villain sports a black leather jacket, an ostentatious gold medallion, and a watch. He is bearded and holds a large gun. While at one level this clearly suggests the fight between good and evil, as an image it works on a number of levels and can be seen to speak of the vulnerability of "tradition" and the motherland in the face of the Western Other. Mother, as a fount of love, protection, traditional morality, and Indian culture, is rendered speechless and helpless by an aggressive West but remains nevertheless a proud, statuesque figure, stalwartly awaiting her trial by fire—which of course can only test and prove her purity and ultimate impregnability.

I will argue in this essay that mainstream Hindi cinema is a central arena for the definition and celebration of a modern Indian identity, working to negotiate notions of traditional and modern India. This operates on the level both of form and of structuring content. It does not, however, operate in a vacuum: films are both one element within the "zone of cultural debate" of "public culture"[2] and themselves arenas of contestation and debate, their meanings in the process of constant negotiation. Audiences are moved (or move) through a film, and that process is as important as any individual images, however potent, that erupt in its course.

Most of the work that has already been done on mainstream Indian cinema has been concerned with either outlining a history or describing themes and their relationship to Indian society.[3] The 1981 issue of *Indian International Centre Quarterly*, inspired by Barthes and early structuralism, invited a number of academics from various disciplines to write on popular cinema, with some interesting results. The journal was an early attempt—and still one of the most successful—to uncover a "grammar" of Hindi cinema and to offer a sociological context.

Finding a model through which one can discuss the intertextuality of Hindi cinema, however, has proved more difficult. Films are complex texts: they are always read and produced in relation to other texts and discourses—other films, mythology, popular art, gossip, and so on. It is important to recognize that film imagery is both fed by and feeds other representations and that films should be placed within their wider context. In an earlier essay I attempted to focus on such representations and their interrelationships in the case of a single film, *Mother India* (1957, producer and director Mehboob Khan), the most successful film of Indian cinema history and in many ways the quintessential Indian film.[4] The film is not simply watched, but is also talked about, is used as a reference, and has assumed mythic status within Indian popular consciousness. That essay was a (necessarily partial) uncovering of some of the other stories and imagery that open onto, and through which a mainstream Indian audience might read, the film. These range from the imagery and rhetoric of nationalism to ideas current in Indian society about female chastity, from other films and books to gossip about film stars. I suggested that the film should be seen as an arena within which a number of discourses about female chastity, modern nationalism, and morality intersect and feed upon each other, with significant political effects, and that this broader text offers fissured, contradictory, and partial representations and identifications. Difficult areas may be spoken of indirectly or erupt in unexpected ways inside or outside the central body of the film text. I was particularly interested in tracing ideas about tradition, modernity, and the West that emerge through the web of texts and stories about Mother India, including, in particular, the gossip surrounding the stars Nargis and Raj Kapoor.

In the present essay I approach the question of intertextuality from another angle. If other films are important texts through which any one film is produced and read, one needs to understand something about genre and the system of repetition and difference within and against which individual films operate.[5] Basing my work on considerable discussion with filmmakers who were working in Bombay in the late 1970s and early 1980s as well as on reflections from audiences and analysis of a large number of films of that period, I have attempted to outline something of this system. It is important to stress that in outlining such an "ideal" model: (1) I am not making claims for every film: the system represents a set of structural concerns or ground rules, internalized by both filmmakers and audience, that any individual film plays both with and against; and (2) any film is always a lot *more* than this system: in particular, films work importantly through visual and aural rhetoric and offer complex identifications and positionings.

I begin with some consideration of the formal conventions of the Hindi film as a genre and move on to develop in more detail a broader framework that is central to its system of verisimilitude. I argue that the films are involved in the construction of Indian identity in three ways: in the notion of a set of Indian conventions of film form that are markedly different from Hollywood or other cinemas; in the films' use of nationalistic or patriotic themes; and through the operation of an ideal moral universe. By this I mean that the films are centrally structured around contradictions, conflicts, and tensions primarily within the domains of kinship and sexuality, and that it is an expectation of Hindi film as a genre—in accordance with the conventions of melodrama—that these conflicts are resolved within the parameters of an ideal moral universe. This defines, somewhat rigidly, paradigms of "good" and "bad" (or expected and unacceptable) forms of behavior and requires that the forces of good triumph over evil.[6]

In this essay I attempt to uncover the terms of that universe and to show

how it is involved in constructing a modern Indian identity. I suggest that the figure of the Mother largely defines (and usually concretely embodies) the field of good, that of the Villain, the field of bad. What is particularly significant is the way in which the good-evil opposition becomes subtly conflated with another set of ideas: good with associations of the traditional, that which is Indian; bad with those of the nontraditional and the "non-Indian." This means that the ideal moral universe becomes integrally bound up with a discourse on traditionalism and nationalism and, in particular, that ideas about kinship and sexuality feed directly into notions about national identity. I will argue that through operation of this moral universe the films construct an Other—a cold, calculating, rapacious, but exotic West/outsider—which has implications for the construction of notions of Indian-ness.[7] The narrative function of the hero is to mediate between these two poles. In this operation certain elements of the "nontraditional" can become "legitimated" and incorporated within the "traditional"—that is, connotations of, for example, love marriage or women driving motorbikes can gradually be shifted through careful negotiation of the contexts within which they appear.[8] Thus, films—including texts such as film-star gossip—are an important locus for the ongoing negotiation and transformation of a sense of "modern" Indian traditionalism. For many years sociologists have recognized the relevance of Indian films to an understanding of the process of "modernizing" India. Thus, as long ago as 1964, Singer went to Madras with "two tentative research plans, both designed to explore the ways in which cultural traditions are modernised"; the second of them was to study "how modern cultural media, especially the films, were becoming vehicles for the cultivation of new regional and national identities."[9] His model was one of adaptation and selective assimilation into a continually evolving core of traditions: "making Indian society more 'modern' without making it any less Indian."[10] While this model lacked the sophistication of more recent work on ideology and discourse theories, the notion of a constant, gradual, almost imperceptible transformation was useful, although he never followed through his intention of studying films.

In focusing on a period from the mid-1970s to the early 1980s, I am concerned with a period of particularly marked transition within Hindi cinema. The ground rules of the moral universe against which the filmmakers of that period pushed were very much the ideal system from the late 1950s to the mid-1970s. The result of their pushing at these boundaries has meant some significant shifts, particularly of certain of the associations of the key terms.

The underlying logic of the system as a framework within which negotiation can take place, however, is still more or less intact today.

Films and National Identity

The literature on Indian cinema has frequently asserted the national importance of Hindi cinema. For example, the Hindi of the films is said to be "the nearest [India] has yet got toward evolving a language which has flexibility, simplicity and a quality which can best be described as communicable"[11]—and, throughout the country, is understood more widely than the unwieldly government bureaucratic Hindi. Equally, the appeal of film songs and film stars is said to transcend linguistic boundaries and regional loyalties: "The film stars are, in a sense, the most Indian of Indian citizens"[12] and:

> The movies seem to be the single most powerful force in the formation of mass culture. The popularity and tremendous appeal of films and film music to the majority of Indians is a prime example. . . . With the cinema have come new concepts of speech, dress, life-style, values, family relationships, dance and music.[13]

It has been claimed that "the unconscious assimilation of [film] Hindi is really a factor in national integration"[14] and also, more jokingly, that Hindi films are "the only unifying thing about India."[15] Whatever the truth of these grand claims, at a very obvious level Hindi films are clearly important in establishing a sense of national identity.

First, all mainstream Indian cinema has shown an amazing resistance to Hollywood cultural imperialism. Since Indian cinema has always had its own vast distribution markets capable of sustaining the industry, its conventions were able to develop without conforming to the expectations of wider international audiences. Thus, traditional entertainment forms, notably village dramatizations of the mythological epics and also, more directly, the urban nineteenth- and twentieth-century Parsee theater with its adaptations of Shakespeare and Victorian melodrama, inflected this development, interacting, of course, with many other developments.[16]

Bombay filmmakers frequently stress that they aim to make films that differ in both format and content from Western films, that there is a definite skill to making films for the Indian audience, that this audience has specific needs and expectations, and that to compare Hindi films to those of the West—or those of Indian "art" cinema—is irrelevant. No successful Bombay filmmaker simply copies Western films. Of course, most borrow openly both story ideas and sometimes complete sequences from Hollywood, Hong

Kong, and other foreign cinemas, but borrowings must always be integrated with Indian filmmaking conventions if the film is to work with the Indian audience. No close copy of Hollywood has ever been a hit. Filmmakers say that the essence of "Indianization" lies in the way that the story line is developed; the crucial necessity for emotion (Western films are sometimes referred to as "cold"); and the skillful blending and integration of songs, dances, fights, and other entertainments within the film. There is also the more obvious "Indianization" of values and other content, including reference to aspects of Indian life with which audiences will identify.[17]

A form has evolved in which narrative is comparatively loose and fragmented, realism irrelevant, psychological characterization disregarded, elaborate dialogues prized, music essential, and both the emotional involvement of the audience and the pleasures of sheer spectacle privileged throughout the three-hour duration of the entertainment. Crucially, it involves the skillful blending of various modes—song and dance, fights, comedy, melodrama, romance, and more—into an integrated whole that moves its audience.

Second, Hindi cinema deals overtly with nationalistic themes, playing upon patriotic motifs (directly and via symbol and metaphor) and—throughout its history—anti-British sentiment. The first films of D. G. Phalke were attempts to celebrate and "teach" Indian mythology in the way that Western cinema had celebrated Christian myth. It was allegedly after seeing *The Life of Christ* that Phalke decided to make *Raja Harischandra* (King Harischandra; 1913, producer and director D. G. Phalke), an episode of the *Ramayana*, as India's first dramatized film.[18] A decade and a half later, Himansu Rai left a successful career with UFA, the major film production company in Germany between the wars, to set up Bombay Talkies in order, he claimed, to bring international glory to the heritage of India and to put his knowledge and skills to use in the service of India.[19] Throughout the thirties and forties, the genres of mythological, fantasy, and stunt film were often used as frameworks for stories that were frankly allegories about the freedom struggle—the subterfuge being necessary because the British ruthlessly censored all references to the independence movement. Thus, for example, a film in which a hero or heroine rescued a people oppressed by a wicked tyrant who had usurped his brother's kingdom would apparently be recognized as subversive by audiences but could escape the attentions of the censors.[20] In the seventies and eighties a number of films, notably those produced by, directed by, and starring Manoj Kumar (as "Mr. Bharat") as well as the later films of Manmohan Desai, played more blatantly—and chauvinistically—on patriotic sentiment.

The films are also, however, at a more fundamental (and less overt) level, about defining and celebrating a modern national identity. This relates to the modus operandi of Hindi cinema, in particular its conventions of verisimilitude. While its conventions of "realism" and "acceptability" are somewhat different from norms of much Western cinema, it is certainly not the case that anything goes. According to filmmakers and the trade press, there is a firm sense of local realism and logic beyond which the material is rejected as "unbelievable":

> The criteria of verisimilitude appear to be closer to the films' roots in mythological drama and refer primarily to a film's skill in manipulating the rules of the film's moral universe. Thus one is more likely to hear accusations of 'unbelievability' if the codes of, for example, ideal kinship behaviour are ineptly transgressed (i.e. a son kills his mother, or a father knowingly and callously causes his son to suffer) than if a hero is a superman who single-handedly knocks out a dozen burly henchmen and then bursts into song.[21]

Thus, filmmakers ascribe the failure of *Jaanbaaz* (1986, producer and director Feroz Khan) almost completely to the fact that the central hero and his father were depicted smoking, drinking, and discussing women together—behaviors that are, it is claimed, unbelievable and unrealistic.

Hindi films are structured according to the rules of melodrama, which require a universe clearly divided between good/morality and evil/decadence.[22] The emphasis of the film is on *how* things will happen, not *what* will happen next, on a moral ordering to be (temporarily) resolved rather than an enigma to be solved through tight narrative denouement. The Hindi film can be regarded as a moral fable that involves its audience largely through the puzzle of resolving some (apparently irresolvable) disorder in the ideal moral universe. A central preoccupation among filmmakers is whether or not their audience will accept a certain representation or narrative outcome—that is, they operate with an explicit concept of their audience's imposing constraints on their filmmaking. Thus, the moral universe within which the films operate is a form of self-censorship based not, like the Hays Code of Hollywood in the 1930s and 1940s, on any ideology of social responsibility or concern about the public image of the film industry, but on a firm belief that the audience will simply boycott a film that is "immoral" or clumsily transgresses the moral code.

Films are developed in script sessions that usually involve one or two screenplay writers, often a separate dialogue writer, and usually the director or producer or both as well. These are often sumptuous affairs, held in five-star hotels or glamorous holiday resorts. Considerable time and energy are spent in discussing what is or is not acceptable and devising screenplay ideas that will please their audience. It is common to hear in script-development sessions phrases such as "our audiences will not accept . . ." and "they'll burn the cinemas down if we show . . ." There is much discussion of other films—Hollywood, Indian classics, and recent Indian releases—and postmortems on recent successes and failures are a topic of keen interest. Discussions of films that flop frequently adduce evidence that the box-office failure is related to unskilled transgression of the moral universe. Thus, for example, one of the most tenacious rules of Hindi cinema, according to filmmakers, is that it is "impossible" to make a film in which a protagonist's real mother is villainous or even semivillainous, and the industry was aghast at the temerity of one filmmaker who, in 1981, produced *Kaaren* (Reason; producer Gopi Rohra, director B. R. Ishara), in which a hero killed his mother, who was a prostitute. The film proved their point by folding after three days, for apparently no audience would watch a film that violated the rules of Hindi cinema so boldly and ineptly. (How far this is true is probably not ascertainable and is anyway irrelevant here. The point is that discussion of the possible reasons for the film's failure went no further.) In fact, very few filmmakers actually watch films with the mainstream audiences and there is none of the formalized audience research that takes place in Hollywood.

Although the filmmakers often explain that their perceived constraints are based on the fact that their audience is conservative and will not accept being shocked, there is no need to be so patronizing. The avid consumption of gossip about film stars alone suggests that audiences derive great pleasure from being shocked in certain contexts.[23] It is important to stress that the ideal moral universe is not necessarily believed by anyone: it is a construct of the filmmakers, with the connivance of their audience, and is as much a product of the history of Indian cinema and the genre conventions it has evolved as of other discourses in Indian society.

The Hindi film audience expects a drama that puts a universe of firmly understood—and difficult to question—rules into crisis and then resolves this crisis within the moral order. This means that transgressions must either be punished or, more excitingly, made "acceptable," that is, be rigorously justified by, for example, an appeal to humane justice, a mythological precedent, or a perceptible contradiction within the terms of the moral code itself. It appears that pleasure is derived from the image of a dangerously broken taboo erupting within a system that provides the reassuring knowledge that it will be safely resolved. If the filmmaker steps outside the moral universe to construct the resolution, however, the film is said to have cheated, to be inept, to be unconvincing, and to be a failure. Particular pleasure—both for audiences and for filmmakers in script sessions—derives from a filmmaker's proposing new ways of bending the comparatively inflexible system, which means that values and meanings are continually being negotiated on the fringes (and the total system undergoing gradual change so that certain taboos of ten or fifteen years ago are more acceptable now). I will now look more closely at this process, with illustrations from a number of films, centrally *Deewar* (The wall; 1975, producer Gulshan Rai, director Yash Chopra), a key film of the 1970s.

The Moral Universe: Mothers and Villains

The two poles of the Hindi film universe can be broadly characterized as follows. In the area of good or morality certain ideal modes of social relations and associated behaviors prevail. Foremost among these are a respect for kinship ties and obligations—usually referred to as kinship "emotion" and considered "natural" to the blood relationship—and an important stress on controlled sexuality. Although the latter has been considerably modified in recent years—since the mid-1980s chastity is no longer so important, even for heroines—casual sexual liaisons are still not completely acceptable. The principles are extended to various nonkin relationships when these are expressed in a kinship idiom. Thus a respect for "emotional" bonds between male friends (such male friendship being known as *dostana* and talked of as, although conceptually distinct from, a brother relationship) is ideal behavior, and the ideal friend is expected to sacrifice his female love or his life (and frequently both) for his buddy.[24] Respect for superiors, again expressed in a kinship idiom (echoing relations between wives and husbands, children and parents, younger and elder brothers and their wives), is also central to notions of ideal behavior.

Certain other attitudes are similarly important: a passive acquiescence to fate (*kismet, naseeb*) or "God's will," deference toward religion and religious practice, religious and communal tolerance, love of one's country, and respect for justice, honesty, and principles. The thrust of these values is to construct a world in which selfish desire and individualism are overruled by emotional bonds and generosity of spirit (heart, *dil*), but both are overruled by social duties and strictures (principles, *usool*). One of the highest accolades (which legitimizes many transgressions) is that a person has "heart"; this implies that the person is able to love and give unconditionally. The very highest accolade, however, is that a person has both heart and principles and that the latter—respect for duty to society and the community—is placed above duty that is linked (contaminated) with emotion (feelings for kin and peers).

The field of badness or immorality is effectively defined as the converse of the good and moral: it is a place in which there is no respect for kinship duties or emotion, in which the family has broken down, in which sexuality is uncontrolled, in which there is treachery between "friends" and no respect for superiors. Fate and religion are flouted, material gain is stressed, there is defiant rejection of one's country and culture and active perpetration of injustice and dishonesty. It demarcates a set of social relationships that are selfish, calculating, and exploitative, in which people are ruthless, greedy, and without compassion and have neither principles nor emotion nor, of course, heart.

Reading broadly across the body of Hindi cinema, two archetypal figures emerge: the Mother and the Villain. In them the opposing values of good and evil are most centrally condensed. This is not to say that every film involves an actual mother figure, nor that such a character is always an unblemished paragon, nor that the degrees of villainy are not negotiable. As ideal types, however, they have evolved through the history of the genre we know as Hindi cinema and are now implicitly figures against which concrete actions represented in individual films take on meaning. They are, of course, also underpinned by reference to two key figures of Hindu mythology: Sita and Raavana, who have also frequently appeared in films; the abduction of Sita episode of the *Ramayana* is one of the most popular bases for mythological films.

THE MOTHER

As I mentioned earlier, filmmakers fervently believe that one cannot make a film in which a central mother character is truly villainous. Individual screen mothers may transgress, but in carefully negotiated ways. The ideal mother's only transgression might be that, in her zeal for self-sacrifice, she effectively abandons her family or tries to take fate into her own hands. Thus, in *Amar Akbar Anthony* (1977, producer and director Manmohan Desai) a tuberculosis-ridden mother tries to kill herself so as not to be a burden on the family. In such cases, however, the narrative requires that she be punished (here by being blinded) before resolution of the moral universe is possible.

In the Hindi film, a mother's love for her son is always unquestionable and appears to serve as the prototype of all kinship emotion (or *dil*)—that is, it is an ideally unconditional, self-sacrificing, devoted love considered natural to the blood relationship. Mother is a fount of nurturing benefi- cence and a vulnerable innocent, a protector of her boy child and in need of protection by him (she often appears slightly crippled or blind). She blesses him with her prayers, feeds him homely food, and sometimes mediates be- tween him and his father, and she serves as the focus that keeps the family and home together.

Mother's sexuality must also be firmly controlled, and filmmakers believe not only that any sexual liaison, apart from that (implied) with her husband, is inconceivable, but also that, however villainous the villains, mother can never be raped. Despite the changes in the representation of heroines' sex- uality in recent years, the taboo on raping mother still appears to hold— although her chastity may be threatened. (This seems to be because rape is seen to be as much a contamination of the woman as a crime of the rapist, and mother cannot be defiled.) If her husband is dead, much is made of her placing *malas* (garlands of flowers) around his photograph; if he is alive, of her placing *siimdoor* (vermillion) in the parting of her hair, in reaffir- mation of her *suhaag* (the auspicious state of having a living husband), how- ever badly he may treat her. Although mothers are played by attractive ac- tresses frequently little older than the actors who play their sons, or else by actresses still firmly associated with their earlier roles as desirable heroines (for example, Nirupa Roy, the most frequently recurring mother of the late 1970s and early 1980s, rose to stardom playing seductive goddesses in the mythological films of the 1950s), mother must be placed, in narrative terms, largely outside the realms of sexual desire—and, of course, it is inconceiv- able that the mother-son relationship overtly acknowledge any sexual tinge, despite what appears to read as frankly Oedipal imagery in a fantasy mode.[25]

Mother is invariably depicted praying in the home or in temples, advo- cating humility and nonviolence, preferring folk wisdoms, and passively accepting her fate as the will of God. These may of course be seen as self- evidently traditional practices. The use of the mother figure, however, also points up a metaphor that is never far from the surface in Indian discourses on both femininity and nationalism: mother as motherland, Mother India, Mother Earth. Film imagery and dialogue play explicitly with the metaphor; the epitome of this is a scene of *Amar Akbar Anthony* that showed three adult brothers (one Hindu, one Muslim, one Christian) lying in hospital beds con- nected to their mother by (patently umbilical) plastic tubes through which their blood flowed to her in an emergency blood transfusion. Through windows in the background appeared emblems of the three major religions of the motherland: temple, mosque, and church.

THE VILLAIN

The baroquely grotesque and overblown personae of Hindi screen villains represent the antithesis of all that is valued in the moral order. The characterizations of unremittingly lecherous, treacherous, brutal, and greedy villains are as unabashedly schematic as are those of the mother figures. While mother is moral probity incarnate, the villain, by definition, breaks the most sacred taboos of the ideal moral order.[26]

The villain is centrally the locus of uncontrolled sexuality and ruthless self-interest and an insatiable greed for material gain that overrides all emotion and compassion—no relationship is sacred, be it a kinship bond, a friendship, a working partnership, or a love affair. Villains rarely have family, and if they do, villainy apparently surfaces in every generation and the relationship with family members becomes at best a partnership in crime. The total absence of emotional attachments to family members or respect for elders is most neatly coded in recurrent scenarios of villainous sons smoking and drinking in front of their fathers—behavior that is considered rather shocking and almost certainly taboo even by many of the most "Westernized" people working in the film industry.

The villain rejects religion, lacks respect for mother figures (his own and others' mothers), defies all social and moral authority figures, and violates the traditionally sacred (for example, he may rape or kill in temple precincts or loot a village celebrating the Holi festival). The villain lacks any pride in Indian culture, usually represented either by his being a complete outsider or by his grossly parodied aping of Western mores. He is also a lawbreaker who steals, cheats, and murders, although this appears to be a less significant aspect of his villainy than his moral transgressions, in particular his thoroughgoing lack of compassion or principles: he steals *from the poor*, cheats *children*, deceives *his friends*, kills *his own followers*, and uses brute force and violence sadistically and indiscriminately. Although moral turpitude does know some bounds—he will not rape a mother—the villain's sexuality is otherwise anarchic: he lusts, whores, and rapes indefatigably and mercilessly, a lascivious leer being the sine qua non of an aspiring villain.

The construction of the villain is also subject to certain formal conventions: villains rarely sing or dance, rarely are presented as characters with a life story or mitigating circumstances, and seldom have sympathetic "emotion" associated with them (that is, they neither arouse feelings of sympathy in the audience nor show sympathy themselves). This is not to say that they are not popular with audiences—they have, particularly in recent years, become more or less cult figures and often have the wittiest lines and are associated with the most extravagant spectacle. This reinforces the point that the relationship between film and audience is not a simple one and that film-makers' assertions about the conservatism of the audience are not the whole story. It suggests rather that pleasure for the audience stems from their involvement in a playful manipulation—and successful resolution—of the moral universe. Accordingly, the archetypal villain must always be seen to get his just deserts, either through "fate," as a direct result of his own excesses, at the hands of the hero or heroine, or, of course, (particularly pre-1980s) under the rule of the law. In the late 1980s villainy reached new heights of depravity and violence, and the sheer number of villains in each film proliferated.[27]

One crucial aspect of the Hindi film villain (and one that cannot be apparent to the casual foreign viewer) is the fact that an audience will almost certainly know, at his first appearance, if a character is villainous or heroic. Not only are villain roles consistently played by a very small group of actors who are immediately recognizable and have cult followings as star villains, but there is also a well-developed iconography of villainy: familiar dialogues, settings, gestures, and scenarios recur through the films. Smoking, drinking, and womanizing—in particular visiting *kothas* (song and dance brothels) or keeping dancing girls in the *addha* (villain's den)—are among the most immediate signifiers of depravity.

Hindi film villainy draws on a number of prototypes: the *zamindar* (landowner), the urban underworld king (smuggler, terrorist, drug dealer, or whatever), the *dacoit* (rural outlaw), and various types of *goondas* (urban thugs, small-time crooks, racketeers, and brutish henchmen). Significantly, the villain is repeatedly placed as the outsider: invoking either the West (or "Westernization") as a signifier of moral depravity or, in the case of the *dacoit*, the "tribal." In the 1980s corrupt politicians and police officers (previously a censorship taboo) gradually, through a process of cunning negotiation on the part of filmmakers, found their place in the Hindi film Hall of Villainy.[28]

OPPOSITION

While a number of factors feed in to construct the terms of the mother-villain opposition, Hindu mythology is crucial. Mother is frequently identified with (and likened to) figures of the Hindu pantheon, most notably Sita, who circulates in popular, commonsense currency as the prototype of traditional Indian womanhood. Motifs from the *Ramayana* story of Sita recur throughout the films: the mother with two sons, separation from a husband, threats to the mother's chastity, various kinds of penance, and, often, a perilous escape from fire. On the other hand, the villainy of Raavana, the monstrous king of the *rakshasas* (demons), who abducted Sita, shows many parallels with that of the film villain. Moreover, just as the film villain is repeatedly placed as the outsider, so Raavana was a foreigner, the king of Lanka. The construction of villainy is, however, also fed by current discourses, for example, the fact that *vilayat* (literally, "abroad," but in fact usually a reference to Europe and the West) is commonly talked of as a place where people are cold, unemotional, machinelike, and without family (or callously reject kinship bonds and duties) as well as sexually profligate.

In describing the mother-villain opposition in this way, much is lost of the raw impact of the visual imagery that erupts in the films and appears to derive much of its potency from the indeterminacy of the levels on which it operates. Returning to *Kartavya*, the film with which I began this essay, one finds a fairly standard narrative. The film tells of two brothers, separated when young. The elder (played by Dharamendra) is a forest officer keen to stamp out the destruction and theft of trees and wild animals from India's forests. The younger (played by Vinod Mehra) had been kidnapped and brought up by villains who have become extremely rich through this smuggling operation, which he now helps to run. Their mother, who has come to stay with her elder son, recognizes her lost son (and his kidnapper) halfway through the film. Alongside subplots of romantic interest, family melodrama, and comedy, the film traces the fight between the forest officer, single-minded in his desire to see smuggling stamped out, and the villains, who want to be rid of him. The film culminates in the villains' using mother as a hostage. While the younger brother is ranting and threatening to kill her and set fire to the countryside, the elder pleads with him to put down his gun and recognize his mother and blood brother.

At the most overt level, the film depicts a gross sacrilege within the kinship domain: a son threatens violence toward his own mother. There are, however, other levels on which the film works. Coded within the still image described at the beginning of this essay is a further violation: the "fierce power of chastity" has been rendered impotent.[29] The paragon of controlled female sexuality (coded via white sari, *kangans*, etc.) is at the mercy of the personification of uncontrolled male sexuality (coded via gun and black leather—leather having connotations not only of impurity within the Hindu belief system but also more generally of macho aggressive [if angst-ridden] male sexuality and potency). Various specific cultural associations complement this scenario: there is implicit reference to the widow who commits *sati* (who, dressed in white, is consumed by the flames of her husband's funeral pyre) and to Sita (threatened by Raavana but also given a trial by fire). A number of oppositions suggest themselves: cotton versus leather, sari versus jacket and trousers, white versus black, *kangans* and *suhaagmala* versus watch and gold medallion, controlled sexuality/chastity versus uncontrolled sexuality/male potency, Sita versus Raavana, vulnerability versus power, tradition and motherland versus Westernization and the foreign.

Of course, this uncomfortable moment is resolved, in this case through the younger brother's finally acknowledging his lost mother; being shot by the hero, his brother; killing the master villain, his stepfather; and dying in his mother's arms, stating the wish that in his next life he might be reborn as their son and brother. The moral universe has been reinstated and the disorder quieted through appropriate—if somewhat schematic—negotiation. It is to this process of negotiation that we now turn.

Negotiation

While the central opposition is conceptually clear, each film proposes its own version of dangerous disorder in the moral universe, which it is the work of the film to resolve. The disorder in *Kartavya* was a particularly daring one: what appears to be an incontrovertible villain is the central hero's brother (and central mother's son). In fact, there exists a rather murky area of semivillainy—usually reserved for the focal protagonists' close kin or domestic group—that provides scope for the all-important negotiation and redefinitions of the moral order.

Semivillains fall into three broad categories. The first is members of the key protagonists' domestic unit. These are invariably found in family social dramas and are frequently women (wicked mothers-in-law, aunts, elder brothers' wives; "lazy" daughters-in-law). Their crimes are primarily transgressions of moral ideals of kinship solidarity and support and result from foibles such as jealousy or selfishness. They are generally ultimately repentant, capitulate to the demands of family harmony, and are made to see the error of their ways and reform. They do not, on the whole, arouse audience sympathy.

The second category—usually men, often father figures—is people whose crimes may be both legal and moral but who are allowed the reprieve of mitigating circumstances. Even severe legal transgressions can be excused to some extent if they are committed in the cause of a kinship bond (for example, a father may take to crime through love for his son). Moreover, as we have seen in *Kartavya,* a brother may be morally depraved and transgress the most sacred rules of family love ("emotion") but to some extent be excused because he was brought up by villains and starved of his mother's love. Throughout the late 1970s and 1980s, taking revenge on crimes committed by the hard-core villains became increasingly acceptable as a mitigating circumstance; examples are the father figures in films such as *Deewar* (1975), *Amar Akbar Anthony* (1977), *Naseeb* (1981), and *Qurbani* (1981). Such semivillainous characters are often represented as ultimately contrite but unable to extricate themselves from their past misdeeds and villainous associates.[30] The moral universe requires that they be shown to be repentant and that they be punished, most often by death.

The third category, and the most interesting and significant for the present purposes, is the central heroes and heroines who break the law and associate with villains but whose transgressions are *always* hedged with mitigating circumstances. Crucially, their crimes are primarily legal rather than moral. The hero is always fundamentally a person of "heart" and "emotion," never loses compassion for the good and the poor, and respects the bonds of kinship morality (and is especially loving and dutiful to mother). This figure may have to repent and be punished but has audience sympathy throughout.

It is often seen as somewhat paradoxical that the fictional heroes and heroines of Hindi cinema can transgress some of the central tenets of traditional Indian mores, flaunt clothes and lifestyles that are "Westernized" to a degree that in the friends and acquaintances of much of the Hindi film audience would be quite unacceptable—even scandalous—and yet retain the audience's sympathy and serve unproblematically as the focus of identification. This is not a wholly new development. Throughout the history of Indian cinema, heroes have sometimes been criminals: Ashok Kumar was a thief in the 1940s smash hit *Kismet,* as was Raj Kapoor in the 1950s *Awaara* and Raaj Kumar in the 1960s *Waqt,* to take just a few examples. Moreover, even in the abundant love stories, the very fact that the lovers make their own choice of partner rather than accepting that of their parents marks them as distinctly subversive of traditional mores. This negotiation is crucial to an understanding of change in the Hindi film and the work of the film in constructing shifting notions of "traditional modern" identities.

Clearly, the hero figure, rather than simply embodying good and tradition, functions most often as a mediator between the poles.[31] While a minority of heroes are actually semivillainous, dramatic tension and the emotional involvement of the audience appear to be fueled by the precariousness of the hero's position—so long as this coexists with the knowledge that the moral universe will be safely upheld. The baseline of heroism seems to consist in the fictional character's respecting what are, at present, core values in the domains of kinship and sexuality, and in the part's being played by a star. This, however, means that new meanings and values can be negotiated as certain kinds of transgressions—both marginal moral lapses and superficial signifiers of Westernization—became more ambiguously valued by virtue of association with a figure who is at base heroic.

Amitabh Bachchan's now classic films with Salim-Javed provide masterful examples of this kind of operation and were of undoubted influence in breaking new ground in the seventies and setting the terms for the contemporary era.[32] *Deewar* is the story of a family separated by a moral crisis: two brothers, a smuggler (played by Amitabh Bachchan) and a police officer (Shashi Kapoor), fight on different sides of the law, and their mother is torn between love for her "bad" son and social and moral duty. In this film we find a universe that is unequivocally split. At one pole lies the world of glamorous, dangerous villainy: of gangland *goondas* and suave "gentlemen" smuggler kings who lounge beside luxury hotel swimming pools, whiskey glasses in hand and limousines on call to shuttle between sleek offices in downtown Bombay and lonely moonlit beaches where their boats unload vast hauls of gold bullion from Dubai. In *Deewar* villainy is more diffusely located than was usual, and the film anticipates the multivillain films of the 1980s: there are at least three separate groups of villains (with varying degrees of sophistication), but society itself is also constructed as an urban jungle, a locus of all-pervasive corruption and a source of danger.

The visual styles of the scenes of this world alternate between the garish kitsch of conventional Hindi film villainy (bright lights, lurid color, and overtly erotic spectacle—for example, the *kotha* dancing girl) and something of the codes of two foreign genres: kung fu (the idiom of many of the fights) and the Hollywood thriller, with its dark, shadowy, blue-lit urban jungle, fights in deserted hangars and warehouses, dockland gangs, car headlights on a rainy night following a murder attempt, and smoky bars where prostitutes hang out. These scenes construct a world of paranoia, loneliness, deception, hard-boiled cynicism, and (male) angst close to the clichés of film noir. Western jazz music (or Muzak) is often used as a mood sound track.

At the other pole lies the world of *usool* (principles)—of tradition, religion, and the law—centrally that of the innocent, humble, vulnerable, nurturing mother, who accepts as her fate that exploitation and abuse are the rewards of honest toil and denounces violence and retaliation. Her joy in life is to look after her sons (and at one time her husband); dressed almost throughout the film in white saris, she is a model of controlled sexuality. Most importantly, she accepts that whatever the personal sacrifice, her duties as an *aurat* (woman) come before her emotions as a *maa* (mother). When she has given her "good" son, the dutifully honest police officer Ravi, her blessings before he sets out to kill her favorite son, the renegade Vijay, she leaves to meet Vijay at the temple, saying, "Aurat apna farz nibha chuki. Ab maa apne bete ka intezaar karne jaa rahi hai" (The woman has done her duty. Now the mother is going off to await her son). Much is made of Ravi's humble lifestyle and meager salary. He quotes his role model from the *Mahabharata*: Arjuna, who slayed his own brother on the battlefield in obedience to Krishna's commands. Ravi takes lessons in traditional wisdom from an elderly schoolteacher, protects and cherishes his mother, and coyly courts his demure middle-class girlfriend through flowers-and-sunshine love songs set in a pretty hill station.[33] The visual style and motifs of this world are primarily those of Hindi film melodrama: romantic songs and dances (eroticism displaced onto aspects of camera work and spectacular mise-en-scéne), interludes of comedy (Ravi as a rather bumbling joker), police stations with pictures of Gandhi on the walls, hospital dramas, scenes in temples, and numerous images of domesticity (eating, cooking, praying in the home). Ravi is also, at one particularly emotional moment, associated with the tune of the Indian national anthem.

The narrative structure can be simply schematized thus:

Order: Happy family with principles and strong emotional bonds.

Disorder: Villains (with no principles or emotions) force father to sacrifice his principles for his emotional attachment to the family. Society spurns them and the family is split.

Order: Villainy (lack of principles and emotion) is punished. Mother and good son sacrifice their emotional attachment (to Vijay) for their principles (duty to society). Society rewards them.

Thus, there are two levels of opposition: the conflict between good (those with principles and emotion) and bad (those with neither), in which good must triumph; and the conflict within the domain of good between principles and emotion, in which principles (duty) must triumph.

Narrative events clearly depict the victory of good over bad: villainy and the nontraditional are destroyed (killed or arrested) by the forces of law and tradition. Interestingly, the message is also reiterated on the level of the structural organization of the film's visual modes themselves, and visual style is an important signifying element. Thus the film uses motifs and quotations from foreign film genres (kung fu and Hollywood) only in scenes of the nontraditional, as surface signifiers of glamorous exotic villainy. As order is restored to the moral universe, these modes are gradually taken over by Hindi family melodrama, and the final resolution is played out wholly within this idiom, with tears, temples, and a mother-son deathbed reunion. The last image of the film is of a police convention paying homage to the mother.

This description, however, neglects the role of Vijay, the "bad" brother, whose function is not only to provide the testing ground for the principles-versus-emotion opposition in the domain of good but also to mediate between the two worlds. The central dynamic of the character hinges on a tension between his exemplary "cool" (he is sophisticated, tough, dangerous, and powerful) and his ingenuous sentimentality or "heart" (he is a desperately loyal and loving son and brother). Throughout the film, Vijay does things the "conservative" Indian audience is said to disapprove of: he smokes, drinks whiskey, has a liaison with a prostitute, wears fashionable Western clothes, drives sleek foreign cars, takes the law into his own hands, refuses (until the end) to accompany his mother to the temple, criticizes his father, and makes hundreds of thousands of "black" rupees as leader of Bombay's most notorious smuggling gang.

While Vijay is, in terms of the moral universe, bad enough to merit punishment and death, he is also good enough to be the focal hero, to remain his mother's favorite, and to die in her arms in the temple, with her blessings. Filmmakers discussing the effectiveness of this negotiation invariably pointed out that the prime extenuating factor was the central place given in the film to Vijay's love for his mother. A flashback to his poverty-stricken mother, struggling to support her two young sons, accompanies—and "justifies"—his first temptation to join the smuggling gang; he spends much of his money on expensive presents for her; he is heartbroken when she leaves him; and in his dying moments his only thought is to rejoin her in the temple. His crimes are mitigated by being presented as fired by desire for revenge on a corrupt society, especially as it had been particularly harsh on his beloved mother; although he is hardly a Robin Hood, his crimes are committed not principally out of selfish greed but to benefit others. He is presented largely as a victim of fate who carries the burden of a monstrously unfair tattoo on his arm ("My Father Is a Thief," tattooed to taunt him by enemies of his father), who knows no peace of mind (*shanti*) and so mis-guidedly rejects the law and honesty as impractical and inadequate.[34]

Whatever his transgressions, the baseline of heroism is respected through-out: not only is the role played by one who is unequivocally a star, but the character of Vijay has "heart." He honors the canons of ideal behavior in the kinship domain and, unlike hard-core villains, values family relationships; he is not only an ideal son but also an exemplary elder brother (as a child he had worked so that his brother could be educated). The uncontrolled sexuality signified by his affair with an ex-prostitute, Anita, is recuperated when, to-ward the end of the film, she reveals that she is pregnant. Vijay immediately suggests that he marry her, relinquishing his life of crime, and give himself up to the police so that his son will not have the stigma of a criminal father. Anita, as a potential mother, abruptly stops drinking, and the films reveals that tucked away in her wardrobe of flowery minidresses and skimpy tops is a red wedding sari—remnant of a "shattered dream" of her mother's. She is not just a whore with a heart of gold but, after all, a good girl who, with the aid of a red sari, marriage, and motherhood, can be exonerated and elevated to Hindi film heroinedom provided, of course, that she dies—which she does, with full audience sympathy.

Although the narrative may punish Vijay's villainy (by death) and recu-perate certain aspects of it (by his change of heart—he finally visits the tem-ple), there is no reason to believe that this overrides the fact that the film of-fers a succession of vivid images in which nontraditional behaviors are associated with a supremely charismatic hero figure and star who was, at the time, an undoubted figure of sympathy and adoration. Furthermore, throughout the film the mother's favorite son was Vijay rather than his bro-ther Ravi, who more obviously embodied traditional heroic values.

The effect of such play with the moral universe was undoubtedly to shift certain key associations around a "modern" Indian identity within the films in the 1970s. In particular, it explored a new model of male heroism that was powerful, aggressive, defiant, self-respecting, sophisticated, successful, and at home with the accoutrements of a Westernized lifestyle, yet still respectful of traditional values. *Deewar* itself includes a number of other models of masculinity—father, teacher, policeman—but each is shown to be patently deficient. Father is, for most of the film, a significant absence (alluded to from time to time by images of moving trains), an inadequate, displaced masculinity, cowardly and passive. The elderly teacher is humble, principled, and wise but poverty-stricken and downtrodden. While Ravi is many of the things that traditional Indian heroes should be—dutiful, soft and romantic but strong—it is still Vijay who has the greater share of his mother's love. While tough masculinity had been seen in Hindi cinema before Amitabh, it was rarely in a central hero figure and in, for example, *Mother India*, it was the mother, Radha, who was the focus of audience sympathy, not her rebellious son Birjoo.

In the context of Hindi cinema of the 1970s, the Vijay persona, and *Deewar*, did much to sweep away the cult of the soft romantic hero, and in fact paved the way for more radical challenges of traditional authority. Amitabh's next success with Salim-Javed, *Trishul* (Trident; 1978, producer Gulshan Rai, director Yash Chopra), went one step further and roused considerable controversy because the angry young man, an illegitimate son seeking to avenge his mother's honor, addressed his wayward father as "my illegitimate" father (that is, he refused him the respect due to one's father according to traditional mores). Again by clever negotiation of the characters and situations the transgression was made acceptable. One suspects that it was out of these, now comparatively mild, breakthroughs that the films of the 1980s, in which heroes directly challenge both father figures and a corrupt patriarchal law, have become possible. Finally, *Deewar* must be seen as part of a trend throughout the 1970s in which overtly Westernized lifestyles and, most notably, less than virtuous heroines become increasingly acceptable as hero figures.

Films and Wider Circulation of Meanings

It would, of course, be absurd to claim that films alone shift values and meanings: there is always (at least) a double movement in which play with the terms of the films' moral universe becomes acceptable, pleasurable, or necessary because of other factors currently operating within the sociopolitical arena. I have argued that Hindi film imagery is part of a regime of representation that constructs—and changes—the meanings accruing to "India" and the "West," "traditional" and "modern," and that the negotiation of the moral universe, in particular the play with the hero or heroine, is central. But the images that films use also have preexisting associations, the audience is vast and heterogeneous, and readings are inflected by other discourses that impinge on the films and are part of the popular preconscious.

In using the format of the moral story, filmmakers are drawing on a well-worn tradition within Indian popular culture: not only that of the key epics, the *Ramayana* and the *Mahabharata* (to which filmmakers quite consciously refer)[35] but also that of more apparently peripheral forms, for example, the *karni bharni* (reap as you sow) poster calendars. These wall charts were popular throughout India until the late 1970s, but are still found in some rural areas today. They depict, graphically—and somewhat gruesomely—the appropriate punishment for various kinds of misdeed as meted out by Vishnu, the protector of dharma. Miscreants range from the "false speaker" to the black marketeer, from the "overloader of animals" (whose fate is to have both arms cut off and pull a rickshaw containing a whip-cracking human monster) to the counterfeiter (who is savaged by sharklike monsters). Significantly, most of these transgressions are not primarily legal crimes but focus on areas familiar from the arena of film villainy: lack of compassion, violence, deceit and hypocrisy, abrogation of public duty, and uncontrolled sexuality. Most interesting is the considerable overlap with film iconography. Thus the counterfeiter, dressed in Western collar and tie, sits with cigarette in one hand, drink in the other, at a table stacked high with bundles of banknotes. The tax defaulter flaunts the crucial status symbol—a telephone—and lounges on a bed against ornate cushions beside a neat flower arrangement (connotations of controlled nature, sophistication, and luxury) and an exotic painting of ships in the moonlight (with perhaps connotations of the glamorous world of smuggling).

While the *karni bharni* tradition feeds into the films, the films feed back into the iconography of the calendar artists. Images of Hindi film villainy also circulate more widely throughout popular culture and consciousness and inspire both the mythology that has grown up around smugglers and the Bombay underworld and that around *dacoits*. Thus it is claimed that film imagery has influenced the present-day appearance of the real *dacoits* operating in the Chambal Valley. According to Sunil Dutt, Chambal *dacoits* rarely rode horses or carried guns before his film *Mujhe Jeene Do* (1961). Meanwhile, the *dacoit* became so glamorous an image in the early 1980s that in Mussoorie, a popular hill resort, Indian tourists would frequent photographers' stalls to pose for their photographs in *dacoit* outfits—cowboy-style fringed jackets, turbans, moustaches, guns—clearly inspired by film imagery.

The issue of intertextuality is obviously crucial, but one of the central questions to consider in discussing the notion of public culture is how to describe all the forces in play within the arena. My essay on *Mother India* made one type of foray into this territory. One could of course repeat the exercise with *Deewar*, which would involve citing not only the references to other and earlier films (including *Mother India*) and the personae built up around the stars, their liaisons, and the gossip about their "private" lives, but also references to a variety of mythologies of decadent Otherness, from the *karni bharni* calendars to the media mythology surrounding Haji Mastaan, Bombay's notorious and highly glamorized smuggler king of the mid-1970s. One would also, of course, need to situate the film in a social, political, and historical context, notably that of the months leading up to Indira Gandhi's 1975 declaration of a state of emergency. It would also be relevant to look at the whole era of transition referred to in this essay in the context of a political shift from a state nationalism broadly modeled on a family morality to its breakdown into regionalism and the legitimation of communalism—like a family with rebellious sons.

If one takes on board the full implications of intertextuality, however, one inevitably recognizes that writing can ever be only a partial uncovering, and in the final analysis there is an infinite regress of context. In focusing here on the assumptions and perceived constraints within which the filmmakers work, I have tried to outline one aspect of these other texts and also to understand something of the mechanism by which the arena of public culture operates as a zone of debate. Films are in no sense a simple reflection of the wider society, but are produced by an apparatus that has its own momentum and logic. The filmmakers are in no simple way in control (even leaving aside debates on auteurship and the death of the author):[36] they are part of this apparatus and are crucially constrained by their internalized systems of rules and by their own perceptions of audience expectations and of other factors in the field. These perceptions are of course underpinned by a more fundamental constraint: the economic context of the film industry within which they work.

The Bombay film industry is an anarchic free market within which filmmakers have to sink or swim. Of course, most are motivated by the desire not only to survive but also to make the large amounts of money that are possible within this system. Almost all films are independent productions financed piecemeal by a combination of private financiers (who extort prohibitive—and illegal—interest rates) and the preselling of rights to distributors in each of the six major territories of India. Power in the system—in the form of control over the final form of the film—does not lie unambiguously with any one group of people but is constantly subject to negotiation between producers, distributors, financiers, directors, writers, stars, and others. The size of the budget of the average Hindi film means that it must make money in most, if not all, of the six territories if it is to make a profit, and therefore the ultimate reference point is invariably beliefs about what pleases audiences. This involves a (mostly knowing) exploitation of crude populist sentiment and a model of a heterogeneous audience to which films have to cater by putting in elements for everybody—failing which the distributors for any territory that has been ignored will opt out or apply pressure. Thus the apparent "national integration" that the films promote can be seen as a direct effect of the economic pressures of the industry.[37]

From the earliest days filmmakers knew that one of the most certain ways of appealing to a pan-Indian audience was to draw on the mythological epics. Filmmakers have also known, however, that a successful film must mark both repetitions and differences from other films. Some filmmakers appear to understand better than some of their so-called intellectual critics how genre operates:

> People seem to like the same thing again and again, so I repeat it . . . but you always have to give them something different, too. . . . There can be no such thing as a formula film—if there was, everybody would be making nothing but hits.[38]

We have seen that one element of "difference" has involved pushing the boundaries of the moral framework, thereby connecting with some of the key concerns of a society in transition in a postcolonial world, concerns about changes in moral values matched with an ambivalent attitude to the Western world. Thus we see an apparent paradox of the Hindi film: it is at once founded upon remarkable cultural specificity (epic texts and uniquely Indian symbolism) but also strikes chords that make it the most popular cinema throughout much of the developing world. It would appear that it was not simply the fact that the tales of the *Ramayana* and *Mahabharata* were familiar throughout India that ensured their suitability but the fact that, as moral fables, they offered the framework for melodrama, within which the perennial battle between good and evil could become the arena in which the "modern" can be constantly negotiated.

Notes

1. *Suhaagmala*: marriage necklace; *kangan*: wedding bangles. A white sari is usually worn by widows and is a signifier of controlled sexuality.

2. Arjun Appadurai and Carol A. Breckenridge, "Why Public Culture?" *Public Culture* 1, no. 1 (Fall 1988): 6.

3. For history, see Eric Barnouw and S. Krishnaswamy, *Indian Film* (New York: Oxford University Press, 1980 [1963]), and Firoze Rangoonwalla, *Indian Cinema Past and Present* (New Delhi: Clarion, 1983). For themes and their relationship to society, see Aruna Vasudev and Philippe Lenglet, eds., *Indian Cinema Superbazaar* (New Delhi: Vikas, 1983); and Sudhir Kakar, "The Ties That Bind," and Ashis Nandy, "The Popular Hindi Film, Ideology and First Principles," both in *Indian Popular Cinema*, ed. Pradip Krishen, *Indian International Centre Quarterly* 8, no. 1 (1981).

4. Rosie Thomas, "Sanctity and Scandal: The Mythologisation of Mother India," *Quarterly Review of Film and Video* 4, no. 3 (1989).

5. Stephen Neale, *Genre* (London: British Film Institute, 1980).

6. As Douglas Sirk, master of Hollywood melodrama, put it, melodrama as a form requires the "deux ex machina of the happy end." This does not, however, preclude its strength lying in "the amount of dust the story raises along the road, a cloud of overdetermined irreconcilables which put up a resistance to being neatly settled in the last five minutes" (Laura Mulvey, "On Sirk and Melodrama" *Movie,* no. 25 [1977-78]).

7. I am not suggesting that the Occidental Other is a simple reversal of the Oriental Other. Said himself argued that there was no such thing as Occidentalism (*Orientalism* [London: Routledge and Kegan Paul, 1978]). Gayatri Spivak makes the important point that the play of power relations already in the field means that it is a different experience for the West to see itself marginalized within Indian representations than for India to see itself constantly so positioned within colonial (and neocolonial) discourse (in *Europe and Its Others,* vol. 1, ed. F. Barker et al. [Essex: University of Essex, 1984], p. 128). The concept does seem useful, however, in pointing up some of the unspoken assumptions within Indian popular culture about Indianness (and non-Indianness).

8. Riding a motorized two-wheeler would appear to brand a woman as "fast," and even in Indian cities (apart from Pune, for mainly historical reasons) few women will risk their reputations in this way. Women on scooters were also a recurrent image in saucy popular calendar art in the 1960s and 1970s. Gradually, through the early 1980s, filmmakers played with placing heroines on motorbikes; a notable breakthrough was Hema Malini, the "dream girl" of the industry, in *Naseeb* (Destiny; 1981, producer and director Manmohan Desai).

9. M. Singer, *When a Great Tradition Modernises* (London: Pall Mall, 1972), p. 247.

10. Ibid., p. 270.

11. *Statesman,* July 7, 1958, quoted in Barnouw and Krishnaswamy, *Indian Cinema,* 1963 edition.

12. Kobita Sarkar, *Indian Cinema Today* (New Delhi: Sterling, 1975), p. 143.

13. M. L. Apte, *Mass Culture, Language and Arts in India* (Bombay: Popular Prakashan, 1978), pp. 9, 25.

14. Sarkar, *Indian Cinema Today,* p. 145.

15. Javed Akhtar, in an interview with the author, February 1981.

16. Information on Parsee theater is drawn from D. Varshey, "Modern Hindi Literature 1850-1900," unpublished Ph.D. thesis, Allahabad University, and R. K. Yagnik, *The Indian Theatre: Its Origins and Later Development under European Influence, with Special Reference to Western India* (London: Allen and Unwin, 1933).

17. For more detailed development of these ideas, see Rosie Thomas, "Indian Cinema, Pleasures and Popularity," *Screen* 26, nos. 3-4 (1985).

18. Barnouw and Krishnaswamy, *Indian Film,* p. 11.

19. Devika Rani, in an interview with the author in Bangalore, January 1989, stressed how important the ideals of the nationalist movement were in motivating Himansu Rai's filmmaking career in India.

20. Barnouw and Krishnaswamy, *Indian Film,* p. 124. See also Behroze Gandhy and Rosie Thomas, "Three Indian Film Stars," in *Stardom: Industry of Desire,* ed. Christine Gledhill (London and New York: Routledge, 1991), for discussion of Fearless Nadia, film censorship, and the nationalist movement.

21. Thomas, "Indian Cinema, Pleasures and Popularity," p. 128.

22. The notion of a moral universe in melodrama is a key concept in Peter Brooks, *The Melodramatic Imagination: Balzac, Henry James, Melodrama and the Mode of Excess* (New Haven, Conn.: Yale University Press, 1976).

23. Hundreds of film-gossip magazines peddling interviews with and scandalous innuendo about stars are published—and make money—in India. They are printed in all languages, al-

though those published in English (*Stardust, Super, Star and Style, Cine Blitz*) are the glossiest—and most salacious.

24. This refers primarily to heroes, but a female "buddy" theme has been attempted at least once: *Patthar ke Sanam* (Promises of stone; 1967, producer and director Raja Nawathe) stars Waheeda Rehman and Mumtaz as two women in love with the same man.

25. For example, the stills from *Kartavya*, where details such as the angle of the gun would seem to speak that which must be consciously denied.

26. The villain, as ideal type, appears to be male. There are of course many villainesses within the dramas, but these tend to be either sidekicks of the villains (and are often present primarily to define their depravity) or less relentlessly evil and more prone to repentance and forgiveness (see discussion on semivillainy).

27. See Madhu Jain, "The Day of the Villain," *India Today*, November 30, 1988.

28. See Rosie Thomas in *World Cinema Since 1945*, ed. William Luhr (New York: Ungar, 1987), pp. 320-21.

29. For further elaboration of the concept of "the fierce power of chastity," see Chris Fuller, "The Divine Couple in South India," *History of Religions* 19, no. 4 (1980): 327.

30. See the description of the *Karni Bharni* wall chart tradition.

31. "Hero figure" refers to both males and females, but during this period the narratives of most films in fact revolve around male hero figures.

32. Salim Khan and Javed Akhtar were a filmwriting duo who emerged in the early 1970s with *Zanjeer* (1973, producer and director Prakash Medra). The film *Chains* established Amitabh's reputation as an "angry young man" and as the superstar of Hindi cinema in the 1970s and early 1980s. The duo went on to write a string of films starring Amitabh that were almost all very big this. They themselves became celebrities and were instrumental in raising the status—and fees—of Bombay screenplay writers.

33. These sections have sometimes been edited out in versions of the film screened in the West.

34. The thrust of the film's overt resolution is to suggest that with men of "principles" around (i.e., Ravi) the law *is* adequate—an uneasy resolution that began to break down in the films of the 1980s.

35. It is common to hear filmmakers say that every film can be traced back to these stories, and even that there are only two stories in the world, the *Ramayana* and the *Mahabharata*.

36. Ronald Barthes, *Image Music Text* (London: Fontana/Collins, 1977).

37. Regional films are produced on much smaller budgets and frequently have state funding.

38. Manmohan Desai in an interview with the author, May 1981.

CHAPTER EIGHT

Repositioning the Body, Practice, Power, and Self in an Indian Martial Art

PHILLIP B. ZARRILLI

In mid-January 1984, after seven months of field research and training in Kerala, India, on the region's martial/medical art, *kalarippayattu*,[1] and a brief two-week stopover in Kuala Lumpur, Malaysia, to visit Ustaz Haji Hamzah Haji Abu's International Kalari-Payat Dynamic Self-Defence Institute,[2] I returned home to Madison, Wisconsin, to receive a copy of the January 11, 1984, issue of *New Thrill* forwarded to me by my Malaysian host. *New Thrill* is a twice-weekly English-language tabloid published in Kuala Lumpur, which, according to its subtitle, "prob[es] the unknown, the mysterious and the exciting" for its presumably young and primarily male Malaysian readership. Framed by moral platitudes and distanced by the veneer of an investigative report, the cover story by "Mai-Pen-Rai" provocatively described the lives of several young Thai prostitutes with sufficient detail to titillate the male Malaysian readers who might either travel to Thailand for sex or at least fantasize about doing so.[3]

I leafed through the tabloid, skimming other stories that probed "the unknown, mysterious, and exciting," including "The [Hollywood] Stars Who Live in Fear" (Olivia Newton-John, Kate Jackson, Robert Redford, and Barbra Streisand); an article about how Jackie Bisset, Raquel Welch, and Joan Crawford were "waitresses while waiting for stardom"; two stories in the "Probe the Unknown" section, "Orgone Energy" and "The Druid Who

Learned to Fly"; and finally an article with the bold headline: "Kalari-Payat: Deadly Art of Locks and Throws." The photographs illustrating the article (Fig. 8.1) included four photographs of me costumed in a karate-style uniform and (honorary) black belt given to me by my Malaysian host, Hamzah (I had been photographed demonstrating four of the traditional *kalarippayattu* poses I learned in Kerala); a head shot of Ustaz Haji Hamzah himself, the mahaguru and founder of this new streetwise self-defense version of *kalarippayattu* in Malaysia; and a photograph of two of Hamzah's Malay-Indian students demonstrating an action-packed *kalarippayattu*-style side kick. When it is performed in a karate-style uniform with the action stopped at the moment of full extension and impact, this kick has all the appearance and glamour of the more familiar karate or kung-fu-style kicks worthy of a Bruce Lee.

Between my first trip to Kerala in 1976 and my last in 1993, *kalarippayattu* practitioners and various producers of culture have presented and represented the martial art in numerous new contexts for a variety of new publics. In addition to the Malaysian tabloid's sensational representation of *kalarippayattu* as a "deadly art of self-defense," among the many other ways *kalarippayattu* has been represented are the following: for a Japanese television/print media audience, as a humorously exotic vehicle through which to sell a vitamin that is touted as "replenish[ing] Vitamin B-1 when your body is all worn out" (Fig. 8.2); for the American television-viewing public watching *PM Magazine*, as an ancient, Orientalized, tradition-bound art through which a (New Age) holistic unity and at-oneness might be achieved; and for Malayali newspaper readers, as an encapsulation of Kerala's cultural, mythohistorical heritage whose story of single-minded devotion and dedication to practice is paralleled by the dedication of today's South Indian Bank (fig. 8.3).

Although such print and visual media representations of *kalarippayattu* are recent developments, the martial art has a long history of being adapted for practice and presentation in a variety of contexts, from the training of the *kathakali* dance-drama performer, to the inclusion of martial techniques in the propitiation of ancestral heroes in Hindu *teyyam* ritual performances in northern Kerala, to its use in training the first Indian (Malayali) circus performers in the late nineteenth century, to staged performances as part of India Festivals throughout the world, to my own use of *kalarippayattu* (along with t'ai chi ch'uan) in training American actors (1993).

Collectively, these examples illustrate how one mode of cultural praxis can take on new and highly divergent meanings in the heteronomous contexts within which *kalarippayattu* is practiced and performed and within

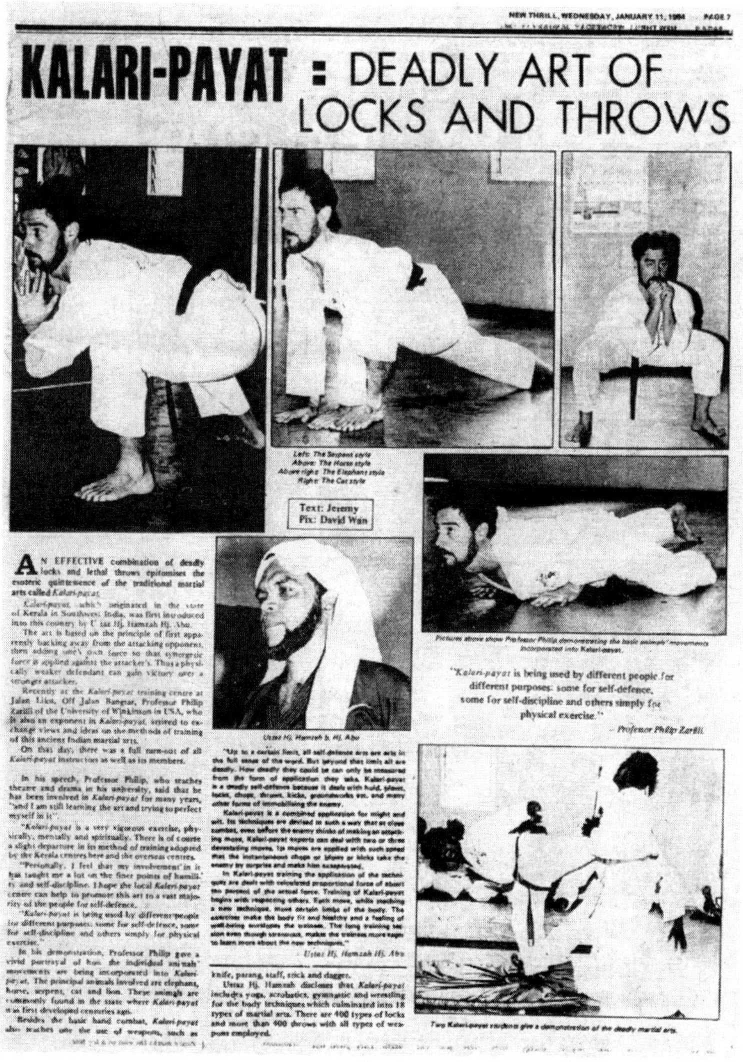

NEW THRILL, WEDNESDAY, JANUARY 11, 1984 PAGE 7

KALARI-PAYAT : DEADLY ART OF LOCKS AND THROWS

Left: The Serpent style
Above: The Horse style
Above right: The Elephant style
Right: The Cat style

Text: Jeremy
Pix: David Wan

AN EFFECTIVE combination of deadly locks and lethal throws epitomises the esoteric quintessence of the traditional martial arts called *Kalari-payat*.

Kalari-payat, which originated in the state of Kerala in Southwest India, was first introduced into this country by Ustaz Hj. Hamzah Hj. Abu.

The art is based on the principle of first apparently backing away from the attacking opponent, then adding one's own force so that synergetic force is applied against the attacker's. Thus a physically weaker defendant can gain victory over a stronger attacker.

Recently at the *Kalari-payat* training centre at Jalan Liku, Off Jalan Bangsar, Professor Philip Zarilli of the University of Wisconsin in USA, who is also an exponent in *Kalari-payat*, arrived to exchange views and ideas on the methods of training of this ancient Indian martial arts.

On that day, there was a full turn-out of all *Kalari-payat* instructors as well as its members.

In his speech, Professor Philip, who teaches theatre and drama in his university, said that he has been involved in *Kalari-payat* for many years, "and I am still learning the art and trying to perfect myself in it".

"*Kalari-payat* is a very vigorous exercise, physically, mentally and spiritually. There is of course a slight departure in its method of training adopted by the Kerala centres here and the overseas centres.

"Personally, I feel that my involvement in it has taught me a lot on the finer points of humility and self-discipline. I hope the local *Kalari-payat* centre can help to promote this art to a vast majority of the people for self-defence.

"*Kalari-payat* is being used by different people for different purposes: some for self-defence, some for self-discipline and others simply for physical exercise."

In his demonstration, Professor Philip gave a vivid portrayal of how the individual animals' movements are being incorporated into *Kalari-payat*. The principal animals involved are elephant, horse, serpent, cat and lion. These animals are commonly found in the state where *Kalari-payat* was first developed centuries ago.

Besides the basic hand combat, *Kalari-payat* also teaches one the use of weapons, such as knife, parang, staff, stick and dagger.

Ustaz Hj. Hamzah discloses that *Kalari-payat* includes yoga, acrobatics, gymnastic and wrestling for the body techniques which culminated into 18 types of martial arts. There are 400 types of locks and more than 400 throws with all types of weapons employed.

Ustaz Hj. Hamzah b. Hj. Abu

"Up to a certain limit, all self-defence arts are arts in the full sense of the word. But beyond that limit all are deadly. How deadly they could be can only be measured from the form of application they take. *Kalari-payat* is a deadly self-defence because it deals with hold, [illegible], locks, chops, thrusts, kicks, [illegible] etc. and many other forms of immobilising the enemy.

Kalari-payat is a combined application for might and wit. Its techniques are devised in such a way that in close combat, even before the enemy thinks of making an attacking move, *Kalari-payat* experts can deal with two or three devastating moves. Its moves are applied with such speed that the instantaneous chops or blows or kicks take the enemy by surprise and make him [illegible].

In *Kalari-payat* training the application of the techniques are dealt with calculated proportional force of about [illegible] percent of the actual force. Training of *Kalari-payat* begins with respecting others. Each move, while teaching a new technique, [illegible] certain limbs of the body. The exercises make the body fit and healthy and a feeling of well-being [illegible] the trainee. The long training session even though strenuous, makes the trainee more eager to learn more about the new techniques."

— *Ustaz Hj. Hamzah Hj. Abu*

Pictures above show Professor Philip demonstrating the basic animals' movements incorporated into Kalari-payat.

"*Kalari-payat* is being used by different people for different purposes: some for self-defence, some for self-discipline and others simply for physical exercise."

— *Professor Philip Zarilli*

Two Kalari-payat students give a demonstration of the deadly martial arts.

Figure 8.1. *New Thrill*'s "Deadly Art of Locks and Throws" with the author in a karate-style uniform demonstrating traditional *kalarippayattu* techniques. Hamzah is pictured in the center and several of his students in the lower right.

which its images are produced.[4] *Kalarippayattu* is being shaped within a set of arenas that South Asian anthropologist Arjun Appadurai and historian Carol Breckenridge call "public culture"—"a zone of cultural debate . . . characterized as an arena where other types, forms, and domains of culture

Figure 8.2. Sathyan Narayanan competing with Japanese actor Nadaka-san in the Aoi
advertising campaign for Alinamin-A.

are encountering, interrogating and contesting each other in new and unexpected ways" (1988: 6). The public culture terrain that *kalarippayattu* inhabits in the late twentieth century is contested by an increasingly diverse group
of "producers of culture and their audiences," many of whom make use of
the mass media in shaping their version of martial practice (ibid.: 6-7).

What interests me about this is the dynamic and shifting relationship
between the body, bodily practice(s), knowledge, power, agency, and the

Figure 8.3. Advertisement for the South Indian Bank featuring *kalarippayattu* sword and shield and emphasizing *kalarippayattu* as a traditional path to self-discipline.

practitioner's "self" or identity *as well as* the discourses and images of the body and practice created to represent this shifting relationship. In each context of its presentation or representation, the *kalarippayattu* practitioner's body is being repositioned for the practitioner, teacher, and cultural consumers, thereby making available quite different images, discourses of power and agency, experiences, knowledge, and meanings for them all.

I will begin with a general discussion of the relationship between the body, practice, power, knowledge, agency, and self. I will then briefly describe two "traditional" paradigmatic ways in which this relationship was historically configured in *kalarippayattu* practice. Finally, I will focus specifically on how this relationship is being played out in one of these newer contexts—the emergence of what I will call a transnational "self-defense" paradigm of martial practice exemplified by Ustaz Hamzah's version of *kalarippayattu*.

The Body, Practice, Agency, Power, and "Self"

I begin this study with the body. First, I turn to the body because *kalarippayattu* practitioners insist that practice "begins with the body." As a Muslim master told me, "He who wants to become a master must possess complete knowledge of the body." Second, I begin with the body because of the recent interdisciplinary reevaluation of the bodily basis of meaning.[5] Given the West's historical privileging of such "inscribing practices" as hermeneutics and texts, social scientist Paul Connerton has argued for the necessity of recognizing the constitutive importance of "incorporating practices," that is, how the body is, and therefore how experience and meaning are, "culturally shaped in its actual practices and behaviours" (1989: 104). Anthropologist Michael Jackson has argued persuasively and passionately for bringing the body and lived experience back into anthropological discourse so that culture will no longer be viewed as disembodied (1989)—a view similar to that expressed by Margaret Drewal (1991) in that both insist upon a more processual, phenomenological, performative view of the constitution of meaning and experience than previous anthropologies of the body that tended to "interpret embodied experience in terms of cognitive and linguistic models of meaning" (Jackson 1989: 122). Finally, I begin with the body because my own experience of practicing and teaching this bodily-based discipline have convinced me that it is only through the body-in-practice that experience and meaning are generated for the practitioner.

Martial arts, like other techniques of disciplining the body such as aerobics, weight training, contact improvisation,[6] and so on may be considered "technologies" [of the body] in Foucault's sense, that is, practices through which "humans develop knowledge about themselves" (1988: 18). Psychophysiological techniques are practiced in order for the practitioner to be transformed to attain a certain normative or idealized relationship between the "self," "agency," and "power"; that is, the practitioner's "self" ideally is reconstituted through long-term practice to achieve agency and power that can be deployed personally, socially, aesthetically, performatively, and cosmologically. Such a transformation can only be actualized through the body-in-practice.

As cultural theorist Richard Johnson asserts, "subjectivities are produced, not given, and are therefore the objects of inquiry, not the premises or starting points" (1986: 44). Following both Johnson and anthropologist Dorrine Kondo's thoughtful ethnographic study of the self,[7] I bracket "self," "agency," and "power" with quotation marks to suggest the problems with Western essentialization and reification of all three, and in order to emphasize that all three should always be considered provisionally; that is, all three are dynamically "crafted" in the constantly unfolding temporal creation of the self in particular contexts.[8] As Kondo asserts regarding self/identity, I would assert that self as well as agency and power are all three "nodal points repositioned in different contexts. Selves [agency, and power], in this view, can be seen as rhetorical figures and performative assertions enacted in specific situations within fields of power, history, and culture" (1990: 304). The martial arts are techniques of bodily practice that allow an individual to gain agency or power *within certain specific contexts.*

Although the self is always in the process of being crafted and is therefore provisional, I would agree with medical anthropologists Lock and Scheper-Hughes that it is

> reasonable to assume that all humans are endowed with a self-consciousness of mind and body, with an internal body image, and with what neurologists have identified as the proprioceptive or sixth sense, our sense of body self-awareness, of mind-body integration, and of being-in-the-world as separate and apart from other human beings. (1990: 57)[9]

It is through this experience-generating body-self in practice that one's self/identity, agency, and power may be transformed. As Johnson points out, however, the "who I am" shaped in practice cannot be divorced from the "who we are"; that is, individual experience and collective identity form a dialectic that *is* the arena through which the "self" is forged *in practice* (1986: 44).

Through their bodily-based techniques, practitioners of disciplines like the martial arts attain three context-specific types of socially circumscribed abilities—they learn, in Foucault's words, "to produce, transform, or manipulate things," that is, they obtain agency; to "determine the conduct of individuals and submit them to certain ends or domination," that is, they obtain power(s); and "to transform themselves in order to attain a certain state," that is, they create a self (1988: 18). Simultaneously, through their practice the body becomes a semiotic system producing certain context-specific "signs, meanings, symbols, or signification" (ibid.).

By assuming that power and agency, like self, are provisional and always context-specific, I seek to avoid the type of reification of both, which, as critics have pointed out, plagued Foucault's thinking on the subject (Keat 1986: 30). Power is certainly manifest when it is exercised on a particular body in a particular context; "power" comes into being as it is practiced most vividly in terrifying aspects of torture (Scarry 1985). It is locatable as it happens. But power also exists as a set of context-specific discursive fields of possibilities. A manifestation of a particular type of power in a particular context is read as "power-full" through an implicit discourse of power that allows interpretation of the event. Between each discourse of power and the exercise of that power there exists what might be called a "dance of the possible"— the possibility that that discourse will actually be exercised on a body. It is this "dance" that accounts for the "agency" inherent in discourses of power. The elocutionary force of such discourses is lodged in the *possibility* (or probability) of the exercise of that power in a specific context by a specific practitioner. To the extent that the possibility of the exercise of a particular power is assumed to be present in a discourse of power, that discourse may itself constrain or influence behavior, actions, and so on.[10]

To summarize my argument thus far, depending upon how a particular individual is positioned within a system of practice within a particular sociohistorical location, the martial arts are one technology of the body through which self, agency, and power are, in Kondo's terms, "crafted" and that "offer culturally, historically specific pathways to self-realization as well as to domination" (1990: 305). I will turn now to a discussion of several configurations of the relationship between self, agency, power, and practice of *kalarippayattu* among traditional practitioners in Kerala and then examine how the body, agency, and power have been repositioned by practitioners according to the modern "self-defense" paradigm of martial practice.[11]

Historicizing *Kalarippayattu*

From at least the twelfth century A.D., *kalarippayattu* was practiced throughout Kerala and contiguous parts of Coorg (Kodagu) District, Karnataka, in southwestern coastal India. Reflecting the early Tamil *sangam*-age notion of battle as the ritual battlefield of one's honor, the practice of *kalarippayattu* was especially associated with subgroups of Nayar (females as well as males at least until the onset of menses). It was the right and duty of Nayar males to serve as soldiers and healers at the behest of the village head (*desa vali*), district ruler (*nadu vali*), or *raja,* having vowed to serve him to death as part of his retinue. Along with Nayars, Cattar (or Yatra) Brahmans, Christians, Muslims, and one subgroup of the Ilava caste (given the special title of *chekor*) learned, taught, and practiced all aspects of the art.

Kalarippayattu declined after the introduction of firearms but survived under the tutelege of a few masters in scattered regions of north and central Kerala. During the modern era *kalarippayattu* was first brought to general public attention during the 1920s in a wave of rediscovery of indigenous arts; despite increasing public awareness within the north Malabar region, however, *kalarippayattu* continued to be little known as a practical martial and healing art to the general public in Kerala and in India as late as 1976 when I began field research.

The current history and practice of *kalarippayattu* cannot be considered apart from the emergence of other Asian martial and self-defense arts as a global form of cosmopolitanism, a phenomenon attributable to the spread of popular martial arts films and other forms of popular literature on the martial arts. V. Pandian summarized the situation in India:

> Ever since the mid-70's, when Bruce Lee took the moviegoing public by storm with his exploits in *Enter the Dragon,* there has been a virtual renaissance of the martial arts. (1983a)

> In recent times, moviegoers—particularly in India—have been enthralled by the amazing feats performed by exponents of the martial arts. In fact . . . Bruce Lee and Liu Chia Hui have become household names in India. (1983b)

Although as early as 1933 Dr. M. H. S. Barodawalla was awarded his black belt after studying karate, judo, and jujitsu in Japan, it was not until the 1970s and the influx of martial arts films from abroad that Indian students traveled east in large numbers to take up training and returned to open karate or karate-style schools throughout the subcontinent. By the early 1980s karate-style fight scenes had become ubiquitous in popular Indian films; karate stories complete with action-packed photographs of brick breaking and gang fights had become regular fare in newspapers and popular magazines; karate schools could be found not only in major cities but also in small towns and villages throughout India; and statewide police forces were receiving regular training in karate.[12] Within Kerala, practitioners of *kalarippayattu* must compete with teachers of karate, kung fu, and modern composite forms of self-defense for students as well as for the attention of their publics.

Two Traditional Paradigms of Self, Practice, Power, and Agency

Among the *kalarippayattu* practitioners who position themselves as maintainers of their traditional techniques, two paradigmatic figures inform how they interpret the relationship between self, practice, agency, and power. First is the royal sage. Barbara Stoller-Miller describes Kalidasa's heroic kings as "royal sages":

> The king's spiritual power is equal to his martial strength and moral superiority. He is a sage (*rsi*) by virtue of his discipline (*yoga*), austerity (*tapas*), and knowledge of sacred law (*dharma*). . . . The ideal royal sage is a figure of enormous physical strength and energy who also has the power to control his senses." (1984: 8-9)

Among the heroic princes of the *Mahabharata*, it is Arjuna who most definitively embodies this particular model of the heroic royal sage in his accomplishment of superior self-control by undergoing extensive practice of yoga and *tapas*. This is most evident when Arjuna gains access to the esoteric, magical powers of the weapon known as Pasupata with which he could conquer his enemies. In contrast to the subtleties of the paradigm of the royal sage embodied in Arjuna, there is the contrasting paradigm of practice and power embodied by his brother, Bhima. Bhima is associated with the raw power of physical and muscular strength, exemplified in the fact that he engaged most often in hands-on combat, especially wrestling and grappling—techniques that were considered the "lowest" of fighting techniques.[13]

Reflecting assumptions that inform the paradigmatic figure of the royal sage, the vast majority of training in traditional *kalari* in Kerala requires months of practice of the preliminary physical culture exercises and breathing techniques, which leads to superior self-control. Attaining self-control begins by discovering and taming the physical or gross body (*sthula-sarira*), discovered through practice of exercises and receipt of full-body massage. The exercises include a vast array of poses, steps, jumps, kicks, and leg exercises performed in increasingly complex and faster combinations back and forth across the *kalari* floor. Repetitious practice of these outer forms "in due time" eventually is understood to render the external body flexible (*meivalakkam*) and, as one master said, "flowing (*olukku*) like a river." Gradually the student begins to manifest physical, mental, and behavioral signs resulting from "correct" practice.[14] At first the exercises are "that which is external" (*bahyamayatu*). Like the practice of hatha yoga, daily practice of these basic forms leads to extraordinary control, and eventually turns the student inward—the exercises eventually become "that which is internal" (*andarikamayatu*). Another master explained the progress: "First the outer forms, then the inner secrets."

Assuming basic principles of the Ayurvedic medical system and of tantric yoga, many practitioners still agree that accomplishment achieved through long-term practice in these psychophysical exercises, massage, and related breathing and meditation techniques (1) makes the body so fluid that there is a healthful congruence of the body's humors; (2) establishes an intuitive and practical knowledge of the body's vital points (*marmmam*) used in fighting (*prayogam*) and in treating injuries (Zarrilli 1992a, 1992b); and (3) leads the practitioner from the outside inward to discovery of the esoteric subtle body associated with tantrism, purifies this subtle body, and awakens the internal vital energy (*prana-vayu*) that becomes manifest as power (*sakti*) in combat as well as medical practice (Zarrilli 1989a, 1989b). According to this particular paradigm of practice, the bodymind-in-practice is the vehicle through which power (*sakti*) is awakened and becomes manifest. Practice of more esoteric psychophysiological and meditation techniques such as attaining accomplishment in *mantra*, the devotional attitude of the individual practitioner, as well as traditional ritual practices all provide complementary paths to enhancing the power(s) at one's disposal. The logical culmination of the royal sage's manifestation of power (*sakti*) is when he attains accomplishment in esoteric powers that allow him to attack an opponent's body's vital spots by simply pointing or looking (Zarrilli 1992b).

According to this discourse, power is *substantive* as well as constituted in relationships. The individual practitioner disciplined himself psychophysiologically in order to substantively actualize *within* his bodymind a certain kind and degree of power (*sakti*).[15] His ability to exercise that power was constrained, however, by the network of hierarchically ordered divine/human relationships within which he lived and attempted to exercise his powers. Whether a *particular* practitioner gained access to particular techniques through which to raise, manifest, and manipulate *sakti* of a particular sort has always depended upon the practitioner's location within the social hierarchy within the place of practice—that is, one's "subject-position" is "crafted within relations of [social] power" (Kondo 1990: 300).[16]

Each of these practices—psychophysiological, psychomental, magical, ritual, and so on—allows the practitioner to actualize some degree of power. As J. Richardson Freeman notes regarding sacred power in Northern Kerala, power (*sakti*) "is differentially understood as it applies to different functions, actors, and contexts," and its meaning "emerges only pragmatically, in practice" (1991: 706). Cosmologically and pragmatically, the practitioner's power is *relative* to his ability to exercise his power in practice. What is common to all manifestations of power (*sakti*) in Northern Kerala is the recognition that *sakti* "is not so much one of specific attributes as of degree: *sakti* operates where there is some peculiarly *heightened efficacy* in evidence" (ibid.).

Borrowing the concept of the shifting subject position from feminist theory (Kondo 1990), the traditional *kalarippayattu* practitioner might be thought of as inhabiting a subject/power position that is relatively unstable. From the point of view of the practitioner, since power is not absolute but a matter of degree, one's own powers shift according to one's own readiness to actualize such power, and in response to the (social, political, ritual, and cosmological) forces impinging on one's ability to exercise power.

Existing side by side with this paradigm of the royal sage who in his most ideal embodiment is able to raise and actualize powers (*sakti*) through meditation, austerities, and so on is the paradigm of brute strength (*balam*) embodied by Bhima. Power (*sakti*) is certainly manifest in the physical strength generated by a Bhima-like practitioner, and through such strength one obtains agency and exercises power. Such manifestations of power-in-strength are, however, both limited to contexts within which this more limited degree of power can be exercised and "tainted" by the implicit lack of self-control embodied by a Bhima. The most extreme example of this potentially uncontrollable state is vividly witnessed in Bhima's disembowelment of Dushasana when he drinks his blood in retribution for Dushasana's violation of Draupadi. This state of excessive "fury" is performatively represented in genres like *yakshagana* or *kathakali* when Bhima assumes a transformed state—he embodies fury (*raudra*).

Arjuna's state of absolute self-control and distance exemplified by his expertise in archery and Bhima's extreme state of fury and blood lust constitute a bipolar continuum between which traditional martial practitioners could configure their relationship between self, agency, power, and behavior.

Revisioning *Kalarippayattu*

Like a number of his contemporaries born into families with a tradition of practicing *kalarippayattu*, Ustaz Hamzah followed in the footsteps of both his father and his grandfather and, in 1948, at the age of six, took his first lesson in *kalarippayattu* on the same day he took his first class in a traditional Muslim school. In a special training space at his family home in central Kerala's Malappuram District, his first teacher (Master Kunnachan Veetil Bavo from Andathode, Malappuram District, Kerala), his father, his grandfather, and all the other adult males of the family gathered to bless both him and his father's sister's son, who was also beginning training. Hamzah remembers the way in which his training began: applying oil to his body, putting on the long cloth (*kacca*) wrapped around his waist and hips to support his navel region, receiving a light massage to his whole body, and then performing a few preliminary exercises. To mark this largely ceremonial occasion there were readings from the Koran, and a goat was slaughtered for a family feast. Thereafter, in the mornings he received his religious education and in the evenings his martial training.

Between the ages of six and fifteen, Hamzah trained under eleven different teachers including Muslims, Christians, and Hindus. Hamzah describes himself as "crazy for *kalarippayattu*"—so crazy that he began to pay masters to come to his house to teach him the specific techniques he wanted to learn. Just before leaving for Malaysia at the age of sixteen in 1958, he learned a few of the most secretive *kalarippayattu* techniques—location, attack, and defense of some of the vital spots (*marmmam*) (Zarrilli 1992a, 1992b).

After growing up in village Kerala where martial arts other than *kalarippayattu* were virtually unknown until the 1970s, Hamzah describes how at first he was "spellbound by the number of martial arts practised" in Kuala Lumpur—the indigenous Malaysian art of *silat*, as well as such well-known martial arts as Chinese kung fu, Japanese judo, Korean tae kwan do, various forms of karate, and so forth. Hamzah saw these arts at demonstrations and in their training halls as well as in their representations in popular magazines and films. After two years of exposure to these other martial arts in Kuala Lumpur, Hamzah concluded that "*kalarippayattu* was far superior to" them all.

For Hamzah, like millions of others caught up in migrations prompted by an increasingly global economy, the landscape of his imagination and his lived reality were altered by his move to Kuala Lumpur. Anthropologist Arjun Appadurai uses the term *ethnoscape* to describe "the changing social, territorial, and cultural reproduction of group identity" that is characteristic of relocations like Hamzah's (1991: 191):

> The landscapes of group identity—the ethnoscapes—around the world are no longer familiar anthropological objects, insofar as groups are no longer tightly territorialized, spatially bounded, historically unselfconscious, or culturally homogenous.
>
> By *ethnoscape*, I mean the landscape of persons who make up the shifting world in which we live: tourists, immigrants, refugees, exiles, guest-workers, and other moving groups and persons. (ibid.: 191-92)

Amidst this shifting, intercultural experience, the martial art of Hamzah's youth was juxtaposed with a global concatenation of images, discourses, and paradigms of martial practice available to him in Kuala Lumpur—an experience through which Hamzah began to revision the *kalarippayattu* of his youth. From the many images, discourses, and paradigms of martial practice available to him from both Kerala and Kuala Lumpur, the principal one that crystallized Hamzah's revisioning of *kalarippayattu* may be characterized as a practical, streetwise self-defense paradigm of the cosmopolitan "man of action." This paradigm is graphically represented in the ubiquitous figure of the martial arts practitioner displaying his strength, expertise, power, and agency as he executes an extended high kick or fights off multiple attackers. Hamzah became convinced that if *kalarippayattu* were reinvented to fit this self-defense paradigm, it could compete for attention and students in the cosmopolitan Kuala Lumpur martial arts marketplace.

From Revisioning to Practice: "Reelaborating" *Kalarippayattu* for a New Public

In 1960 Hamzah began a long process of "reelaborating" *kalarippayattu* for a new Kuala Lumpur public that led to the 1974 opening of the first *kalarippayattu* training center outside of Kerala, India. I have borrowed theater semiotician Patrice Pavis's term *reelaboration* to describe the process of transformation that takes place when a tradition or practice is altered for a new context (1989: 38).[17] In this instance, Hamzah gradually reelaborated all aspects of *kalarippayattu* for a more global, cosmopolitan public, including its organization, pedagogical structure, techniques, accoutrements of practice, and the narrative and images used to present and represent the art. This process of reelaboration and transformation repositioned not only the practitioner's body but also the notions of agency and power implicit in that body's practice. By the time of my visit in 1983, both Hamzah's style and his narrative about its development had become crystallized as a practice and as a history. It is the story of the invention of this new style that I now relate.

In 1960, when Hamzah decided to bring *kalarippayattu* to this new public, he returned to Kerala for eleven months of intensive training under three different teachers. It was then that he became "enlightened in [the practical aspects of] *kalarippayattu.*" During this trip and when he returned again in 1965 and 1967, Hamzah learned more than one hundred locks, releases, and counters to weapons attacks; how to fight off two, three, or four opponents at a time; and numerous disarming tactics. Focusing his attention exclusively on practical applications for fighting—especially such techniques as locks and escapes—he took no interest in the preliminary psychophysical exercises, the advanced weapons training so often seen in today's stage demonstrations and popular Malayalam films, or the more esoteric ritual or meditational dimensions of *kalarippayattu* practice associated with the figure of the royal sage.

Before he began to train his first students in 1974, Hamzah reorganized *kalarippayattu* to make it "international." He purged it of what he perceived to be its local, outmoded parochial aspects—its preliminary psychophysical exercises, massage system, and modes of breathing control—associated with the paradigm of the royal sage. In turn, he foregrounded the *kalarippayattu* techniques he thought would appeal to his new cosmopolitan public: those used in practical fights and for self-defense, and those associated with the raw strength and power of a Bhima. Hamzah is very clear about his reasons for instituting this change:

> [Martial artists] show off [what they know] in Malaysia, and they were interested in this.
>
> If a diamond is kept in the ground, people will ignore it. They will only be interested in a polished and cut stone. *Kalarippayattu* is like that. There would have been no interest in the old style of this martial art. Today people will not be interested in the [body control] exercises. People want to learn things very fast. If I followed the Kerala style [of teaching], people would leave after two weeks. I don't think this would work [in Kuala Lumpur].
>
> In Kerala, the teachers are very protective. Some are angry with me for bringing [all these practical techniques] out into the open and making them available to all. The thinking in Kerala is very short-sighted. People in Kerala only know their own world and not the world outside. I felt it was my duty to teach what I know and help people believe in *kalarippayattu*'s greatness. (Hamzah 1983)

Hamzah's emerging vision of *kalarippayattu* shaped the raw strength and power of a Bhima into an urban, cosmopolitan, streetwise art in which precision, speed of execution and learning, and practical application in a street encounter were most important. Consequently, Hamzah separated specific poses and steps from their original context as part of longer body-exercise sequences that in the traditional context are understood to lead to healthful congruence of the humors and recombined them for purely offensive or defensive purposes. He joined these basic stances and steps with more advanced *kalarippayattu* empty-hand techniques including locks, throws, releases, and tricks—techniques that, "if you're really in a fight," allow you to "counter or cheat an opponent."

To these *kalarippayattu* techniques, Hamzah also added approximately one hundred throws he learned when he studied Indian wrestling during one of his return trips to Kerala—a tradition associated in particular with Bhima and Hanuman. He organized all these combinations and sequences of moves specifically for self-defense, counterattack, or disarming an opponent in five major categories: locks, blows, throws, steps, and "general dynamic techniques," or combinations.

Hamzah crafted a narrative to describe his reconstituted *kalarippayattu,* proclaiming that all its techniques are

> based on actual attack and counter-attacks from the very beginning with no imaginary movements or punches in the air. KALARI-PAYAT is a direct method of combat. Each one of the thousands of Kalari-Payat techniques is a complete finishing tactic, which enables the person to get into the enemy and put him under control. . . . Kalari-Payat is a training to fight with the arts of chops, blows, kicks, punches, squeezes, locks, throws, sweeps breaking technique, fallen-down [*sic*] techniques and steps, movings and pressure-point tactics also vital-point attacks, all methods of sticks, all ranges of weapons, swords, shields, axe, daggers, ropes, etc. and all releasing techniques.
>   Kalari-Payat . . . is taught strictly for self-defence. . . [and is] aimed to equip its practitioner with devastating combat tactics that can apply in real defence. (Hamzah n.d.: 1)

Hamzah organized these techniques so that self-defense, traditionally deferred until very late in *kalarippayattu* training, is systematically taught from the first day of practice.[18]

By organizing his training around this practical self-defense paradigm, Hamzah reshaped the constraints on when and to whom one should teach the more dangerous and secretive empty-hand aspects of the art. Among many teachers in Kerala, empty-hand techniques were taught last for three reasons: (1) students had to prepare their bodyminds from a young age through the elaborate, graded exercises so that they would be able to intuitively respond to an attack with an appropriate defense; (2) empty-hand techniques were extraordinarily dangerous and part of learning the location of and attacks to the vital spots (*marmmam*); and (3) masters only gave this secret knowledge to their most advanced and trusted students. The vital spots were secret since penetration led to death, a maiming injury, or, at the very least, an intense pain that shocks the entire system and may initiate a serious long-term illness (Zarrilli 1992a, 1992b).

Thus Hamzah separated the long-term psychophysiological effects of practice from the practical, fighting applications—a repositioning of the body in relation to the experience of practice that emphasizes not so much the long-term health benefits of practice, but the short-term usefulness of its techniques to fighting.

Hamzah also organized his techniques into a hierarchically ordered and visually marked set of ranks based on the *dan* grade model used in many modern Japanese and Korean martial disciplines (Draeger 1974; see table 8.1). Students wear white karate-style uniforms embroidered with the most visible symbol associated with *kalarippayattu* in Kerala—the sword and shield.[19]

Table 8.1.*Yellow-belt syllabus,* International Kalari-Payat Dynamic Self-Defence Institute World Headquarters, Malaysia

A. *Locks*		B. *Blows*	
1.	Wrist belt	1.	Palm heel-one
2.	Hand lock-one	2.	Neck chop-one
3.	Wrist twist-one	3.	Proper nose-one
4.	Hair lock-one	4.	Knuckle chin
5.	Elbow ring-one	5.	Side heel
6.	Eagle lock-one	6.	Hammer blow
'7.	Leg scissor	7.	Light finger
8.	Hair strangle	8.	Middle jab
9.	Ankle break-one	9.	Strangle chop
10.	Elbow twin-one	10.	Front kick m-one
11.	Rear twist	11.	Front kick m-two
12.	Strangle close	12.	Instep temple-one
13.	Body lock-one	13.	Instep temple-two
14.	Helpless-one	14.	Instep arm
15.	Elbow break-one	15.	Helmet blow

C. *General dynamic techniques*	
1.	Physical, mental, and health training
2.	Counter set—one, two, and three
3.	All style steps and moving one and two
4.	Eagle fly and triple kicks
5.	Step punches, chokes, and kicks
6.	Chumadadi one
7.	Tiger attack one
8.	Multiple weapons defenses

Hamzah's marking and ordering of training may be contrasted with dress in traditional *kalari,* where students wear either the long, hand-wide red cloth (*kacca*) or the briefer and less cumbersome to wrap white *lengoti* (see fig. 8.2). Both provide an important degree of support for the region known as the "root of the navel" (*nabhi mula*) while leaving the practitioner's body completely exposed so that oil can be liberally applied to promote health-giving stimulation of the bodily humors and saps during exercise. The virtually unclothed body can move fluidly, unencumbered by potentially restrictive clothing. These traditional *kalarippayattu*-wrapped cloths are unmarked and give no sign of relative rank.[20]

The karate-style belted uniform covers the entire body, precludes application of traditional oils, and makes performing the body-control exercises difficult since to some degree it inhibits *kalarippayattu*'s free-flowing movements. In self-defense forms where the karate-style uniform is used, many throws are based on grasping the opponent by the upper jacket. Unlike the unmarked *kalarippayattu* cloths, the karate belt marks the rank a practitioner holds. Perhaps most important, for many young men the karate uniform is associated with a cinema-generated image of the martial arts expert—a man of action like Bruce Lee with a taut, tough, tight body who controls the world around him.

Just as the clothing of traditional *kalarippayattu* students is unmarked, so is their progress through training visibly unmarked. Advancement is a gradual process that depends on a master's intuitive reading of a student's progress not only in physical execution of techniques, but also in spiritual and behavioral terms. A master is said to "know [each student's] mind from the countenance of his face" (*mukhabhavattil ninnu manassilakkam*). Consequently, advancement is not literally marked by external signs that are worn, but is demonstrated in what techniques a student is allowed to practice.

Hamzah's students advance through the graded ranks, hierarchically ordered by belt color—white (beginner), yellow, green, red, brown, and black (first through eighth *dan*)—and pass a formal examination covering a printed syllabus for each.[21] Passing an examination permits the student to wear the next higher grade belt and to move on to the more advanced set of techniques the student must master to obtain the next belt.

To pass a belt examination a student must perform the requisite locks, blows, multiple defenses, throws, or steps. For example, the green belt examination consists of sixteen locks scored up to five points each and five multiple defenses scored up to four points each for a total possible 100 points. Two judges (holders of a black belt) score each technique. A student who scores between 95 and 100 receives a special A-level grade; 90 to 95 is A level, 80 to 90 B level, 70 to 80 C level. The minimum passing grade is C. A student who receives three C's in moving up the ranks will "never be permitted to become an instructor." A student who fails an exam is permitted to retake the examination after one month.[22] To obtain a black belt the student must also submit an essay demonstrating understanding of the art. These essays usually include at least passing reference to the behavioral, moral, health, and spiritual aspects of practice.

Malaysian students, like many of their Kerala counterparts, pay a monthly fee (in 1983, thirty dollars for regular classes held three days per week and fifty dollars for special classes in which they receive more individual attention). But unlike students in Kerala, those in Malaysia are also charged an examination fee for each rank test (yellow, twenty dollars; green, thirty dollars; red, forty dollars; brown, fifty dollars; first-*dan* black, one hundred twenty dollars; second-*dan* black, two hundred dollars; third-*dan* black, three hundred dollars; fourth- to eighth-*dan* black, four hundred to eight hundred dollars). It takes approximately four to six months for the typical student to progress sufficiently to pass a rank test. In Hamzah's system it is possible for some students to receive a first-*dan* black belt in as little as eighteen months. When one passes one becomes a subinstructor. Only those with advanced *dan* black belts are permitted to teach independently, and the title "mahaguru" is given to those who pass the eighth-*dan* black belt examination.

Although Hamzah also learned some special breath-control/meditational techniques[23] and some treatments and revival techniques that were traditionally considered an essential part of a master's repertoire of skills, he no longer pratices any of these techniques. If injuries occur, instead of giving treatments himself with *kalarippayattu*'s traditional hands-on medical treatments (*kalari cikitsa*), he says he "prefer[s] to go to the hospital because it is faster and more effective than the traditional therapy. Ayurvedic treatments just take too long. It was fine for that age, but it is just too slow for today's world."

While Hamzah's version of *kalarippayattu* is the first I know to have fully conformed to a transnational self-defense paradigm, it is by no means the only one. A number of other practitioner/teachers in Kerala and throughout India have either transformed *kalarippayattu* itself into a form of self-defense similar to Hamzah's or borrowed parts of it to create new hybrids.[24]

Over the years Hamzah's system has slowly gained public attention and a healthy number of students in Malaysia. In 1985 he reported having three hundred students in his six Kalari Payat centers in West Malaysia, some of which are branches located in the tea estates where large populations of South Indians reside. Students range in age from ten to forty and are primarily long-term South Indian immigrants to Malaysia. Public recognition from the Malaysian government has included demonstrations at national cultural days, and Film Nagara made a short film on Kalari Payat. An invitation was issued to Hamzah to corepresent Malaysia at the International Martial Arts

Demonstration organized by the Singapore Martial Arts Instructors Association in 1986.

Hamzah's reorganization of *kalarippayattu* into a graded, ranked system that can be taught quickly and with practical results, as well as his representations of *kalarippayattu*, make three interrelated appeals: the first is to a youthful, modern, fast-paced, cosmopolitan sensibility, that is, the art is effective and can be learned and used quickly; the second is "scientific," that is, he represents practice as systematically organized so that the student will not waste time; and the third is "international," that is, by being "international," Hamzah's *kalarippayattu* can cross cultural and national boundaries. It is a paradigm of practice that is intended to be geographically interchangeable. By deemphasizing local, territorially specific, indigenous aspects of practice, martial practice transcends "specific territorial boundaries and identities" (Appadurai 1991: 192). The transnational territory that Hamzah's *kalarippayattu* inhabits is itself a newly created and imagined territory—a theatricalized cosmopolitan space inhabited by a character common to martial arts action films, the man of action.

Images of the *Kalarippayattu* "Man in Action": Clean Bowling Over the Jet-Set Generation

Like any creative businessman, Hamzah knew he had to garner publicity for his enterprise to succeed. In 1974 Hamzah put his first students through an intensive three-month course at the conclusion of which he staged a two-hour demonstration to attract attention. At the same time, he mounted a massive publicity campaign for the first-stage demonstration. Since then he has regularly produced his own brochures and advertisements.

Hamzah places ads in a variety of publications including the English-language *Movieland*, a popular film magazine.[25] Typical of other issues, the April 1981 edition features numerous photographs and articles on American television reruns ("Ex-Brunette Loni Hits"; "WKRP's Other Woman Jan Smithers Fought to Keep Playing Shy Bailey"; "Nancy Allen the Actress with the Very Sensually Shaped Figure"), Tamil and Hindi films with shorts on various stars, and semisensational color-photo cover stories such as Padmini Kolhapure as "the girl who stunned India with a kiss."[26] In this issue Hamzah's advertisement for his self-defense institute appears below a photograph of an embrace between Tamil actors Rajnikanth and Madhavi in their new film, *Thillu Mullu*, and next to an ad for the health medicine Rejuvenal. Hamzah's advertisements always feature an action-filled photograph of an empty-hand or weapons technique, usually of one combatant fighting off multiple attackers, one of them caught in a mid-air leap, kick, attack, or defense. Advertisement copy includes a variety of come-ons aimed at specific groups of potential students or employers. Most important is the appeal to the young man about town enamored of the James Bond- or Bruce Lee-type figure: "defend yourself in times of danger and surprise attacks." For the image-conscious young man, the ad promises that he can "build a strong healthy body." Appealing to a modern, fast-paced lifestyle, one can enroll in "'crash training' available for people on the move." Hamzah also provides "special rates for ladies and children" and invites the "attention [of] all movie producers and directors: stunt services and dynamic fighting techniques can be provided."

The adjacent ad for Rejuvenal, a "preparation [that] contains some vitamins and herbs . . . manufactured in West Germany," appeals to the same type of energetic, active life-on-the-go audience Hamzah addresses. In terms that might just as easily have been written about his *kalarippayattu* classes, Rejuvenal claims to "help you in health and vitality . . . to lead a healthy, vigorous, and active life . . . [restore] robustness and [maintain] vitality . . . [relieve] irritability, lack of concentration, unrest and general debility."

Hamzah continuously recycles his version of the origins and practice of *kalarippayattu* through all available media. The *Malay Mail* of August 31, 1985, featured a two-page color photo spread in the Saturday "Lifestyle" section sandwiched between the day's television schedule and reviews of two fantasy/adventure films, *Mad Max beyond Thunderdome* and *Buckaraoo Banzai*. In addition to history, this article included student testimonials about the benefits of practice. Ten-year-old David Amirthajar Samuel, the youngest in the class, tells how "this training is good for me as I feel healthier now and it has also built up my stamina," while Raja Mohammed "has become a bolder person since taking up lessons." The mahaguru himself is featured in a two-page color photo/text insert that presents a capsule biography of his training and the story of how he introduced the art to Malaysia.

An important journalistic leitmotiv is establishing *kalarippayattu*'s superiority to karate. This strategy is illustrated in articles covering the 1986 visit of twenty-four-year-old Malayali black-belt karate teacher K. T. Hakeem, who came to take a crash course in Hamzah's version of *kalarippayattu*. Hakeem's story was featured in two publications, the April 30, 1986, issue of *Malaysian Post* and the June 15-21, 1986, issue of *Weekend Review* published by the Hindustan Times Press, New Delhi. Both articles featured action photographs of the young, mustachioed Malayali male executing a high kick while fighting off attackers. The *Malaysian Post* headlines claim that Kalari Payat puts karate "in the shade," while the *Weekend Review* article sells Hakeem as a "new star on [the] *kalari* horizon." Both articles tell how Hakeem decided to "'give something extra' to those who got trained [in karate] under him": "he thought a dash of *kalari* training would enable them to face any challenging situation with true grit and sure-fire success." The newspaper accounts emphasize how extraordinary it is that Hakeem left his native Kerala, home of *kalarippayattu*, to study the art in Malaysia with Hamzah, "the Mahaguru who had modernised [*kalarippayattu*] and introduced a few innovations which included a grading system and a uniform. The jet-set generations were clean-bowled over by all these" (*Weekend Review*).

As seen in the *New Thrill* photo spread covering my visit, my presence in Kuala Lumpur proved an equal catalyst for publicity. At a special belt-grading function to which a number of reporters and photographers had been invited, I performed a few basic *kalarippayattu* exercises and one practical application of a basic technique in which I threw one of Hamzah's advanced black-belt students. My performance of this escape was well documented by the photographer and became the subject of several feature stories.

Both Hakeem and I were multivalent symbols for Hamzah. Hakeem, as a Malayali holding a black belt in karate, decided to submit himself to *kalarippayattu* training under Hamzah, which could be read as the wayward native Malayali who went outside his own culture to study karate returning "home" to a better art of self-defense. As a karate master, Hakeem already could be read as a man embodying action controlling his world. By studying *kalarippayattu* he would be even better able to exert such control and display himself as a man of action. As an American I could be read as one of the modern, cosmopolitan, self-assured, men of the world who is trained in self-defense and therefore able to control his world. This is the image embodied in such popular action-film figures as James Bond, Bruce Lee, Chuck Norris, and their popular Asian-cinema counterparts.[27] These dynamic male figures vanquish their opponents with techniques choreographed from an eclectic variety of Asian and Western fighting techniques. As a scholar, I implicitly legitimized the importance and study of self-defense, and Hamzah's *kalarippayattu* specifically. Even though I am not an expert, as a practitioner trained in Kerala I could also be read as embodying the tradition of which they were a part. Although our styles were totally different, nevertheless we ostensibly practiced the "same art." My presence pointed backward to the place of *kalarippayattu's* origins in Kerala and forward to the cosmopolitan present. Hamzah's intuitive insistence that I show "at least one practical tactic" provided the essential link between the traditional exercises I knew and Hamzah's practically oriented modern self-defense form. My demonstration was a sign of "authentic" practice (self-defense) that valorized his own. Besides, it was good theater, and it made for good publicity.

Reading the Presentations and Representations: Issues of Power, Control, Sex, Violence, and Virility

The *New Thrill* tabloid picture spread in which I appeared, with its hyped-up title, "Deadly Art of Locks and Throws," is one obvious print-media example of what Richard Schechner has called the theatricalization of news—a phenomenon on the increase "because the public and those who exploit the public want increased theatricalization, which means simplification, quick arousal, and satisfactory resolution of the excitement" (1985: 318). Titillating headlines and photographs arouse the (male) reader's curiosity and draw him into the world of the tabloid, where short "news" stories simplify complex issues. A series of short, simplified sets of visual and print images are juxtaposed one against another. Much like the 1984 issue in which I appeared, the June 21, 1980, issue of *New Thrill* featured reports about a "striptease queen," criminal violence, a ghost story, and *kalarippayattu.*

As the eye travels from one image or brief narrative to the next, the sets of images and texts demand to be read intertextually for the possible meanings created by their juxtaposition. The tabloid, like its mass-media counterparts, quickly juxtaposes and thereby links virility, sex, violence, and the supernatural.[28] In these brief, spectacularized narratives, all four realms share a test of a man's personal and interpersonal boundaries and behaviors. Virility, sex, violence, and the supernatural are all concerned with power—with who controls what and whom. All four invite the male reader to vicariously enter the fantasy (if not the actuality) of arousal associated with each dangerous encounter with an other. Each arousal provides its own brand of "excitement," and the excitement is present in the encounter with what remains other, and is therefore unknown and mysterious. The image of the male projected here, and supported in many of the popular action-packed martial arts movies, is a highly gendered fantasy in which the "virile" man controls his environment and all those around him either by the force of attraction, or literally by exercising force. These representations of sex, violence, and the supernatural take the male reader outside his normative social and interpersonal boundaries and appear to be as potentially exciting as they are dangerous.

The image of the male that emerges from these pages is that of a controlling figure—the virile, self-confident man in control. He is usually pictured in action, with a taut, attractive, and powerful physique, and is described as energetic, dynamic, and therefore "healthy." If he can control his body and confront physical danger, he should be able to control everything in his world. To envision oneself as a Bruce Lee or a Hakeem, executing a dynamic high kick, is to enter the fantasy, if not the actuality, of having power and control over one's environment. This man of action is what Appadurai calls a "mediascape": an "image-centered, narrative-based account of strips of reality" offering "a series of elements (such as characters, plots and textual forms) out of which scripts can be formed of imagined lives" (1990: 9).

The repackaging, mediation, and transnationalization of *kalarippayattu* to fit the cosmopolitan self-defense paradigm has transformed it from a complex, embedded, local (martial, therapeutic, and fighting) art whose powers are ritually, ethically, spiritually, and socially circumscribed into a spectacular and melodramatic one whose powers are either decontextualized or recontextualized.[29] In these short, mediated image/texts, each arena within which power is asserted is divorced from its complex local context. Indigenous arts like *kalarippayattu*, or a spiritual art like Master Tan's control of spirits residing in banana trees, were traditionally grounded in their local context. One experienced such arts and their practitioners not through a mediated representation of them, but either immediately, within the local context where the master demonstrated his powers in practice, or through performative means of celebrating the warrior's heroic demeanor like ballads, dramas, or dances. A particular master's power and control were experienced and understood within a hierarchy of interactive spheres of power operative in the local setting.

Although this melodramatic subtext does not have the same fully schematized narrative found in most modern martial-arts action films, the same basic elements are present: danger, attack, defense, control, and power.[30] This schematic subtextual melodrama lies behind the resonance and articulation of the representations of *kalarippayattu* exemplified by Hamzah's commodified self-defense version of the art pitched to the modern martial arts marketplace and present in virtually every popular martial arts magazine, including the American monthlies *Black Belt* and *Inside Kung-Fu*. The circles of signification embed and interpenetrate all the "traditional" versions of the Asian martial arts in their contemporary self-defense guises, in which distinctions between arts, cultures, and histories are erased.

In the case of *kalarippayattu*, its characteristics as an Indian discipline for the development of the bodymind and all the requisite powers necessary to enter combat as part of one's duty (dharma) are erased. Both the bodymind per se and the results of its long-term development toward a particular type of accomplishment and cultivation of internal powers are repositioned. The transnational melodramatic subtext replicated in films, action photographs, and action narratives locate the very real issues of power, fear, control, and attack in the individual male's fantasy world and outside the constraints of the traditional social and ethical context.

The highly circumscribed boundaries that were intended to contain the exercise of power and control in the local context are, in modern media, blurred in their facile juxtaposition of images. Cultural producers interested in attracting and titillating their readers and viewers are not concerned with articulating the ethics of practice that circumscribed the exercise of power in a particular locale. The suggestive titles and photographic images of masters of self-defense dynamically fighting off three opponents are divorced from a contextualizing narrative that might situate the potential exercise of violence within a particular context and thereby circumscribe it. Titles like "Deadly Art of Locks and Throws" foreground and theatricalize violence rather than explore the elements of self- and social control that ideally circumscribe violent acts. As Joshua Meyrowitz asserts in *No Sense of Place*, modern media's blurring of "distinctions between here and there, live and mediated, and personal and public" is contributing to an increasing sense of placelessness, to the divorce of mediated meanings from the particularity of their present, lived context (1985: 308). This decontextualization of images of the exercise of power and control removes the clear boundaries of responsibility that could circumscribe the potential exercise of power to do violence.

Ideals, Images, and Intent

As Foucault points out, central to any technology of the self or power are "modes of training and modification of individuals, not only in the obvious sense of acquiring certain skills but also in the sense of acquiring certain attitudes" (1988: 198). While exploiting every media possibility for presenting his form of self-defense through images that contribute to the representation of the practitioner as a physically fit, confident, dynamic man on the go, able to control his environment and to do so violently, Hamzah simultaneously asserts the fundamental ethical principle that governs the more traditional paradigms of practice he was taught in his own training as a young boy, a principle intended to constrain the potential for violence of the self-defense practitioner. He insists that all of his students observe

> the oath that had to be taken privately with one's master and one's own god: I promise I will not misuse this and will only use it for self-defense. If I misuse it I will face the displeasure of my master and will be dismissed from further training.

When a student fills out an application form for admission to training, the student and two sponsors promise to abide by the rules and regulations and conditions stipulated by the International Kalari-Payat Dynamic Self-Defence Institute. The student agrees to a statement saying:

> I also understand that this art is to be used for the sole purpose of self-defence and not for any purpose of evil design. And if any evil deed motivated by evil design is done by me then the entire responsibility is with me and I shall solely bear the consequence thereof.
>
> Persons who have any criminal record or with misconduct are not allowed to continue the training.

Students ideally achieve not only the ability to defend themselves with potentially deadly force, but also the moral authority not to misuse the power they have acquired.

Hamzah's students speak and write with great conviction about how their practice of the art has helped them. In his required three-hundred-word essay for the first-*dan* black belt exam of 1981, one student reflected on the multiple benefits of his three years of training:

> I have found [the training] to be an excellent form of physical fitness and self-defence. In the beginners class, I had minor problems like body aching and over-tiredness, but eventually with continued practise I began to feel better, strong, and more eager to keep on practising. I passed my different belt gradings in stages from white to yellow, green, red, and then to brown belt. By now my legs and hands ha[d] become stronger and powerful and they have turned into a lethal weapon. I have never had the opportunity to test my self-defence skill since I have never indulged myself in any form of violence and since I would walk away or talk myself out of any fight even if the odds were to my credit. By the practise of Kalari, I have learned to control myself, my movements and to respect others. Kalari Payat teaches you to be prepared to defen[d] yourself from sudden attacks, it gives you patience, the ability to be punctual, to have confidence in what you do and discipline. It also frees us from chronic illness.

The 1977 testimony of another student also belies the image he and other black belts create in action photographs featured in newspaper stories and in advertisements for the school:

> Before I started practising I was hot tempered, aggressive, bulky and hunchy in shape. But now I have found that patience and calmness are two beautiful aspects of life. Moreover my body is well formed and I am always looking forward enthusiastically to life. I can firmly say that this art builds one up not only in physique but also in character.

Echoing both of his fellow students, another black-belt candidate wrote in 1979:

> After a few years a Kalari-Payat exponent changes for the better in both physique and character. He becomes humble and is able to think more clearly. He is confident of himself and gentle in the treatment of others around him.

These testimonies self-consciously speak of pacification of violent temperaments, of calm and self-control. Read against the assertive, aggressive, violent images of the cosmopolitan man of action, they clearly reflect the ambiguity implicit in practicing a bodily discipline like the martial arts, which can serve equally as a pathway to self-realization or to domination. It is a slippery path that is constantly being negotiated by each teacher in every arena of training and practice.

Notes

I conducted field research in Kerala in 1976-77, 1980, 1983, 1985, 1988, and 1989. While I was there I trained practically under Gurukkal Govindakutty Nair at the C. V. N. Kalari, Trivandrum. In 1989 I also trained under the auspices of the Kerala Kalarippayattu Academy (Cannannore), C. Mohammed Sherif, director. I wish to acknowledge with thanks support provided by a Fulbright Fellowship (1976-77), Senior Research Fellowships from the American Institute of Indian Studies (1980, 1983, 1988), the University of Wisconsin-Madison Graduate School (1980, 1983, 1985, 1988), the Richard Carley Hunt Memorial Postdoctoral Fellowship from the Wenner-Gren Foundation for Anthropological Research (1985), and a Senior Research Fellowship from the Social Science Research Council (1985). This essay is part of my forthcoming comprehensive study of *kalarippayattu, "When the Body Becomes All Eyes," Paradigms and Discourses of Practice and Power in Kalarippayattu, South Indian Martial and Medical Art.*

1. In Malayalam, *kalari* means "place, open space, threshing floor, battlefield" (Burrow and Emeneau 1961: 98). It derives from the Tamil *kalam* meaning "arena, area for dramatic, gladitorial, or gymnastic exhibitions, assembly, place of work or business" (ibid.). In Malayalam *kalari* also idiomatically refers to that special place where martial exercises (*payattu*) are taught. The root of the Malayalam *payattu* is the Tamil *payil,* "to become trained, accustomed, practice," while its nominative form means "practice, habit, words" (ibid.: 265). In Malayalam *payil* becomes *payiluka,* "to learn, speak," *payattuka* "to exercise in arms, practice," and finally *payattu* has the idiomatic meaning of martial exercise or "trick" (ibid.).

Although the Tamil roots of both *kalari* and *payattu* are antique and can be traced to as early as the first century A.D. (Burrow and Emeneau 1961; Burrow 1947), their specific idiomatic Malayalam meanings may be no older than the eleventh or twelfth century, when it is probable that the systems of martial practice assumed a structure and style akin to those extant today. Belying the assumption that the compound itself might have an equally antique use as the singular *kalari* and *payattu*, the *Malayalam Lexicon* notes that the earliest use of the compound *kalarippayattu* is in Ulloor Parameswaram's early-twentieth-century drama *Amba*.

Although M. D. Raghavan (1947) suggested that *kalari* was derived from the Sanskrit *khalurika*, Burrow has conclusively demonstrated that *khalurika* ("parade ground, arena") and its Sanskrit root, *khala-* ("threshing floor") are Dravidian loan words (1947; also 1946). According to the *St. Petersburg Lexicon*, the first occurrence of *khalurika* is Hemacandra's *Abhidanacintamani*, dated about the twelfth century.

2. In 1983 Hamzah was the only individual who had established a viable permanent center for *kalarippayattu* training outside India. Hamzah initiated our correspondence in 1980 when he responded to an article I had written on *kalarippayattu* that appeared in *TDR: The Drama Review* (Zarrilli 1979).

3. The pen name Mai-Pen-Rai is an atypical Malay name that is not likely to be known to the Malay reader except among those who frequent Thailand. For those who do frequently cross the border, Southeast Asian anthropologist Mary Grow informs me that *mai pen rai* ("never mind; it doesn't matter") is a typical saying through which Thais express their cultural ideal of "cool-heartedness." At least among those who have visited Hatyai, the irony of the use of "never mind" as a pen name for a story on prostitution should be obvious.

4. I have chosen to use the phrase "mode of cultural praxis" rather than "genre of cultural performance." When Milton Singer first proposed the category "cultural performance," he applied it to discrete items of performance including plays, concerts, and lectures as well as prayers, ritual readings, recitations, rites, and festivals, all of which encapsulate and exhibit "elementary constituents of the culture" (1972: 7). The postmodern turn in anthropological studies has problematized the modernist notion of culture as a relatively stable category, as well as of cultural performances as "encapsulating" "elementary constituents." Such a notion implies an essence fixed within boundaries rather than the fluid process of creating meaning characteristic of any act of performance, or of cultural praxis. For a recent discussion of the implications behind this more processual/performative view of culture, see Drewal (1991).

5. In addition to the studies discussed here, see also the important work of linguistic philosophers Lakoff and Johnson (1980); M. Johnson (1987); Lakoff (1987).

6. See Cynthia J. Novack's recent ethnographic study on contact improvisation (1990).

7. Kondo problematizes our Western notion of self as "unitary substance and consciousness," and in its singular place situates the self as plurally located according to context (1990: 304). On the relationship between self and person, see also the earlier, if problematic, studies of Shweder and LeVine (1984), White and Kirkpatrick (1985), Mauss (1973), and Carrithers, Collins, and Lake (1985).

8. Given this processual view of the ongoing temporal constitution of the self, and therefore of experience and meaning, the "body" too must be viewed as provisional. Such a notion has been advanced by feminist theorists like Judith Butler, who asserts that the body is "a variable boundary, a surface whose permeability is politically regulated" (1989).

Although *bodies, body images,* and *representations of the body* appear to us to be static objects with fixed significations, in this emergent, processual sense, one's own "body," like the "self," is constantly being made. This does not mean that at certain points in the history of one's relationship to one's own body, an individual never treats his or her body, or its image, as an object. Certainly such objectification is one part of our experience of our bodies in the image of our body reflected back to us in our mirrors, or those representations of our body in our memories, recollections, and imagination.

9. This sense of the "individual body-self" is distinguished from "the social concept of the

individual as 'person,' a construct of jural rights and moral accountability," which is a "uniquely Western notion of the individual as a quasi-sacred, legal, moral, and psychological entity whose rights are limited only by the rights of other equally autonomous individuals" (Lock and Scheper-Hughes 1990: 57).

10. The "problem" with disciplines in which agency and power are potentially generated and/or exercised is that there is always the implicit danger that the practitioner might transgress the socially circumscribed boundaries within which that power is ideally constrained. This is as true of the individual martial arts practitioner within a school as it is of the nuclear-age threat of a Dr. Strangelove.

11. Although I use the word *reposition*, I do not wish to suggest that there is a stable, originary position.

12. For example, see Eddie Fernandes's March 21, 1982, *Indian Express* story entitled "The Bruce Lees of India," and Arun Katiyar's four-page special feature complete with dynamic, action-packed photographs, "Enter the Super Corps!" reported in *Bombay* 4, no. 21 (June-July 1983).

13. There is an obvious Sanskritic bias in this hierarchical ordering of martial techniques. According to Sanskritic texts, bow and arrow were considered the "highest" attainment of the martial practitioner, while wrestling and grappling were the "lowest"—a ranking that reflects the transmission of pollution associated with touching and distance. Since one can kill an enemy from the greatest distance with the bow and arrow, one can kill without becoming polluted. The Tamil emphasis on power's being transmitted through sacred swords is reflected in *kalarippayattu*'s emphasis on sword and shield as its premier weapons.

14. Given the wide variety of styles of *kalarippayattu* practiced, what is or is not "correct" practice is open to the individual interpretation and authority of the master of every *kalari*.

15. In the context of South Asia, I would argue with Kondo's assertion that power is not "some essential substance . . . which some people have and some people do not" (1990: 307). There power *is* decidedly substantive, and the raison d'être for *kalarippayattu* and other such *sakti*-raising arts is to accumulate access to powers in practice.

16. The well-known story of the low-caste Ekalavya who, unable to study the martial arts because of his low birth, secretly learned by observing Drona teaching Arjuna illustrates this fact. When Drona discovered Ekalavya, he requested of him his *dakshina* or "gifts"—his right thumb, thus rendering the low-caste Ekalavya unable to best Drona's most prized high-caste *kshatriya* student, Arjuna.

17. Pavis originally used the "neutralized and somewhat insipid term—*reelaboration*" to describe the process by which "the cultural and theatrical traditions of the source culture are transformed by the needs of the target culture's theatrical and cultural tradition" (1989: 38). While I find the term *reelaboration* apt since it suggests the processual, temporal manner in which adaptation takes place (like Singer's concept of "cultural performance"), Pavis's use of "source" and "target" cultures is somewhat problematic since it assumes an objectivist metaphysics by implying that "source" and "target" cultures are discrete, bounded entities, and that one moves self-consciously from one to the other "knowing" what the "source" culture is and how it is distinct from the "target" culture. Because of his life experience, Hamzah is inhabiting an intercultural ethnoscape; there is no target "culture," although there definitely is a target public.

18. Although Hamzah teaches applications from the first day of training, specific knowledge of the vital spots is still preserved for the most advanced students.

19. In contrast to the pride of place given to bow and arrow in the Dhanur Vedic tradition (*Agnipurana* 249-52), in *kalarippayattu* the practitioner was to die by his sword. See the Gangadharan translation (1985).

20. The only difference that marks masters and older practitioners from students has more

to do with modesty associated with age than the hierarchy of rank. While they are teaching and when they are not exercising themselves, most masters will wear either a cotton towel or everyday *muntu* wrapped around their waist.

21. Young girls traditionally trained in *kalarippayattu* up until the onset of menses; young girls still train along with young boys in a few *kalari* today. Hamzah invites women to train in his modern style, and even advertises special self-defense classes for women. There were, however, no women at the classes I attended while I was in Kuala Lumpur in 1983.

22. The Kerala Kalarippayat Association has instituted annual competitions among students of member *kalari*. Students compete for awards in the preliminary exercises and weapons practice. The weapons are wielded only with students from the same school. There is no freestyle competition. Senior masters serve as judges and make awards based on style and form. Although student participants train hard for the annual competition, the awards per se are not linked to advancement within a particular *kalari*.

23. Hamzah learned special breath-control/meditation techniques for two months. He was required to be celibate, fast, and completely separate himself from the material world. In the first stage of meditation he was required to sit still, focusing his eyes straight ahead and his mind on God. From this simple sitting exercise he progressed to more complex forms.

24. For example, Higgins Master, a Christian of Trichur who traces his family lineage of practice to the royal family of Cochin in whose service they taught and fought, teaches a rough and ready hands-on style of *kalarippayattu* in which preliminary exercises are seldom taught and emphasis is on empty-hand techniques, especially locks, throws, and applications to the vital spots. He even calls his style of practice "Bhima" style.

Two other innovators located in the capital city, Tiruvanathapuram, are Renshi K. Mohanan and Balachandran Master, each of whom has fashioned his own composite self-defense style. Mohanan is founder, director, and "chief controller" of kaju-kado karate, a combination of *karate* (ka-), *judo* (-ju-), *kalari* (-ka-), and *aikido* (-do). Trained as a youth in *kalarippayattu* in college, he took up the "rough, very practical, full contact" Japanese karate. He devised a composite style that he feels is effective for street fighting. Balachandran Master established the Indian School of Martial Arts, which combines Tamil (*ati murai*) techniques and some *kalarippayattu* with boxing and karate-style self-defense techniques he learned in the Indian armed forces. A very hard style of practice, Balachandran combines the trappings of modern self-defense training (uniforms, etc.) with traditional *kalari* rituals.

25. Likewise, others aim their representations of martial practice to the young, male, cosmopolitan audience. Srinivasan advertises his classes with flyers that invite the reader to "defend yourself on the streets." Articles on Srinivasan have appeared in English-language Indian film glossies including the *Sun*. V. Arvind's 1983 article "Master of the Games" appears opposite a three-quarter-page photo spread of eleven models entitled "Aren't They Cool?" The caption reads: "Beauty is not skin deep—it takes lots of guts as well to stand in a freezing sea and make it look as though there's a heatwave on. But that's what fifteen beauty queen hopefuls did on Brighton beach in the run-up to the combined Miss England, Miss Wales and Miss Scotland contests. The finals, of course, will be indoors."

26. The cover story title refers to how Padmini, "sweet 16 and never been kissed . . . decided that Prince Charles was just too, too desirable to be allowed to pass by without a pair of cherry-red lips being pressed against his cheek. So the star of India's film industry — 'Kiss Oomph' to her fans—stepped forward in the Bombay Studios and kissed her hero." The story comes complete with a color photograph of Padmini and Prince Charles.

27. A special subgenre of Malayalam films dating from the 1960s is the ballad films whose stories are usually taken from the northern ballads (*vatakkan pattukal*) of the old Malabar region of Kerala. These ballads sing the deeds of *kalarippayattu*-trained heroes and heroines trained in traditional *kalari* techniques to fight duels to the death. Similar in their cinematic

treatment of war and combat to other Indian-cinema religious and epic films, these films differ from their contemporary representations of fighting in their idealization and glorification of the larger-than-life martial deeds of traditional heroes. Although they are choreographed by traditional masters, the *kalarippayattu* techniques shown in these Malayalam ballad films are sequences designed not to give an accurate representation of the subtleties of interior practice but to emphasize the superhuman feats of the hero. For a detailed discussion, see Zarrilli 1994.

Part of the reason that *kalarippayattu* has an image problem with many young Malayali males today is that the cinematic representations of the traditional martial art in the ballad films does not fit their expectations of how a martial art should look and enable one to fight. Fighting with outmoded weapons appears anachronistic and far from the type of image they hope to actualize by training in a modern martial art.

28. In the Malaysian example, "the unknown" is an important fourth text and set of images serially joined to the other three. They are self-consciously joined under the tabloid's banner of exploring the "unknown, mysterious, and exciting."

29. Other contemporary contexts such as the demonstration stage are also transforming *kalarippayattu* in radical, though different, ways. The emphasis in some *kalari* today on training students exclusively for stage demonstrations has made their style of *kalarippayattu* into a beautiful, fluid, dancelike art; for those most interested in the art as a martial art, however, this style has lost its raison d'être.

30. Although spectacle and melodrama were both an important part of the subtext of many traditional genres of cultural performance through which Kerala culture represented the heroic spirit of the *kalarippayattu*-trained warrior to itself, they were still embedded within a socio-cultural fabric that ideally restrained and constrained the powers of the practitioner.

Social and ethical constraints are always ideal constructions. One of the two most important quasi-historical/mythological heroes sung about in Kerala's northern ballads is Tacholi Otenan. Although practitioners were instructed never to use the most secret art of attacking the body's vital spots unless their life was in danger, one of the ballads glorifies Tacholi's subduing of a recalcitrant young woman, Kunki, by attacking her *marmmam* and apparently raping her as well. After she is subdued, she becomes pregnant and bears his child. In the context of the medieval hierarchy of social and legal constraints, Tacholi had been commissioned by the local ruler to collect taxes due from the young woman's father, who wished his recalcitrant daughter to be tamed. Both male authority figures approved of Tacholi's "taming" of Kunki.

References

Alter, Joseph S. 1992. *The Wrestler's Body: Identity and Ideology in North India.* Berkeley: University of California Press.

Appadurai, Arjun. 1990. Disjuncture and Difference in the Global Cultural Economy. *Public Culture* 2 (2): 1-24.

———. 1991. "Global Ethnoscapes: Notes and Queries for a Transnational Anthropology." In *Recapturing Anthropology*, edited by Richard G. Fox, pp. 191-210. Santa Fe: School of American Research Press.

Appadurai, Arjun, and Carol A. Breckenridge. 1988. Why Public Culture? *Public Culture*, 1 (1): 5-9.

Arvind, V. 1983. Master of the Games. *Sun* 6 (45) : 16-17.

Bruner, Edward M. 1986. "Ethnography as Narrative." In *The Anthropology of Experience*, edited by Victor W. Turner and Edward M. Bruner, pp. 139-55. Urbana: University of Illinois Press.

Burrow, T. 1946. Loanwords in Sanskrit. *Transactions of the Philological Society.*

———. 1947. Dravidian Studies VII: Further Dravidian Words in Sanskrit. *Bulletin of the School of Oriental and African Studies*, no. 12, part 1, 365-96.

Burrow, T., and M. B. Emeneau. 1961. *A Dravidian Etymological Dictionary.* Oxford: Clarendon.

Butler, Judith. 1989. *Gender Trouble.* London: Routledge.

Carrithers, M., S. Collins, and S. Lukes. 1985. *The Category of the Person.* Cambridge: Cambridge University Press.

Connerton, Paul. 1989. *How Societies Remember.* Cambridge: Cambridge University Press.

Draeger, Donn F. 1974. *Modern Bujutsu and Budo.* New York: Weatherhill.

Drewal, Margaret. 1991. The State of Research on Performance in Africa. *African Studies Review* 34 (3): 1-64.

Fernandes, Eddie. 1982. The Bruce Lees of India. *Indian Express,* March 21.

Fiske, John. 1989. *Understanding Popular Culture.* Boston: Unwin Hyman.

Foucault, Michel. 1988. "Technologies of the Self." In *Technologies of the Self: A Seminar with Michel Foucault,* edited by Luther H. Martin. Amherst: University of Massachusetts Press.

Freeman, J. Richardson. 1991. "Purity and Violence: Sacred Power in the Teyyam Worship of Malabar." Unpublished Ph.D. dissertation, University of Pennsylvania.

Gangadharan, N., trans. 1985. *The Agnipurana,* Parts I and II. Delhi: Motilal Banarsidass.

Hamzah, Ustaz Haji. 1983. Personal interview by Phillip Zarrilli.

————. n.d. Kalari-Payat Institute promotional brochure.

Hart, George L. 1975. *The Poems of Ancient Tamil.* Berkeley: University of California Press.

————. 1979. *Poets of the Tamil Anthologies: Ancient Poems of Love and War.* Princeton, N.J.: Princeton University Press.

Hobsbawm, Eric, and Terence Ranger, eds. 1983. *The Invention of Tradition.* Cambridge: Cambridge University Press.

Jackson, Michael. 1989. *Paths toward a Clearing: Radical Empiricism and Ethnographic Inquiry.* Bloomington: Indiana University Press.

Johnson, Mark. 1987. *The Body in the Mind.* Chicago: University of Chicago Press.

Johnson, Richard. 1986. What Is Cultural Studies Anyway? *Social Text* 16: 38-80.

Kailasapathy, K. 1968. *Tamil Heroic Poetry.* Oxford: Clarendon.

Katiyar, Arun. 1983. Enter the Super Corps! *Bombay* 4 (21): 40-43.

Keat, Russell. 1986. The Human Body in Social Theory: Reich, Foucault, and the Repressive Hypothesis. *Radical Philosophy,* no. 42: 24-32.

Kondo, Dorrine K. 1990. *Crafting Selves.* Chicago: University of Chicago Press.

Lakoff, George. 1987. *Women, Fire, and Dangerous Things.* Chicago: University of Chicago Press.

Lakoff, George, and Mark Johnson. 1980. *Metaphors We Live By.* Chicago: University of Chicago Press.

Lock, M., and N. Scheper-Hughes. 1990. "A Critical-Interpretive Approach in Medical Anthropology: Rituals and Routines of Discipline and Dissent." In *Medical Anthropology: Contemporary Theory and Method,* edited by T. M. Johnson and C. F. Sargent, pp. 47-72. New York: Praeger.

Mauss, M. 1973. Techniques of the Body. *Economy and Society* 2 (1): 70-88.

Meyrowitz, Joshua. 1985. *No Sense of Place.* New York: Oxford University Press.

Novack, Cynthia J. 1990. *Sharing the Dance: Contact Improvisation and American Culture.* Madison: University of Wisconsin Press.

Pandian V. 1983a. Fire Without, Calm Within. *Indian Express,* September 4.

————. 1983b. A Force to Reckon With. *Indian Express,* September 18.

Pavis, Patrice. 1989. Dancing with *Faust:* A Semiotician's Reflections on Barba's Mise-en-Scene. *TDR: A Journal of Performance Studies* 33 (3): 37-57.

Raghavan, M. D. 1947. *Folk Plays and Dances of Kerala.* Trichur: Mangalodayan.

Scarry, Elaine. 1985. *The Body in Pain.* Oxford: Oxford University Press.

Schechner, Richard. 1985. "News, Sex, and Performance Theory." In *Between Theater and Anthropology*. Philadelphia: University of Pennsylvania Press.

Sheets-Johnstone, Maxine, ed. 1992. *Giving the Body Its Due*. Albany: SUNY Press.

Shweder, Richard A., and Robert A. LeVine. 1984. *Culture Theory: Essays on Mind, Self, and Emotion*. London: Cambridge University Press.

Singer, Milton. 1972. *When a Great Tradition Modernizes*. New York: Praeger.

Stoller-Miller, Barbara. 1984. *Theatre of Memory: The Plays of Kalidasa*. New York: Columbia University Press.

T.K.A.M. 1986. New Star on Kalari Horizon. *Weekend Review*, June 15-21, p. 15.

White, Geoffrey, and John Kirkpatrick, eds. 1985. *Person, Self and Experience: Exploring Pacific Ethnopsychologies*. Berkeley: University of California Press.

Zarrilli, Phillip B. 1979. Kalarippayatt, Martial Art of Kerala. *Drama Review* 23 (2): 113-24.

———. 1984. "Doing the Exercise": The In-Body Transmission of Performance Knowledge in a Traditional Martial Art. *Asian Theatre Journal* 1 (2): 191-206.

———. 1989a. Three Bodies of Practice in a Traditional South Indian Martial Art. *Social Science and Medicine* 28 (12): 1289-1310.

———. 1989b. "Between Text and Embodied Practice: Writing and Reading in a South Indian Martial Tradition." In *Shastric Tradition in Indian Arts*, edited by A. L. Dallapiccola, pp. 415-24. Stuttgart: Franz Steiner.

———. 1992a. To Heal and/or To Harm: The Vital Spots (*Marmmam/Varmam*) in Two South Indian Martial Traditions. Part I: Focus on Kerala's *Kalarippayattu. Journal of Asian Martial Arts* 1 (1): 36-67.

———. 1992b. To Heal and/or To Harm: The Vital Spots (*Marmmam/Varmam*) in Two South Indian Martial Traditions. Part II: Focus on the Tamil Art, *Varma Ati. Journal of Asian Martial Arts* 1 (2): 1-15.

———. 1994. "When the Body Becomes All Eyes": Paradigms and Discourses of Practice and Power in *Kalarippayattu*, the Martial and Medical Tradition of Kerala. Unpublished manuscript.

Zarrilli, Phillip, ed. 1993. *Asian Martial Arts in Actor Training*. Madison, Wis.: Center for South Asia.

CHAPTER NINE

Nation, Economy, and Tradition Displayed

The Indian Crafts Museum, New Delhi

PAUL GREENOUGH

Artisans—household-based hand manufacturers of useful and decorative commodities for domestic, ritual, and tourist consumption—make up only a small proportion of India's workforce, but the proportion has been steady for twenty years, and it is likely that India has more artisans today than any other nation in the world.[1] A huge rural demand for articles of everyday utility is met by potters, smiths, weavers, and dozens of other artists, while the mostly urban middle and upper classes require at least a sprinkling of handmade artifacts as an expression of their nationalist-modernist taste. Vigorous marketing has made handmade Indian goods, especially cotton and silk textiles and ready-made garments, familiar in the West. It is fitting, then, that in the Indian capital there is a state-supported crafts museum that is "among the most prominent of the forces behind what are variously known as Indian handicrafts, 'folk art' or 'popular art'" and that has "defined criteria of excellence by determining what should be preserved and encouraged."[2] Indeed, the crafts museum is dedicated to the preservation of the country's rich craft traditions. But its most ambitious mission is to raise the incomes of India's artisans, most of whom come from low-caste, tribal, and ex-untouchable backgrounds and are desperately poor. It tries to do this by, on the one hand, exhorting artisans to maintain quality by persevering with traditional materials and designs and, on the other hand, by stirring up demand among tourists and city dwellers by displaying outstanding craft objects and by drawing attention to master artisans whose public demonstrations in New Delhi exemplify practical genius. These exhortations, exhibitions, and demonstrations are enveloped by a complex set of ideas about India's artistic traditions, its economic trajectory, and its national uniqueness, ideas whose contradictory claims swirl around the museum's modest institutional presence.

When New Delhites seek out-of-doors leisure, they stream to the city's eastern edge, where parks, statues, monuments, and restored ruins as well as edifices of law, sport, science, and culture stud the planned terrain (fig. 9.1). The low, mock-rustic buildings of the crafts museum, located at the busy intersection of Bhairon Marg with Mathura Road, are juxtaposed in one direction with the glass and stone pyramids of the modern National Fairgrounds and in the other with the looming turrets of the medieval Purana Qila or Old Fort (fig. 9.2). The fairgrounds (dating from 1972) are configured as a grid to represent the twenty-six Indian states and territories, each of which has built an exhibition hall (Panjab Bhavan, for example); these physical arrangements assert the theme of unity in diversity, so crucial to the Nehruvian national ideal. The Old Fort, a sixteenth-century palace begun by the Mughal Humayun and completed by the Afghan Sher Shah, is even more dramatic, and its battlements can be seen from nearly anywhere in the city.[3] Directly adjoining the Old Fort and a short distance from the fairgrounds is the National Zoo (established 1957), from which animal sounds float across to the crafts museum. The zoo, filled mostly with animals from the Indian subcontinent, is one of a handful in the country. Other nearby sites—the National Gallery of Modern Art, the Supreme Court, the National Theatre, and the National Stadium—help to complete this quarter of the capital.

The public spaces, institutions, and monuments that surround the crafts museum are tame. Families arrive together, share snacks and soft drinks, take photographs. Peopled in daytime by young and old who stroll the paths with guards in the background, the zoo, fort, and fairgrounds are nearly deserted in the evening. Yet this tameness is another word for order. These urban sites allude to threats that the Indian state has struggled to subdue—medieval despotism in the case of the Old Fort, wild beasts in the case of the zoo, rebellion and secession in the case of the fairgrounds. They concentrate the national patrimony, evoke the rise and fall of earlier regimes, and reinscribe a narrative of struggles against foreign oppressors. Like similar institutions in capitals elsewhere, they amplify an elite version of the national heritage and

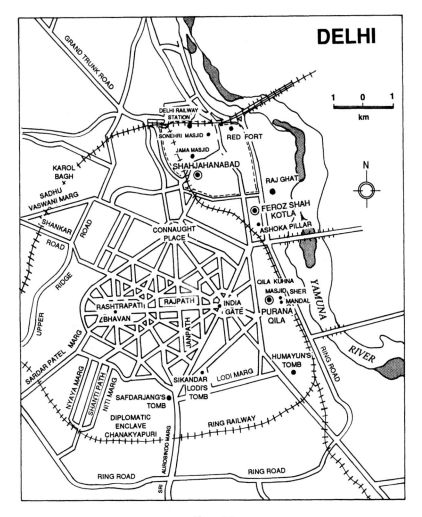

Figure 9.1.

burnish without irony the saga of the freedom struggle[4]—this despite increasingly violent separatist conflicts and a spreading concern among minorities about their rights as citizens.

The crafts museum's formal title is the National Handicrafts and Handlooms Museum; it was established in the mid-1950s.[5] As the name suggests, hand-loomed cloth (*khadi*) had a privileged place in the museum's conception, reflecting the unique role of hand spinning and weaving in nationalist practice as well as the hard-headed realization that weavers make up the

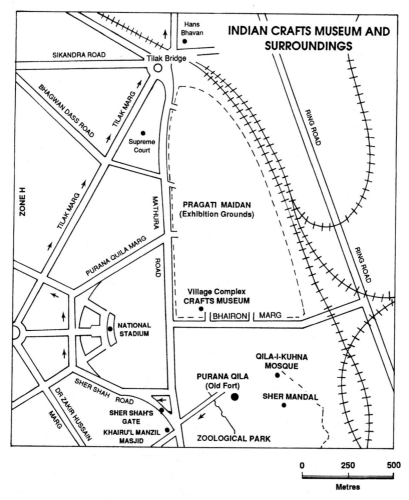

Figure 9.2.

largest proportion of artisans in the country and continue to be displaced by mills.[6] Underlying advocacy of a revived artisan sector are several unspoken assumptions: that handmade goods in rural India will continue to be in demand despite industrial substitutes; that urban consumers can be weaned away from certain kinds of factory-made goods; that both rural and urban demand will increase if artisans adhere to their craft traditions. Museum staff frankly disparage innovation and confront visiting artisans with examples of past excellence in every medium; at the same time, the museum tries to shape urban demand by instructing middle-class taste and teaching the elements of crafts to schoolchildren. Further, like museums in other national capitals, the crafts museum serves both to naturalize the nation and to strengthen the nation's position in the international system. To realize the former aim, it co-opts and then tries to smooth out India's vast regional and local artisanal variations. To realize the latter, it sends outstanding artisans abroad on missions of cultural diplomacy, for example, controversial Festivals of India. The overt promotional goals and the implicit diplomatic ambitions are thus situated in relation to four cross-cutting themes: the economic betterment of poor artisans; shifting demand for handcrafted goods; elite practices of cultural revival and preservation; and propagation of the national idea domestically and abroad. As will be readily seen, the museum functions in a terrain of cultural contestation.[7]

Jostling of Crafts in the Capital

The crafts museum has no monopoly on the sale of handcrafts in the capital. Craft retailing is a very visible part of New Delhi's economy, and private merchants, voluntary associations, and other state institutions all have a stake in the very practices of design, production, and promotion that the museum tries to affect. Shopping for crafts is an agreeable activity for Indian and foreign tourists. Guidebooks to the city offer shopping tips, and in every sizable hotel a foyer shop sells, among other things, handwoven clothes and block-printed scarves, replicas of Mughal miniatures, brass utensils and cast-bronze deities, appliquéd cloth with tiny embedded mirrors, ivory chessmen, sandalwood statues, cotton dhurries, leather bags, and lacquered boxes. Visitors are accosted on the street by craft peddlers, and they stumble over craft goods spread along the road by vendors; street haggling for handmade articles is the norm. At the north end of Janpath, a major street in the commercial center, a labyrinthine Central Cottage Industries Emporium sells handmade artifacts from all over India at fixed prices. At Connaught Place, a focus for tourism, banking, and travel services, the Gandhi Ashram Khadi Bhandar and the All India Handloom Fabrics Marketing Corporation are major *khadi* outlets. Numerous nearby shops sell silks, gems, silver, ivory, and woolens. Bespoke tailors work up *sherwanis, kurtas,* and *salwar-kameez* (forms of North Indian dress) in a matter of hours. Along Baba Kharak Singh Marg more than a dozen state craft emporiums specialize in regional products—*bidri*-ware from Andhra Pradesh, jewelry and gemstones from Rajasthan, sandalwood from Karnataka, inlaid marble and brocades from Uttar Pradesh, rugs and lacquerware from Kashmir, and so on. A vibrant trade in gems, jewels, and horn and leather goods is carried on at the Tibetan Market, while other specialists are found more distantly: the silversmiths of Chandni Chowk, the antique shops of Sunder Nagar Bazaar, the Tibet House emporium on Lodi Road, and the tony boutiques in Hauz Khas Village. Foreign tourists find a last opportunity at Indira Gandhi airport, where sandal-scented soap, filigreed gold, and kilo-sized packets of tea bound in brocade are sold for foreign exchange.

Both Indian and foreign tourists revel in this abundance, but tourism does not drive New Delhi's market in crafts. The city's artistic, professional, and bureaucratic elites have long favored folk paintings, sculptures, and carvings as elements of household decor, while upper-class women have worn handprinted garments since the 1950s as an affirmation of Indianness. In recent years the taste for native arts and crafts has spread more widely in the monied middle class. Folk is *chic.* Ready-to-wear shops sell garments that look traditional—*desi* textures, shapes, and colors—but the cuts are frequently more "designed," the cloth and dyes are improved, and the cost is much greater than for similar articles only a few years ago.[8] The situation is similar with regard to household furnishings. In bourgeois homes there may be two channels of taste: in one room a handwoven rug, a rustic wooden chest, and a printed or painted *pichwai* with mythological scenes hanging on the wall; in another room an impressionist print, chromed Bauhaus chairs, and a plastic-encased stereo and television system. Handmade and factory-made items are sometimes mixed in the same space, and craft artifacts are asked to serve novel purposes: an antique, lattice-carved window from Rajasthan is turned into a coffee table, while a bronze lamp in the shape of the goddess Lakshmi is drafted to be an ashtray.[9] Purists deplore such practices, but eclecticism in New Delhi keeps pace with a global consumption style that creolizes commodities of every provenance.

Many factors create taste in New Delhi, and the crafts museum is only one voice among many. Further, compared to attendance at the National Museum (of art and archaeology), the National Gallery of Modern Art, or the Gandhi Museum, attendance at the crafts museum is light. The travel agents, airlines, and hotel chains that book thousands of tourists each year neglect the crafts museum in their brochures, while New Delhi guidebooks give it only a few lines. Visitors are directed instead to the gardens and mosques of medieval dynasts, to Agra's monuments and to son et lumière under the walls of the Red Fort. Tourists' expectations aside, it may be that the sheer ubiquity of crafts in New Delhi explains why few Indians seek out the crafts museum. Then again, craft articles often come from the village, and those with village origins may want to put the associations behind them. Whether for these reasons, or because it lacks spectacle, or because it is unfamiliar as an institutional type, or because the goods it sells must be negotiated for face to face with the artisans who make them and know their worth, the crafts museum draws modest attendance. Nonetheless, the museum offers a striking example of state intervention on behalf of the working poor; in so doing, however, the state involves itself in numerous cultural and institutional dilemmas.

The Galleries

Visitors to the crafts museum encounter three attractions: the galleries, which exhibit a sizable collection of new and old craft artifacts; the village complex, which displays vernacular architectural styles; and the craft demonstration area, where artisans publicly make and sell their wares. These three areas retrace the movement in museum practice from a more traditional arrangement of exhibits according to a fixed taxonomy, to the embedding of exhibits in lifelike ensembles or dioramas, to the contemporary approach that asks visitors to produce their own knowledge and pleasure by interacting with the exhibits—in this case with living artisans.

The galleries are the principal focus. Designed and built in the early 1970s by the architect Charles Correa, they suggest at first glance a North Indian village. Their dun and terra-cotta-colored structures lie low to the ground around garden courtyards with generous sight lines toward the looming Purana Qila. Oxcarts, clay sculptures, and brass vessels are scattered about. The effect is so rustic that first-time visitors have been known to ask, "Where is the museum?" Late in 1991 nearly seven thousand square meters of additional gallery space were opened.[10]

The core of the collection was assembled in 1956 by the All India Handicrafts Board for "preserving outstanding specimens of Indian handcrafts as source material for initiating study, research, documentation, reproduction and development" and for "disseminating information about the history of crafts as well as their production techniques."[11] This was a bold preservationist concept, although the core collection was neglected in the museum's first premises near Janpath in the late 1960s.[12] The collection was transported to the present site in 1974; it was given an accessions budget and has grown steadily. The museum now possesses nearly thirty thousand examples of metal icons, lamps, incense burners, ritual accessories, wood carvings, painted wood, papier-maché articles, dolls, toys, puppets, masks, folk and tribal paintings, terra-cottas, ivories, playing cards, metal inlay work, jewelry, cane and bamboo artifacts, and many other crafts, as well as a large cross section of cotton and silk textiles. These are displayed in three exhibit spaces or "courts"—the Village Court, the Temple Court, and the Darbar Court—that suggest the interiors of generic households, temples, and palaces respectively.

Attached to the galleries is a library holding ten thousand books and articles, a slide collection, a small conservation laboratory, and a research and documentation unit that photographs, dates, and catalogs artifacts before they are installed. Because curatorial practice is so evidently professional, the visitor might assume that the craft museum's values were equivalent to those of art museums elsewhere. But the collection is not justified by the values of high art. Significantly, the crafts museum is placed under the Ministry of Textiles and not the Ministry of Human Resources, which takes responsibility for the capital's major art and archeology museums. There are some important differences to note. For one thing, craft museum exhibits are intended not to illustrate changing artistic themes, genres, styles, and media through time, but to demonstrate the static equivalence in form and function between the present and the past: "the collection truly reflects the 'continuing conditions' of Indian craftsmanship [and] both old and new pieces of the Indian heritage have been displayed side by side to demonstrate the high level of skill that has survived in India."[13] It is evidence of *continuity* and *survival* within India's material tradition, rather than innovation, that determines whether an artifact is an acceptable addition to the collection. Second, the primary intended audience is not connoisseurs or art historians or even the public at large, but visiting artisans. The current director has expressed his hope that the museum will become "a university for craftsmen," and he refers to the collection as a "reference tool" for artisans. The latter are admonished, however, that their skills rarely equal those of the best in the past.[14] Craft museum staff thus take a more didactic line with producers than is the case in most art museums. Third, while the nearby National Museum (of art and archaeology) is forbidden by its rules to buy works by living artists, the crafts museum adds some two thousand pieces each year, old and new just as it likes. The chief criterion is not age, authorship, or provenance but quality: "any piece that satisfies the proof of exquisiteness of craftsmanship, conception, device, or design."[15] Fourth, the cosmopolitan concept of fragile and costly "masterpieces," ringed by security and exhibited with awe, is barely acknowledged. The majority of the craft museum's pieces are anonymous; only a small part of the collection is kept behind glass; and more than three-quarters is always on exhibit—a high proportion compared to fine art museums, where the bulk of the holdings is shielded from the light of day. Finally, in addition to collecting artifacts, museum staff systematically collect information about the artisans who produce them. Special questionnaires and file folders have been designed for this purpose, and a National Craftspersons Directory, now being compiled, will include data about thousands of artisans and their work, techniques, and careers.[16]

The museum holds workshops from time to time to bring together practitioners of the same craft from different parts of the country. For example, a workshop to improve bronze-mirror making was held in March 1988; village and tribal smiths from seven states attended. After studying outstanding examples in the museum's reference collection, the visiting artisans experimented to discover the surest means of transferring fine details from wax forms to the cast bronze objects.[17] Such workshops have no precedent in traditional India, and this is a clear example of the museum's role in acknowledging and then homogenizing regional traditions under the auspices of the new nation. Yet artisans eagerly participate; they consider it an honor and they heed the message that improvements in quality will translate into higher prices. Extensive contacts with artisans from all over India sometimes bring museum staff face to face with the last representative of a particular craft technique; in these cases the museum's preservationist motives may become particularly clear. After documenting the artisan's technical skills, the museum has been known to arrange a pension and even to find an apprentice to preserve the moribund craft for another generation.

In a counterpoint to exhorting artisans, museum staff freely criticize the urban middle class for its ignorance of authentic design and fine workmanship. The middle class, it is said, naively consumes the tricked-up goods that bazaar dealers fob off on them. Hence the museum instructs middle- and upper-class taste by holding several exhibitions each year. A select group of New Delhi opinion leaders, including the diplomatic corps (who can create trends abroad), is invited. The museum prepares well-illustrated catalogs, and other publications about specialized genres appear from time to time. To reach the coming generation, the museum invites students to tour the galleries and observe artisans at work. In so-called creativity workshops master artisans demonstrate the rudiments of their crafts, after which students are invited to try their hand. A peculiarity is that while the students are encouraged to indulge in "free expression," the artisan-instructors are constrained. A cultural divide yawns: on the one side, spontaneity and creativity, on the other, only traditional discipline. The museum's justification is that urban children in India, like their Western counterparts, are born under the sign of the machine and know crafts only as a limited number of "hobbies." They must be encouraged to experiment freely whereas artisans must shun novelty, for they are heirs of a timeless tradition.[18]

As I noted earlier, urban demand for craft goods arises more from the compulsions of fashion than from need. There is little made by hand in India that cannot be mass produced; hence demand must be primed by representing handmade goods as stylish and enviable. The museum is reluctant to do this too overtly, although entrepreneurs are happy enough to take up the task. But what accounts for the continuing demand for handicrafts in *rural* India? The partition of the museum artifact collection into the Darbar, Village, and Temple Courts suggests three poles of demand. Yet it is simple to point out that India's princes are no more, that the real *darbar* in the sense of a class of princely and landed magnates who commission luxury dress, jewelry, household furnishings, harnessware, and weapons has long since been swept away. Similarly, the village demand for crafts, in the sense of a ready market for humble items of utility, while still enormous, has been deeply eroded by substitutes made of plastic, paper, aluminum, nylon, rubber, and glass. No one who can afford a plastic bucket is eager to carry water in a clay pot, and rising rural incomes imply that ever greater numbers of villagers will buy factory-made goods. If village demand is stagnant or shrinking and *darbari* demand is exhausted, then only temple demand—in the sense of handmade articles required for ritual performance—remains. The Temple Court illustrates the context of use for these articles, and museum staff are committed to the idea that production for Hindu ritual exceeds production for daily use in importance. A museum brochure observes that

> the function of art and craft in providing a livelihood, even today in India, is often surpassed by its more important function on major ritual events such as birth, initiation, marriage, [and] death as well as annual and seasonal festivals. Here both the craftsman and his craft serve as significant ritual contributors in the ceremonies. On all these occasions an assortment of textiles and garments, vessels and utensils, toys, games, props and furniture is used. What is noteworthy, however, is that the same object used for mundane purposes attains a ritual value, a sacrosanctity, which then elevates the craft, and consequently its maker, to the realm of the sacred. These are therefore not items of "craft" made for the sole purpose of marketing; in reality, they form an integral part of the socio-religious order of traditional and contemporary village and tribal India.[19]

This legitimation of the artisans' role in domestic ritual suggests that there is a basement of demand despite the long decline in India's craft traditions:

Hindu ritual will always require a residual set of artisan skills. Like koshering in the Jewish tradition or the preparation of chrism (consecrated oil) for Catholic sacraments, some practices are too sacred to be mechanized. It is these skills and practices that the museum celebrates. Yet emphasizing the integral role of artisans in a living religion has its social consequences: because Hindu ritual stabilizes and naturalizes caste differences, the artisans who supply ritually necessary craft articles help shore up a profoundly conservative socioreligious order. This suggests yet another reason for the state to support the crafts museum.[20]

The Village Complex

The second focus of the museum is the village complex, a cluster of fourteen huts and their courtyards on six acres in the open air (fig. 9.3). The complex dates from the 1972 Asian fair, when craftsmen arrived in New Delhi with the necessary wood, tile, thatch, and stone. Each hut displays the architectural style of a regional ethnic group in a particular state or territory.[21] A few huts are built to scale, but most are full size. The interiors are partially furnished, and the exteriors are decorated with paintings and folk designs. Attached courtyards are furnished with farm tools and simple machines (waterwheels, grain mortars) as well as nets, boats, wagons, and storage vessels; some of these are anchored to the site with wire and bolts. It is obvious that house forms, decorative motifs, and agricultural implements are strikingly diverse in different parts of India, yet once again it is the museum's purpose with this permanent exhibit to establish the unity of the nation in diversity.

A museum brochure states that "in every hut, items of day-to-day life are displayed in order to recreate the cultural contexts in which they were actually used before they become museum pieces locked behind glass cases,"[22] thus criticizing older exhibition practices and identifying the crafts museum with a modern duty to contextualize artifacts. On the other hand, the further observation that the huts in the village complex "are not reconstructed to the extent of showing smoke stains on the kitchen walls and a just extinguished *hukkah* [hookah] beside a *charpoy* [rope bed], because it is understood that fake reconstruction of a village would be as bad as [the] intensivecare unit-display of art objects in glass cases" betrays some uneasiness.[23] Broaching the idea of "fake reconstruction" calls into question the ontological status of the village complex; if the village is not an aggregation

Figure 9.3. Kulu hut (Himachal Pradesh) constructed of stone blocks with tile roof and wooden veranda. Village complex, Indian crafts museum. Photo by P. Greenough.

of "fakes," what *is* it? One guidebook suggests that in the village complex the tourist can "visit rural India without leaving Delhi," an illusion that is never sustained: no one lives in the complex, nothing is in use.[24] Yet it is not a Potemkin village, either, in the sense of an architecture of facades thrown up for a transient political effect.[25] Nor is it, like Hauz Khas Village in South Delhi, a historic settlement burnished with paint and plaster for leisure-class consumption. Perhaps the best analogy is with the dioramas in a natural history museum, where assemblages of faux trees, plants, and animals are set into microterrains that reconstruct ecological relationships. The value of this mode of exhibition lies in the marked contrast: the visitor's movement past a series of frozen vistas reveals the complex diversity of an observed nature. The diorama analogy works well for the village complex, especially if we substitute *nation* for *nature*—except that the dominant species in a diorama, in this case human beings, is missing from the ghostly huts. It helps to know, then, that when the village complex was built in 1972, artisans were seated in the courtyards where they made craft objects for visitors' appreciative gaze. These artisans, or rather their successors, have long since been removed to the crafts demonstration area, which is the third focus of the museum.

The Crafts Demonstration Area

A sign that says "This Way to the Master Craftsmen" directs visitors to a partly arcaded square where up to thirty artisans, both men and women, ply their skills for visitors.[26] The artisans are selected by museum staff on the basis of prior acquaintance or are recommended through a network of known artisans, emporium managers, and scholars. Artisans are invited to New Delhi for a month, provided transportation and lodging, and given seventy rupees (about two dollars) a day for food and expenses; more than two hundred artisans participate annually.[27] Artisans bring their own tools and raw materials; potters and smiths, who need help with firing and smelting, are allowed to bring assistants. These arrangements continue year round except in the hottest months. The museum is popular with visiting artisans, who can earn significant amounts. By village standards museum customers are wealthy, and because each visiting artisan makes and sells a unique product, there is little competition. Further, because customers are assured that they are observing *master* artists, the propensity to haggle is limited. Visiting artisans determine their own prices, but the transactions are recorded by museum staff.[28]

The diverse colors, textures, persons, and activities in the crafts demonstration area offer visitors a dense, informal, and visually rich experience. The artisans are staggeringly skillful, and most are eager to demonstrate their skills. They enjoy being photographed.[29] Tourists clearly experience the artisans at work as a kind of entertainment, and in this setting production becomes consumption. In some cases artisans are entertainers, as for example the flute makers who warble on bamboo pipes and the puppet makers who stage little dramas accompanied by dialogue, songs, and drumming. That entertainment and sales are central aspects of the visitor-artisan encounter is glossed over by the museum staff, who emphasize more transcendent meanings. A museum brochure implies that the chance to observe the artisans at work redeems tourists' industrial-age alienation and gains them access to a higher consciousness:

> The [crafts] demonstration programme provides its visitors an opportunity to see the craftsman's creations unfold before them. Unlike assembly line production, where the factory worker has little or no conception of the object he is producing, the craftsperson possesses a unified view of his creation. The nature of the materials and techniques, the design and its execution, the socio-religious context and purpose of creation are all engrained in his consciousness. To see a craftsman at work is therefore like seeing the universe take place in front of one's eyes.[30]

The literal sense of this is that the demonstration area is a cosmogonic space. Art historical studies confirm that artisanship was intended by Hindu theorists to be approached as a yogic discipline in which the artisan visualized the form and invoked appropriate deities as preliminaries to fabrication.[31] While this idea is elaborated in *sastras* and may well describe the artisan's consciousness when he or she is making objects for ritual use, it seems unlikely that it captures the artisan's mentality in the worldly arena of a New Delhi museum. The *Shilpa Sastras* explicitly forbid artisans to make objects under the gaze of laypeople.[32] Further, it is unlikely that visitors to the demonstration area know that they are participating in cosmogonic processes; uninformed of Hindu artistic theory, most walk about restlessly as if they were perusing animals in a zoo. On the other hand, ritual practices need not be self-consciously solemn, nor do they flatly contradict the mundane, and transcendence may be there for those who have eyes to see it in the artisans' labors. One cannot follow the artisan's conjurer-like gestures—which give to every object a pleasing iconographic surface and adapt even flaws in the medium to an overall design—without sensing that higher purposes are being served.

In many cases, artisans at the museum are making their first visit to New Delhi. They reside in dormitories on the grounds, but language barriers divide them, and they tend to sort themselves by craft and comprehension: Hindi-speaking potters fraternize with Hindi-speaking potters. Some have art school certificates, but most are trained by village masters. Whatever their origins, they are well aware that an entire institution has been established to recognize them and their work. They bask in the unusual esteem, and local artisans from the Delhi vicinity come after hours to meet them. There is pronounced institutional concern for their welfare: guards are posted to protect them, the museum staff is trained to deal with them fairly, and the director intervenes to settle their disputes.

Physical security is provided only on the grounds of the museum; if artisans venture outside, they face the same hazards as other rustics in the city. The current director, Dr. Jyotindra Jain, narrated the following story.

An illiterate tribal, a maker of decorated terra-cotta roof tiles, was invited to the museum from his village in the Raigarh region of eastern Madhya Pradesh. He had never been in a city before or even on a train, and a museum aide had accompanied him to New Delhi. One evening during his stay, two museum guards obtained country liquor as *prasad* (a token of grace in the form of foodstuffs given by priests to devotees) from a Bhairab temple adjacent to the museum. The guards invited the Raigarhi tile maker and a Gorakhpuri potter to drink. When the potter eventually got up to go about his business, the tile maker followed him. The potter crossed the busy road in front of the museum and got onto a bus, but the tile maker, dizzy with drink, was injured trying to ascend; suddenly he disappeared from the potter's sight. The latter got down and returned to the museum to report the disappearance to the director.

Where had the Raigarhi tile maker gone? For three days the director went from hospital to hospital and even to the city morgue in an effort to find him. A missing-persons bulletin was broadcast over New Delhi television, to no avail. The director became disheartened and wrote out a letter of resignation to his superior, the chief secretary of the Ministry of Industries, acknowledging responsibility and confessing that "it is inappropriate to display human beings as in a zoo." Two days later the tile maker reappeared at the museum. He explained that after he had fallen from the bus, someone had taken him to a hospital; he quickly left, but could not find his way back to the museum. Reasoning that he had arrived from Raigarh by train, he began to follow a nearby set of railway tracks, resolved to walk the nine hundred kilometers home. Unknowingly, however, he had trudged in a circle along the commuter rail line that engirdles the city, ending up before the crafts museum, which he recognized from the traffic light configuration. During this time he had foraged his food, and he offered the director a cucumber tied up in his garment. The director's letter of resignation was rejected by the government.

Context, Survival, and Innovation

Building on the efforts of earlier administrators, the crafts museum has reached a high state of development and influence under Jyotindra Jain, who joined the staff as senior director in 1984.[33] More than anyone else since Verrier Elwin, Jain has won recognition and respect for the artistic skills of low-caste and tribal artisans. His anthropological training and previous museum experience make him a formidable administrator. Jain was born in 1943 in Indore (Madhya Pradesh) and took his B.A. and M.A. degrees in 1963 and 1965 in ancient Indian culture, cultural anthropology, and art from the University of Bombay. He worked for two years as an assistant at the Gujarat Research Society in Bombay and lectured between 1966 and 1969 on Indian culture and art at the university. He then went to Austria and obtained a certificate in ethnographic museology and a Ph.D. in ethnology and Indology from the University of Vienna in 1972. In the mid-1970s he held a visiting professorship in Indian folk and tribal religions and art at the South Asian Institute of Heidelberg University. His first museum appointment was with the Shreyas Folk Museum in Ahmedabad, Gujarat, where he served as director from 1976 to 1978; this was followed in 1979-80 by a readership at the L. D. Institute of Indology of Gujarat, which gave him responsibility for the institute museum. In these years Jain adopted the practice of traveling to villages to observe, collect, and document crafts in situ, relying on photography for a permanent record. Hitherto, Indian folk art museums solicited donations or turned to dealers and third parties for artifacts, but Jain took the position that responsible collecting required museum staff to know exactly where craft objects came from, how they are used, by whom, and for what purposes.

Jain published much of his Gujarat research in articles and monographs in the early 1980s, emphasizing the religious function and semantic significance of craft designs.[34] He also published a catalog, *Folk Art and Culture of Gujarat: Guide to the Shreyas Folk Museum* (1981), that suggested his thinking about the social function of artisanship and the display of craft objects in folk art museums. His guiding idea was to establish the social context of use; "social context" here referred to the end users of craft objects—the patrons, not the artisan-producers.[35] Each object in the Shreyas Museum catalog was thus attributed first to one of six major Gujarati social groups—identified as rulers, pastoralists, Maldharis, farmers, Muslims, and traders—and then to a regional caste group. Photographs illustrate the disposition of objects in situ. In effect, crafts are treated as material signs by which social groups distinguished themselves; it was barely acknowledged that these same material signs had been produced and sold as commodities by other groups to earn a living.

After Jain took up his duties as senior director of the crafts museum in 1984, his museological practices and values underwent a change. On the one hand, he continues to emphasize contexts of use; as noted, craft objects are arranged in the museum's galleries in three "courts"—*darbar*, temple, and village. On the other hand, these artifacts have been collected from all over India, and the collection can hardly claim to represent particular groups residing in particular places. The provenance of individual pieces is noted, but the assemblage that fills a "court" is a composite—the Temple Court, for example, evokes generic Hinduism by declining to explicate sectarian differences. Indeed, the museum's integrative nationalist ideology requires that all temporal specificities and ethnic particularities be subsumed within an encompassing tradition. At the same time, Jain's attention has shifted from craft consumers to producers—to the artisans whose economic uplift is one of the museum's chief concerns. While it may still be plausible to construe crafts in rural Gujarat as exquisite reflections of a stable social order, they are decidedly commodities in New Delhi. In short, in New Delhi the powerful modern forces that affect artisans' well-being cannot be ignored. Jain has to ask himself what the museum's attitude toward nontraditional sources of demand should be. How should artisans be advised in matters of innovation? What overarching historical framework predicts the fate of hand manufacture in an era of industrialization?

In seeking answers to the last of these questions, Jain has available only a limited number of models to describe India's cultural trajectory. On the one hand, there is "modernization theory," which assumes that the arts along with the rest of culture will continually change in relation to science and technology. This theory (which in the West is not so much a theory as a narrow way of looking at the past few centuries of European experience) accepts the disappearance of hand manufacturing as a sign of progress; handcraft production has inevitably lost its economic significance and craft technique finds nurture only within museums and the academy. This theory, like the pressure from foreign capital that underlies it, has never been acceptable in political India, and the elite's discomfort with its implications was evident as early as the Swadeshi era (1905-12), when homemade and handmade alternatives to European industrial products first became identified with nationalism. On the other hand, there is a cultural preservationist model, also from the West, that envisions a halt in the destruction of crafts by widening the public appeal of handmade goods; this is to be done, as the Victorian Arts and Crafts movement had shown, by refining the quality of handcrafts and by mounting a trenchant critique of industrialism.[36] This position has been more acceptable among nationalists, and its most articulate expression is found in the deeply pessimistic works of A. K. Coomaraswamy.[37] Coomaraswamy's ideas have gripped Indian cultural history since the 1920s, and not only Jyotindra Jain but also Pupul Jayakar, Kamaladevi Chattopadhyay, and others centrally involved in the postindependence effort to preserve Indian crafts regularly cite him.

Ananda Kentish Coomaraswamy (1877-1947) argued, in a series of essays published between 1906 and 1927, that traditional craftsmanship in India was tethered by two anchors: the ritual needs of caste society, an organic society that had eschewed egalitarianism and technological change for their own sake; and the profound spiritual discipline of the artist who, when properly appreciated, must be seen to be a ritualist and a *yogin* as well as a skilled artisan.[38] During the nineteenth century, according to Coomaraswamy, both anchors had been ripped loose by secular learning, the industrial system, and the "virus" of competition that held India's elite in thrall. This analysis was to a considerable extent derived by applying the ideas and values of John Ruskin and William Morris and their Victorian colleagues to the colonial setting of India and Ceylon, influences Coomaraswamy openly avowed. But a distinctly un-Arts and Crafts movement theme was Coomaraswamy's attack on the cultural tastes of "Young India," by which he meant the privileged graduates of the colonial educational system; these were the Indians (he uses the term comprehensively to include the Ceylonese) who denigrated traditional arts and crafts and declined to extend the patronage that had been given unbrokenly for centuries. Young India, he said, wore "borrowed plumes," while their adoption of foreign values was culturally impoverishing, for "a single generation of English education suffices to break the threads of tradition and to create a nondescript and superficial being deprived of all roots—a sort of intellectual pariah who does not belong to the East or the West, the past or the future." Consequently, there could only be artistic "decay" and "degradation," despite the efforts of a few traditionalist reformers. Coomaraswamy held that India's modern arts and crafts were at best only "survivals"of a past glory, and he wondered whether "it would not be wiser to accelerate the process of destruction than to attempt to preserve the broken fragments of the great tradition."[39]

Coomaraswamy's despairing analysis resonated with the views of Orientalist reformers like E. B. Havell, and it was substantially accepted by his most important Indian disciple, Mulk Raj Anand.[40] These themes—ancient artistic glory, organic caste solidarity, peasant religiosity, tastelessness among the educated, inevitable artistic decay, the dim prospect of mere survivals—reverberate in the rhetoric of crafts museum publications and are present in Jain's public reflections on the cultural situation of contemporary India.

Coomaraswamy had disputed the necessity of museums in India and was particularly critical of the application of curatorial practices to Indian folk materials. He is prominently quoted in a crafts museum brochure as follows: "Museum objects on the whole were not originally 'treasures' made to be seen in glass cases, but rather common objects of the marketplace that could have been bought and used by any one."[41] This is not, as it might appear, just a questioning of the colonial art museum's presentational *style*, of displays of labeled objects in vitrines; it is also a questioning of the practice of setting objects for display at all. Indigenous art theory had no concept of the exhibit, let alone of the museum. According to Coomaraswamy, handcrafted objects were always made to be used, and aesthetic appreciation of them under conditions of domestic or ritual use was simply the complement of knowledgeable commissioning: "It is the business of the artist *to know how things ought to be made* and to be able [to make them] accordingly, as it is the business of the patron to know *what things ought to be made,* and of the consumer to know what things *have been well and truly made* and to be able to use them after their kind."[42] In this and many other passages, Coomaraswamy contended that Indian arts and crafts had once flourished in a community of knowledgeable and spiritually informed producers, patrons, and consumers. The collapse of these allegedly shared standards during the colonial period, and the desire to reinstate them in part through appropriate museum practices, helps to explain the crafts museum's steady disparagement of the middle-class Indian taste.

Such views and values suggest a course of action for the determined museum director. When Jain arrived at the crafts museum in 1984, he began disassembling glass-case displays, which not only isolated craft objects inappropriately but also, by grouping them higgledy-piggledy with only the most laconic captions giving genre, site, and date, destroyed all reference to original conditions of production and use. His insistence on preserving a wider sense of context make him a scourge of other museum directors, who continued to imitate European practices of more than fifty years earlier. Jain writes:

> As we blindly adopted the archaeological museum concept we forgot that . . . in our case the "past" and the "present" were not so severely divided, and therefore we did not give adequate importance in our Museums to the factors of traditional artistic skills that have survived in abundance till date; the living practices of rituals, festivals, mythology, picture-shows of itinerant story tellers, traditions of performing arts, oral traditions, etc. The question is not that of recalibrating our Museum machinery to bring it on a par with other Museums; but it is imperative that we reconsider the concept of Museum as inherited by us, especially in view of the fact that the Indians themselves never made Museums of fragmented art objects or anything for that matter. . . . We build stone or brick and concrete rectangular boxes for Museum buildings . . . [and] display chopped Buddha heads, decontextualised *yakshis* and architectural fragments inside glass cases with captions that tell nothing: *"Yakshi.* Bharut. 150 B.C." As if the Museum objects had no other context outside these captioned glass cases.[43]

The key terms here are *context* and *survival*, but they have different statuses. While *context* is considered a knowable, existing reality to be found "out there" in India's thousands of villages and capable of being physically registered in photographic traces within the museum's walls, *survival* is a provocative abstraction that derives from a view of historical change in which the disappearance of traditional skills is an inevitable cultural tragedy. The peculiar nature of this tragedy in India is that it has been so drawn out, indeed, that has so far been only partial when compared with the Western world. Because of this, the crafts museum is in a position to slow down, perhaps to halt, and in some cases even to reverse the trend of cultural destruction. Jain says "I am a traditionalist but not a revivalist," although he has occasionally intervened to arrange pensions and to find apprentices to save the last practitioners of dying crafts. This is, in effect, to create a new context—a museum context—of patronage unlike anything known to tradition. Interestingly, Jain does not compare himself to the environmentalist who labors to save an endangered species; he prefers the more homely figure of a neighbor who rallies to support an orphan. His vision is paternal rather than technocratic.

Jain was asked what constitutes an ideal experience for an artisan visiting the museum as part of the regular cycle of one-month appointments. His reply included three elements: first, the artisan would continue to make exactly the same articles in the same way as he or she had done previously in the village; second, the artisan would study the museum's collection to see how technical skills could be improved; third, the artisan would return home resolved to "throw off" the influence of intermediaries who continually demand design changes in the hope of attracting sales. Perhaps the most striking part of his answer is that it does not allow for interaction or learning *among* the artisans while they are together at the museum. Such interaction, however, may be inevitable.

Machihan Sasa is a forty-year-old potter from Lonpui Village in Ukhrul District of the northeastern state of Manipur. He arrived at the crafts museum in late November 1989 with his eight-year-old son and an assistant. Sasa was a handsome, black-haired, literate man whose special talent is hand building and polishing unglazed clay vessels (fig. 9.4). At intervals over a three-week period I watched him prepare his clay by grinding lumps of dry soil carried all the way from Manipur; he rolled out clay slabs on a flat surface and formed these into large round vessels and then decorated, polished, and fired them. His clay-working tools were simple: two wood paddles to beat

Figure 9.4. Manipuri potter Machihan Sasa polishing a large pot in the crafts demonstration area of the crafts museum. Photo by P. Greenough.

the pot inside and outside, a few bamboo strips to scrape the sides, wet rags. The real tools were Sasa's hands, with which he slapped, pinched, and molded the clay as he moved with dancelike movements around it. While he worked, visitors passed by his space to talk, to admire, and give orders for the pots from him that he could not supply at once; one of his best sales methods was to show German tourist B the written order he had already taken from Japanese tourist A.

In the space next to Sasa worked an artisan from Madhya Pradesh named Lakshmi Lohar. He too had come with an assistant. Lohar—a name that signifies ironsmith all over India—had the skill to turn rough metal strips into

Figure 9.5. Manipuri potter Machihan Sasa experimenting with ironwork. Crafts demonstration area of the crafts museum. Photo by P. Greenough.

gazelles, lamp basins, and riders on horses. His control of the red-hot iron, which he held in handmade tongs and tapped with a small hammer on an anvil made from a section of railway line, was superb. His forge, a small hole in the ground filled with burning charcoal and oxygenated by a hand-turned bellows, was a magnet for young children, who repeatedly stuck bamboo swords and wooden spears into the fire while he worked. He never admonished them.

Arriving at the museum early one cold December morning, I found Sasa, the potter, swathed in a muffler and at work in the space usually occupied by Lohar, the smith. Sasa was experimenting with discarded strips of iron wire (fig. 9.5). As I watched, he hammered out a pair of simple handles, which he then attached to the lip of one of his own still-wet clay pots. When I asked why he had done this, he shrugged. Because there is no tradition of metal handles being attached to Manipuri pots, I had witnessed a modest (and undoubtedly stillborn) example of the diffusion of form between media. When

I later pointed this out to Jain, a pained look came over his face, and he remarked that such mutual influences are "a dangerous outcome" of bringing artisans together from different backgrounds. According to Jain, artisans are invited to the crafts museum only for a month because a longer stay would "uproot" them from their environment, "spoil" their technique, and alter their attitude toward sales. On the other hand, Jain acknowledges that large-scale crafts innovations are taking place all over India. In particular, strong pressures are exerted on artisans by craft-emporium managers and dealers to alter their traditional practices, to mix their media, and to ape other artisans' successful designs; it is against these entrepreneurs, who cater to "public tastelessness," that the museum has set its face.

Because it is not a craft object's antiquity but the excellence of its execution that the museum exalts, and because the museum exhibits the best work of the past as an incentive to improve artisans' skills, it will come as no surprise that to achieve parity with the past is considered the pinnacle of achievement. Yet parity can have unintended consequences. The museum occasionally hosts artisans whose skills are so consummate that their work can be mistaken for pieces hundreds of years old. That is, these artisans (wood and ivory carvers in particular) can produce artifacts that are, from a commercial perspective, fakes. Because there is a lucrative market for fake antiquities in India, dealers try to control the output of these artisans, and they occasionally threaten artisans with violence; the artisans sometimes turn to the museum for protection. Although the museum neither seeks out nor encourages faking, it shares with dealers and conoisseurs unbridled admiration for those few artisans who are capable of consistently producing undetectable fakes. There is a massive irony in this situation, which develops directly from the exaltation of tradition and the disparagement of innovation.[44]

Visiting artisans are warned against innovation, but the museum places no restraints on entrepeneurs who make profits from it. Just as the Victoria and Albert Museum in London has been a treasure trove of ideas for generations of English designers, so the craft museum is a magnet for decorators, designers, and entrepreneurs in New Delhi.

One day in December 1989 while I was sitting with Sasa, the Manipuri potter, in the crafts demonstration area, a well-dressed woman arrived with three workmen in tow. She spoke with Sasa for a few minutes, then bought several of his pots and wrote out an order for several more. I fell into conversation with her while Sasa and the three workmen animatedly discussed

Figure 9.6. Kumari, a crafts boutique at Chanakyapuri shopping center, New Delhi, 1989. Photo by P. Greenough.

his work. Monika Das, an upper-class Punjabi, is co-owner of a New Delhi boutique that sells pottery and handwoven woolens to well-to-do customers, mostly women.[45] She is a well-traveled, high-energy businesswoman whose husband directs a tractor factory. Her shop, called Kumari, is designed to suggest a village hut, although this is belied by its plate-glass windows and discreet lighting (fig. 9.6). Kumari is situated in an open parking area in a shopping center in the Chanakyapuri neighborhood of New Delhi—the diplomatic enclave. At Monika's invitation I visited Kumari and found there a wide variety of pots, some glazed, others not, some wheel-thrown and others hand-built, many with exotic surfaces, unusual lusters, and incised designs; all were intended for use as lamp bases or flower pots. The tasteful display of these ceramics, along with pieces of hand-spun art textiles in natural-dyed wools, compared well with similar small shops in New York's Soho and London's Islington.

Monika's pots were fabricated approximately ten miles south of New Delhi on a small "farm"; this term is used in New Delhi to refer to parcels of land obtained from the regional planning authority on which the city's elite build country houses. At the farm was a small pottery that employed a workforce of six; it has specialized buildings for mixing the clay and for molding and glazing the pots. There were two kilns, one English-style, the other *desi*. All of these structures were laid out attractively around a central compound.

Conversation with Monika revealed that her workmen, who were paid a regular wage and not a piecework rate, were all potters by caste and hailed from the Delhi area; she had trained them herself in a variety of local and exotic techniques, including Japanese *raku* glazing.

Monika had a precise sense of her business needs; her clients depended on her for a steady stream of new forms with distinctive designs, colors, and glazes. Her shop was undoubtedly helping to shape bourgeois taste by introducing choice and standards into arenas where they had rarely been seen before. Yet she does not claim to be dealing in "art," and the utilitarian uses of her wares—potting plants, holding up electric lamps—set the outer limit to what she expected to sell. Within this limit, she constantly sought novelty that could be adapted to her small factory. Hence she read cosmopolitan journals on ceramics, invited foreign potters to visit her shop and factory, and sought out ceramics galleries whenever she traveled abroad. Periodically, and for the same reason, she went to the crafts museum to see, discuss, and purchase the work of Indian potters who were otherwise inaccessible, as she was doing the morning I met her. In the exchanges that take place at the museum, two ambitions dovetail: while Monika studies innovations that she can adapt and market, the visiting artisans obtain the prices they want, without being dependent on intermediaries.

Monika Das is by no means a unique figure; in the course of several weeks I met two others with sketchbooks—a young interior decorator and a commercial artist, both New Delhi residents—who regularly come to the museum for design ideas to adapt to their professional needs. When I questioned Jain about this kind of visitor, he again made a pained face, observing that it was their influence as much as that of the craft-emporium dealers that he was trying to keep artisans away from. It is an ironic fact, however, that strict enforcement of the one-month rule suits the designers' and entrepreneurs' need for novelty. Were the crafts museum to limit visiting artisans to one *week*, the entrepreneurs could adapt to the pace. Clearly, the museum's ambition to exhibit timeless forms of craft production is perfectly suited to the capital elites' ongoing need to refurbish their houses, offices, gardens, and clothing with stylish designs and allusions to tradition—ethnic chic.

State Promotion of Indian Craft Traditions

Themes of art and artisanship have played a part in the development of nationalist culture in India since the beginning of the century.[46] The importance of this identification has not faded, and in the government's 1992-97 five-year-plan, one finds the statement that "handicrafts are not only a part of the country's rich cultural heritage but they have also been a unifying factor in the national life."[47] It should come as no surprise, then, that the crafts museum has been a favorite of the ruling Congress Party for decades. Prime Minister Indira Gandhi visited often in the last years of her life, bringing with her dignitaries and diplomats. She took pleasure in conversing with the artisans and demonstrating her knowledge of Madhubani painting, a regional folk style from the Maithila region of the state of Bihar. Madhubani designs were originally daubed on hut walls by Kayastha and Brahman women as decorative elements in agricultural festivals and life-cycle rituals, but during Indira Gandhi's prime ministership the artists were encouraged by the All India Handicrafts Board (now Commission) to shift to painting on paper. Collectors were astonished by the strength of their colors and images, and Madhubani paintings have developed a good market in India and abroad. Motifs from the *Puranas* and vernacular epics, originally intended to secure a goddess's blessing or to ward off evil at a marriage or menarche, appear on the walls of homes and museums in distant countries. Indeed, the cosmopolitan success of Madhubani painting can be taken as a prototype of the global projection of Hindu folk imagery under the patronage of the state.[48]

Efforts by the governments of China, India, Indonesia, Egypt, and Mexico to project a favorable view of their countries abroad became more urgent in the 1980s, when they began to practice cultural diplomacy by projecting essentialized versions of their traditions. In India this included not only the marketing of *khadi* cloth, clothing, and crafts in foreign boutiques and galleries but also the launching of state-sponsored cultural festivals and living folk-art demonstrations. These were variously called *The Festival of India* (Britain and the United States in 1981 and 1985 respectively), *Shilpakar: Continuing Traditions of Indian Craftsmen* (Soviet Union 1986-87), *Indian Craftsmen* (Sweden 1987), *The Tribal Arts of India* (Japan 1988), and *Indien Festspiele* (Germany 1992).[49] Begun under Indira Gandhi, they continued under her successors. The commercial success of the American festival in particular caught the attention of Rajiv Gandhi.[50] The expense of the craft museum's new galleries, the increasing scale of the museum's collections, and the launching of projects like the National Craftpersons Directory become more understandable in light of the fact that handcraft promotion is appreciated at the highest levels of government. In fact, a judgment seems to have been made to project India abroad as a *craft nation*—a global cultural reserve where vital traditions of folk arts and crafts, music, and dance are maintained.

Conclusion

The National Handicrafts and Handlooms Museum in New Delhi is a deceptively simple institution. While it can be perused in an hour, it is not so easy to say what it is or how it works on those who visit it. Its physical plant is modest, overshadowed by the grander structures nearby, and it refers to itself in visual terms that suggest a well-watered village. Its staff eschew the usual ambition of capital-city museums, which is to exhibit masterpieces under conditions of great security. Yet the museum makes an unmistakable set of claims about the importance of artisans and of handmade crafts as continuing elements in Indian culture and in the construction of the Indian nation. Because the museum's parts were assembled at different times and from different motives—the core artifact collection in 1956, the village complex and craft demonstration area in 1972, the new galleries in late 1991—it is impossible to draw out a single explanatory thread or institutional trajectory from its nearly forty-year existence. The museum's very name mixes its metaphors and allusions, and the diverse publics who come to visit—Indian and foreign tourists, prime ministers and diplomats, school-age students, decorators and designers, managers of craft boutiques—respond to different institutional possibilities. This evident diversity makes it clear that the crafts museum, a pillar of India's emerging official national culture, lies within a "terrain of cultural contestation" characterized by organizational fluidity, multiplicity of promises, and social heterogeneity. The director, Jyotindra Jain, has come to terms with these struggling meanings, playfully suggesting that the museum might be called an "imaginary museum."[51]

Three themes in this essay have helped to frame an understanding of the museum's institutional practice: enduring official anxiety about the place of artisans in India's industrializing "economy," ideological concern for the unity and continuity of India's craft "tradition," and the representation of India to its own citizens and to foreigners as a "crafts nation."

The actual effects of the craft museum on artisans' income are unclear and at best indirect. While some artisans have no doubt improved their earnings after giving public demonstrations in New Delhi, the call to a few thousand to visit for a month would seem to have a very diffuse impact on the millions who remain at home. The museum's oft-stated principle that artisans will prosper only by maintaining traditional forms, materials, and designs has a certain plausibility, but it contradicts the conduct of entrepreneurs, who pursue profits by shifting production toward novelty. Museum staff and entrepreneurs alike are intent on shaping the taste of the middle class (now in excess of 100 million), but where the one is constrained by fixed budgets, limited staff, and sunk capital, the other is flexible, risk-oriented, and mobile.

What can be said with more confidence is that the museum has been successful in continuing to link the idea of the unity of the nation with certain preindustrial technologies and associated rituals. The idea of a single religiously necessary and perennial Indian craft tradition, first formulated by A. K. Coomaraswamy in the Swadeshi era, is demonstrably a nationalist myth. But Congress Party governments have drunk deeply of this myth, which has constrained full-tilt industrialization. A space for artisans has been reserved in eight successive five-year plans—a space where handloom, *khadi*, folk arts, *coir*, and numerous other village industries have been allowed to persevere more or less unmolested by industrial competition.[52] From the other direction, massive poverty in rural areas has allowed makers of inexpensive mats, clothes, pottery, and metalware to find local markets for their wares despite the ready availability of industrial substitutes.

Finally, what are the implications of positioning India as a craft nation, a diplomatic project with which the museum has been closely connected? The fate of this image, once it is launched into global cultural space, is hard to predict, although a reputation based on ivory carving, *ikat*, and lost-wax metal-casting technologies *and* on high-quality steel, self-launched satellites, and atomic energy is actually suggestive of the country's rich resources. Most foreigners readily respond to India's handmade goods, whose exquisite designs, colors, and natural materials effortlessly elicit goodwill, and the government's investment in folk crafts may turn out to have been shrewd. It is an investment that continues to spill over onto the crafts museum, which is uniquely able to identify and send abroad an abundance of beautiful artifacts and the talented artisans who make them, and thus to stimulate worldwide admiration.[53]

Notes

The research and interviews for this article date to 1989-91. I thank Katy Bartlett, Carol Breckenridge, Jan Bremen, Richard Burghart, "Monika Das," Jyotindra Jain, Philip Lutgendorf, Dulali Nag, Chris Pinney, Dietmar Rothermund, and the anonymous readers for the University of Minnesota Press for suggestions and materials used in completing this essay. Errors of fact and interpretation are my own. The facilities of the Center for International and Comparative Studies of the University of Iowa and of the South Asian Institute of Heidelberg University are gratefully acknowledged.

1. The number of artisans in India is greatly affected by the definition of *artisan* that is used; in fact, this term is no longer used for statistical purposes. The Planning Commission indicates that in 1991-92 there were 26.4 million workers employed in the so-called traditional industries, including *khadi*-cloth weaving, handloom weaving, village industries such as grain husking and

sugar making, sericulture, handicrafts, and coir fiber processing; see Planning Commission, *Eighth Five Year Plan, 1992-97*, vol. 2, *Sectoral Programmes of Development* (New Delhi, 1992), pp. 132-44 and Statement 6.2, p. 150. The Indian Census includes artisans within the category of the "household industry worker," but it limits itself to counting only those workers whose principal income derives from the home-based production of handcrafted products. Thus, while the census indicates that the number of "household industry workers" increased from 7.7 million in 1981 to 10.4 million in 1991, these numbers are well below those given by the Planning Commission. See *Census of India 1981*, Series I, Part III-A (i) *General Economic Tables*, Table B-3 p. 240, and Appendix IV, pp. 105-7, and *Census of India 1991*, Series 1, Paper 3, *Provisional Population Totals: Workers and Their Distribution*, pp. 33, 193ff., and figure 3.

2. Jim Masselos, review of *National Handicrafts and Handlooms Museum, New Delhi* by Jyotindra Jain and Aarti Aggarwala, *Journal of Asian Studies* 49 (November 1990): 973. In 1989-90 the craft museum employed 150 persons, and its annual budget was approximately 7 million rupees or $350,000 U.S. These details and other information were provided by Dr. Jyotindra Jain, senior director of the crafts museum.

3. A key feature of Luytens and Baker's original (1914) design for New Delhi was a "central vista" running two miles from Government House (subsequently Rashtrapati Bhavan) on Raisina Hill to the Purana Qila (Old Fort); the vista heightens the significance of institutions like the zoo, fairgrounds, and the craft museum that arose later at the Old Fort's base (Gerald Breese, *Urban and Regional Planning for the Delhi-New Delhi Area: Capital for Conquerors and Country* [Princeton, N.J.: Department of Sociology, Princeton University, 1974], pp. 12-15).

4. Despite obvious contrasts, a comparison between the cultural-national-institutional politics of the capitals of India and Quebec is instructive. See Richard Handler, "On Having a Culture: Nationalism and the Preservation of Quebec's *Patrimoine*," in *Objects and Others: Essays on Museums and Material Culture*, ed. George Stocking Jr. (Madison: University of Wisconsin Press, 1985), pp. 192-217.

5. Ajit Mookerjee, *Crafts Museum* (New Delhi: All India Handicrafts Board, 1971), p. 7.

6. Administratively, the crafts museum is placed under the all-India handicrafts commissioner within the Ministry of Textiles; in the early 1950s it was under the Ministry of Commerce and Industry, while in the 1970s it was moved to the Ministry of Foreign Trade. The history of cottage industries, hand-loom revival, and crafts export promotion in India from the 1950s on remains to be written, but it is linked to the efforts of a series of central ministers advised by two powerful women close to the Congress Party leadership, Kamaladevi Chattopadhyay and Pupul Jayakar, and at least one foreign technical adviser, Elizabeth Bayley Willis. See Pupul Jayakar, *The Earthen Drum: An Introduction to the Ritual Arts of Rural India* (New Delhi: National Museum, 1980); L. Chandra and J. Jain, eds., *Dimensions of Indian Art: Pupul Jayakar at Seventy*, 2 vols. (Delhi: Agamkala Prakashan, 1986), esp. 1:xv-xliv; Kamaladevi Chattopadhyay, *The Glory of Indian Handicrafts* (New Delhi: Indian Book Company, 1976); Kamaladevi Chattopadhyay, *Inner Recesses, Outer Spaces: Memoirs* (New Delhi: Navrang, 1986); and Jamila Brijbhusan, *Kamaladevi Chattopadhyay, Portrait of a Rebel* (New Delhi: Abhinav, 1976), pp. 139-48. See also Katherine F. Hacker and Krista Jensen Turnbull, "The Elizabeth Bayley Willis Collection," in the Costume and Textile Study Center exhibition catalog *Courtyard, Bazaar, Temple: Traditions of Textile Expression in India* (Seattle: University of Washington, 1982), p. 9.

7. The concept of a terrain of cultural contestation has been adapted from Arjun Appadurai and Carol Breckenridge, "Why Public Culture?" *Public Culture* 1, no. 1 (Fall 1988): 5-9.

8. The evolution of such clothing is accelerated by official agencies and entrepreneurs, who furnish both weavers and tailors with designs, and by advertisers, who articulate both their exclusivity and their consonance with regional and national traditions. For a careful study of the commercial and cultural practices that link hand-craftsmanship, women's sari fashions, and the

promulgation of regional tradition, see Dulali Nag, "Fashion, Gender and the Bengali Middle Class," *Public Culture* 3, no. 2 (Spring 1991): 93-112.

9. These examples reported by Jyotindra Jain in "Karma of the Coffee-Table," *Times of India*, Sunday Review, May 6, 1990, p. 1.

10. For an account of the new galleries, see Sunil Sethi, "The Rebirth of a Museum," *Sunday Times of India*, December 14, 1991, p. 18.

11. National Handicrafts and Handlooms Museum, *Crafts Museum* brochure, (no date).

12. Sethi, "Rebirth of a Museum."

13. *Crafts Museum* brochure, p. 2. The origins of displayed items are indicated on labels, but the exhibits freely combine artifacts of very different dates and provenances.

14. "Craftsmen [are] increasingly losing touch with their own traditions of materials, techniques, designs and aesthetics of their arts and crafts due to the sudden changes caused by modern industrialization" (Jyotindra Jain, "A Heritage Comes Alive," *Indian Express Weekend*, September 22, 1990, p. 2).

15. *Crafts Museum* brochure, p. 2.

16. These data are organized under the following headings: Name of the craft, craftsperson's name, date and place of birth, father's/husband's name, particulars of family, family's participation in craft, experience, educational qualifications, average income, clientele, detailed note on cultural and historical background, bibliography, description of craft, materials, tools and equipment, process, description of object made, cultural significance of craft. In addition, there is space for photographs and cross-references to items in the crafts museum collection and notations of awards and recognition and participation in the museum's demonstration program.

17. National Handicrafts and Handlooms Museum, "Highlights of the Activities for the Period from January 1988 to December 1988" (mimeo), p. 1.

18. *Crafts Museum* brochure, p. 8. In 1988 alone, twenty-one thousand students from 348 schools, some from as far away as Chandigarh and Dehra Dun, visited the museum (National Handicrafts and Handlooms Museum, "Highlights . . . January 1988 to December 1988," (p. 2).

19. Jyotindra Jain and Aarti Aggarwala, *Museums of India: National Handicrafts and Handlooms Museum, New Delhi* (Ahmedabad: Mapin, 1989), p. 12. Note that Pupul Jayakar refers to handicrafts as "the *ritual* arts of rural India" (*Earthen Drum*). The best ethnographic evidence for the essentially religious functions of Indian artisans comes paradoxically not from peasant castes but from tribal groups conventionally seen as being outside the mainstream of Hindu society. See, for example, Jyotindra Jain, *Painted Myths of Creation: Art and Ritual of an Indian Tribe* (New Delhi: Lalit Kala Akademi, 1984), p. 5.

20. The crafts museum does not exclude non-Hindu artisans or their work from its activities and galleries. Religious and caste differences are rarely acknowledged in museum publications, although caste names are used to identify artisan communities. Many of the artisans come from "scheduled tribes," i.e., they are economocally backward indigenes.

21. At the time of the Asian fair in 1972, all the states and territories were represented; some huts have since deteriorated and been pulled down. The present structures represent Kulu in Himachal Pradesh; Saurashtra and Banni in Gujarat; Madhubani in Bihar; Bhilwara in Rajasthan; West Bengal, the Nicobar Islands, and Kashmir; the Adi Gallong from Arunachal Pradesh; Rabhas from Assam; Ao Nagas from Nagaland; Gadbas from Orissa; Todas from Tamilnadu; and Gonds from Madhya Pradesh. Occasionally a new hut is added to the complex; a "Sarguja hut" was built during 1988. See All India Handicrafts Board, Publicity Branch, *Village Complex (Gram Jhanki)* (New Delhi: Ministry of Industry, n.d.), and National Handicrafts and Handlooms Museum, "Highlights . . . January 1988 to December 1988."

22. Jain and Aggarwala, *Museums of India*, p. 10.

23. Jain, "A Heritage Comes Alive," p. 2.

24. *India: A Travel Survival Kit* (Berkeley, Calif.: Lonely Planet, 1984), p. 142.

25. On "Potemkin villages," see Joseph L. Wieczynski, ed., *Modern Encyclopedia of Russian and Soviet History*, vol. 24 (Gulf Breeze, Fla.: Academic International Press, 1976), pp. 134-35. I am grateful to Steven Hoch for this reference.

26. The artisans spoken of here are the *official* artisans; before the opening of new galleries in December 1991, at least a dozen men could be found daily preparing beams and poles for the new buildings, laying brick, spreading plaster and paint, stringing electrical lines, etc. These were recognizably workmen because of their soiled clothes, their indifference to visitors, their freedom to address each other loudly and to move around the site, whereas the invited craftsmen sat in clean clothes at assigned spaces, producing steadily while conversing with visitors. Next to each official artisan was a neatly lettered sign, not unlike those placed before animals in the zoo, stating the artisan's name, medium, village home, district, and state. Clearly, the crafts museum has the authority to define which artisans are worthy of attention, but one can imagine a slightly different kind of museum that would recognize Delhi masons, electricians, carpenters, and painters.

27. In addition to the regular cycle of demonstrations, special seminars and workshops are held each year; as a result, 245 artisans were in residence at the crafts museum during 1988, and they represented 154 craft traditions; see "Highlights . . . from January 1988 to December 1988."

28. Cash is paid directly to the artisans, and the crafts museum takes no portion from these sales.

29. The photographs accompanying this article were taken by the author with permission.

30. *Crafts Museum* brochure, p. 4.

31. See Ananda K. Coomaraswamy, "Hindu View of Art: Historical," in *The Dance of Shiva* (London: Peter Owen, 1958), pp. 22-34, as well as Mulk Raj Anand, "Principles of Artistic Practice," in *The Hindu View of Art* (London: George Allen and Unwin, 1933), pp.169-86.

32. The prohibition is cited by Coomaraswamy in "Hindu View of Art: Historical," p. 31.

33. The author appreciates Dr. Jain's helpfulness in a series of interviews on April 1, 1989 (Ames, Iowa), December 15, 1989 (New Delhi), December 18, 1989 (Varanasi), January 4, 1990 (New Delhi), and August 16, 1991 (New Delhi).

34. E.g., Jyotindra Jain, *Folk Art and Culture of Rural Gujarat* (Ahmedabad: 1980); Jain, "The Visual Vocabulary of Crafts," *Shilpakar* (Bombay, 1982): 5-20; and Jain, *Painted Myths of Creation: Art and Ritual of an Indian Tribe* (New Delhi: Lalit Kala Akademi, 1984), all of which explicate Gujarati research material.

35. "The objects of the museum have been identified as belonging to a specific community on the basis of their use rather than their manufacture. If a certain type of carved wooden chest is peculiar to the Mer, it has been linked with the Mer rather than the carpenter who has made it" (Jyotindra Jain, comp., *Folk Art and Culture of Gujarat: Guide to the Collection of the Shreyas Folk Museum of Gujarat* [Ahmedabad: Shreyas Prakashan, 1980], p. xi).

36. For a recent survey, see E. Cumming and W. Kaplan, *The Arts and Crafts Movement* (London: Thames and Hudson, 1991).

37. For an appreciation of Coomaraswamy's influence, and for an effort to evaluate some of his mistakes and their sources, see Niharranjan Ray, "The 'Life' of Coomaraswamy: An Interpretation" and Senake Bandaranayake, "Ananda Coomaraswamy and Approaches to the Study of Traditional Sri Lankan Art and Society," both in *Paroksa, Coomaraswamy Centenary Seminar Papers*, ed. Gulam Muhammad Sheikh et al. (New Delhi: Lalit Kala Akademi, 1984), pp. 3-7 and 27-37, respectively.

38. Coomaraswamy's broad historical-cultural views are most apparent in *Medieval Sinhalese Art—Being a Monograph on Medieval Arts and Crafts* (Colombo, 1906; London, 1908), *The Indian Craftsman* (London, 1909), and various essays in *The Dance of Shiva* (London 1924).

A more compact source is A. Coomaraswamy, "Art in Indian Life" *Coomaraswamy: Selected Papers*, vol. 1, ed. R. Lipsey, Bollingen Series 89 (Delhi: Oxford University Press, 1977), pp. 71-100.

39. "What Has India Contributed to Human Welfare?" in *The Dance of Shiva*, pp. 3-21, and "Young India," ibid., pp. 149-67. Non-Hindus have no place in Coomaraswamy's analysis, although the existence of other craft traditions with their own ritual underpinnings is not in doubt. See, for example, Deepak Metha, *A Sociological Study of Gandhian Institutions: Work, Weavers and the Khadi and Village Industries Commission.* Ph.D. dissertation, Department of Sociology, Delhi University, 1989, especially chapter five, which discusses the connections between work and worship in the lives of Muslim weavers in Bara Banki district. Cited in G. Pandey, *The Construction of Communalism in Colonial North India* (Delhi: Oxford University Press, 1990), pp. 97-99.

40. Anand, however, laid more emphasis than Coomaraswamy did on the permanent religiosity of the Indian masses and was therefore more hopeful about the survival of the arts and crafts; see Anand, *Hindu View of Art*, pp. 217-21, and his brief personal memoir, "Coomaraswamy Darshan," in G. Md. Sheikh et al., *Paroksa*. For a careful analysis of the context and impact of the ideas of Coomaraswamy and his contemporary E. B. Havell, among others in the development of a nationalist, Orientalist, and traditionalist reformulation of India's artistic ideologies in the period 1900-20, see Tapati Guha-Thakurta, *The Making of a New 'Indian' Art: Artists, Aesthetics and Nationalism in Bengal, 1850-1920* (Cambridge: Cambridge University Press, 1992), chapters 5-6.

41. *Crafts Museum* brochure, p. 6. I have not been able to trace the source of this quotation.

42. Coomaraswamy, "Art in Indian Life," p. 80, emphasis in the original.

43. Jain, "A Heritage Comes Alive," p. 1.

44. Jain points out, in a related irony, that the government's export controls on antiquities damage the economic interests of the very best contemporary artisans; customs agents cannot distinguish copies that have been "aged" from real antiques and thereby halt the flow of both.

45. The name is a pseudonym.

46. Guha-Thakurta, *The Making of a New 'Indian' Art*.

47. India, Planning Commission, *Eighth Five Year Plan, 1992-97*, vol. 2, *Sectoral Programmes of Development*, p. 141.

48. Madhubani painters, it should be noted, were not originally artisans by background, and their success is not in accord with the crafts museum's emphasis on assisting traditional artisans from low-caste and tribal origins. See Jayakar, *Earthen Drum*, p. 116.

49. The whole cycle of Festivals of India has not yet been examined. The festivals were controversial in India and generated considerable commentary in the New Delhi feuilleton. Richard Kurin has closely analyzed the handicraft and performance aspects of the Festival of India in Washington, D.C., during the summer of 1985 in "Cultural Conservation through Representation: Festival of India Folklife Exhibitions at the Smithsonian Institution," in *Exhibiting Cultures: The Poetics and Politics of Museum Display*, ed. by Ivan Karp and Steven D. Levine (Washington, D.C.: Smithsonian Institution Press, 1991), pp. 315-43.

50. Kurin, "Cultural Conservation," pp. 322-23.

51. "We call [the crafts museum] a Museum because it has been so dubbed for a long time, but in reality it does not behave like one, and while hesitating about assuming a conventional nature and role, it asks many questions about itself, and the end effect emerges as an institution that truly strives for an identity but is in no hurry to find a slotted definition for itself. . . . If we appear to be stranded, we might be called an imaginary museum for the time being" (J. Jain, "A Heritage Comes Alive," pp. 1-2).

52. For a review of the scale and diversity of these programs, see Planning Commission, *Eighth Five Year Plan, 1992-97*, vol. 2, *Sectoral Programmes of Development*, pp. 132-44 and Statement 6.2, p. 150.

53. Regional museums with closely related collections and exhibition goals include the Folk Art Museum and the Bharatya Lok Kala Museum in Udaipur, the Shreyas Folk Museum and the Calico Museum of Textiles in Ahmedabad, the Regional Handicraft Centre and the Gurusaday Museum in Calcutta, and the Bharat Bhavan in Bhopal; a similar institution exists in Bhuvaneshvar.

Contributors

Arjun Appadurai is director of the Chicago Humanities Institute and Barbara E. and Richard J. Franke Professor in the Humanities at the University of Chicago. He is the author of *Worship and Conflict under Colonial Rule: A South Indian Case* (1981), editor of *The Social Life of Things: Commodities in Cultural Perspective* (1986), and author of numerous articles.

Carol A. Breckenridge is a historian of South Asia who teaches at the University of Chicago. She is also the editor of *Public Culture*, a journal of cultural criticism that seeks to shape the debates about global cultural flows and public spheres in a diasporic world. She recently edited a book (with Peter van der Veer) entitled *Orientalism and the Postcolonial Predicament: Perspectives on South Asia*.

Frank F. Conlon is professor of history, South Asian studies, and comparative religion at the University of Washington, where he has been a member of the faculty since 1968. His scholarly research has concentrated on the social history of modern India, and he is the author of *A Caste in a Changing World: The Chitrapur Saraswat Brahmans, 1700-1935* (1977). He has conducted research on the history of Bombay and of the Western Indian region of Maharashtra and at present is working on a study of the life and career of Vishnubuwa Brahmachari, a nineteenth-century Hindu revivalist of Maharashtra.

Sara Dickey is associate professor of anthropology and Asian studies at Bowdoin College in Brunswick, Maine. She has carried out research on film watching, politics, class relations, and domestic service in southern India, and she has worked with women's organizations in India and Sri Lanka. Other publications include *Cinema and the Urban Poor in South India* (1993) and "The Politics of Adulation: Cinema and the Production of Politicians in South India" (1993).

Paul Greenough was educated in India, at Visva Bharati University, and at Columbia University and the University of Chicago. He is the author of *Prosperity and Misery in Modern Bengal: The Famine of 1943-1944* (1982). His research interests include health and social welfare in a broad sense and the role of science and technology in modern South Asia. He teaches history at the University of Iowa.

David Lelyveld is the author of *Aligarh's First Generation: Muslim Solidarity in British India* (1978) and has been an editor of the *Encyclopedia of Asian History* (1988) and the *Journal of Asian Studies*. Formerly associate professor of history at the University of Minnesota, he has also taught at Columbia University and the University of Washington. He is currently working on a book to be entitled *The Fate of Hindustani: Colonial Knowledge and the Project of a National Language*.

Barbara N. Ramusack, professor of history at the University of Cincinnati, is the author of *Princes of India in the Twilight of Empire: The Decline of a Patron-Client Relationship, 1914-1939* and is currently writing a volume on the Indian princes and their states for the New Cambridge History of India. She has also published several articles on the interaction of British feminists and Indian women's organizations, including "Cultural Missionaries, Maternal Imperialists, Feminist Allies: British Women Activists in India, 1865-1945" (1989) and "Embattled Advocates: The Debate over Birth Control in India, 1920-1940" (1990).

Rosie Thomas is senior lecturer in film theory at the University of Westminster and has written extensively on Indian popular cinema. She is also a film and television producer and has produced a number of programs on South Asian issues and on Asian communities in Britain.

Phillip B. Zarrilli is professor of theater and drama, folklore, and South Asian studies at the University of Wisconsin at Madison. His books include *The Kathakali Complex: Actor, Performance, Structure* (1984) and (with Farley Richmond and Darius Swann) *Indian Theatre: Traditions of Performance* (1990). He is currently completing two new books, one on *kalarippayattu*, and another on *kathakali*.

Index